TAKE OFF 1

LEHRBUCH

Verfasser	Willibald Bliemel Anthony Fitzpatrick Jürgen Quetz
Berater	Mary Bianchi, Düsseldorf Dr. Ulrich Brack, Marl David Cunningham, Fürth Eduard von Jan, Frankfurt Wolfgang Plüghan, Brunsbüttel Astrid Rosenkranz, Völklingen Dr. Jörg Rublack, Mannheim
Verlagsredaktion	Dr. Blanca-Maria Rudhart
Umschlag	Atelier Noth & Hauer, Berlin
Zeichnungen	Linden Artists (Valerie Sangster, Jon Davis), London; Hewett Street Studios, London; Dennis Mallet, Amersham; Gabriele Heinisch, Berlin
Fotos	Angelika Fischer (S. 6, 9, 13, 14, 15, 37, 56, 102, 103), Berlin; David Graham (S. 12, 38, 43, 59, 80), Hewett Studios, London
Bildquellen	S. 16: DEWE Werbeagentur GmbH, Hildrizhausen; R.W. Eggert, Düsseldorf; Interfoto, München; S. 17: Cornelsen-Velhagen & Klasing, Berlin; S. 18: Weltbild-Dia, München; S. 21: Bundesministerium für Post- u. Fernmeldewesen, Bonn; S. 27: British Tourist Authority, London; S. 28: British Tourist Authority, London; S. 29: Barnaby's Picture Library, London; S. 37: Punch Publications Ltd, London; S. 39: Essen und Trinken, Hamburg/Ian Cook; S. 41: British Tourist Authority, London; Barnaby's Picture Library, London; S. 43: British Railways Board, Frankfurt; S. 60: Barnaby's Picture Library, London; S. 61: Robinson Clubhotels/A. Tappe; S. 62: „IVB Report", Heiligenhaus; S. 66: Woman's Royal Voluntary Service, London/J. R. Rifkin; S. 68: London Regional Transport, London; Barnaby's Picture Library, London; S. 69: Barnaby's Picture Library, London; „IVB Report", Heiligenhaus; S. 71: Punch Publications Ltd, London; S. 72: British Tourist Authority, London; S. 73: Grand Hotel, Brighton/W. Gardiner; S. 76: British Tourist Authority, London; S. 77: British Tourist Authority, London; S. 78: Punch Publications Ltd, London; S. 79: K F S/Distr. Bulls, Frankfurt; S. 91: Zentrale Farbbild-Agentur, Düsseldorf; Barnaby's Picture Library, London; Artreference, Frankfurt; Interfoto, München; S. 92: Rob Judges; S. 99: Cartoons for Students of English by L. A. Hill and D. A. Mallet, Oxford University Press; S. 100: Peter Brookes/The Sunday Times (7. 12. 75); S. 101: Mirage Music Ltd./Essex Musikvertrieb GmbH, Köln

1. Auflage

14.	13.	12.	11.	10.	Die letzten Ziffern bezeichnen
1997	96	95	94	93	Zahl und Jahr des Druckes.

Bestellnummer 48993

© Cornelsen & Oxford University Press GmbH, Berlin, 1985

Das Werk und seine Teile sind urheberrechtlich geschützt. Jede Verwertung in anderen als den gesetzlich zugelassenen Fällen bedarf deshalb der vorherigen schriftlichen Einwilligung des Verlages.

Satz	Fotosatz Gleißberg & Wittstock, Berlin
Reproduktion	Meisenbach, Bruns & Stauff, Berlin
Druck	gedruckt in HongKong

ISBN 3-8109-4899-3

Vertrieb	Cornelsen Verlag, Berlin

Gedruckt auf chlorfrei gebleichtem Papier ohne Dioxinbelastung der Gewässer.

So arbeiten Sie mit Take Off

Der „rote (= blaue!) Faden"

Auf jeder Seite finden Sie in der linken (= blauen) Spalte Arbeitsanweisungen und grammatische Erklärungen. Diese sollen Ihnen helfen, sich beim Wiederholen zu Hause, aber auch bei Übungen im Unterricht zurechtzufinden.

Die Höraufgaben

Neue Redewendungen werden Ihnen in der Regel zunächst von einer Cassette vorgespielt. Diese Aufnahmen zeigen Ihnen, wie Engländer oder Amerikaner ihre Sprache im Umgang miteinander benutzen.

Grammatikregeln ...

G 1 (a)

... finden Sie:
(1) in einer kurzen „Daumenregel" direkt neben den Übungen, damit Sie immer wissen, worauf Sie achten müssen.
(2) im Grammatikanhang, auf den bei den „Daumenregeln" verwiesen wird, z. B. G 1 (a). Dieser Anhang gibt Ihnen einen Überblick über die in Take Off 1 Unit 0–5 (= blau) und 6–10 (= grün) behandelte Grammatik.
(3) im Arbeitsbuch, und zwar dort in knapper und einprägsamer Form; oft sind es nur „Merkhilfen", die angeboten werden, an die man sich vielleicht leichter erinnern kann als an die Erklärungen in den „Daumenregeln" oder im Anhang des Lehrbuchs.
Lernen Sie deshalb auch nicht unbedingt die Regeln aus dem Lehrbuch auswendig, sondern prägen Sie sich eher die Merkhilfen aus dem Arbeitsbuch ein und machen sich mit den Überblickstafeln des Grammatikanhangs vertraut.

Lern- und Rollenspiele ...

... sind dazu da, daß Sie die neue Sprache auch gleich an anderen Menschen „ausprobieren" können; gehen Sie also herum, sprechen Sie möglichst viele andere Teilnehmer an, und benutzen Sie dabei die neuen Redewendungen. Auch wenn das anfangs etwas ungewohnt sein mag – es macht Spaß, es erhöht Ihre Übungsmöglichkeiten und – auch das ist wichtig – Sie können sprechen, ohne daß Ihnen außer Ihrem Gesprächspartner noch jemand anders zuhört!

Leseverständnis ...

... wird vor allem in den Texten am Ende einer Unit geübt. Lesen Sie diese Texte so, wie Sie auch Texte in deutscher Sprache lesen würden: versuchen Sie, den Gesamtsinn zu erfassen, ohne dabei jedes einzelne Wort verstehen zu wollen (oder gar nachzuschlagen).
Die Aufgaben zu diesen Texten sollen Ihre Aufmerksamkeit auf solche größeren Sinnzusammenhänge lenken. Sie sollen Ihnen helfen, Texte so in den Griff zu bekommen, daß das Lesen Spaß macht.

Die Arbeit zu Hause

▷ AB 4

▷ CC

Benutzen Sie dazu das *Arbeitsbuch*; es enthält eine kleine Einführung in Arbeitstechniken, die Ihnen das Sprachenlernen erleichtern könnten; welche Übung im Arbeitsbuch jeweils für Sie interessant ist, zeigt Ihnen der Verweis am Ende einer Übung im Lehrbuch, z. B. ▷ AB 4 = Übung 4 zur gleichen Unit im Arbeitsbuch.
Wichtig ist auch der *Vokabelteil* im Lehrbuch, an dessen Anfang Hinweise zum Vokabellernen stehen.
Ein *alphabetisches Vokabelregister* hilft Ihnen, Wörter wiederzufinden, die Sie vergessen haben.
Weiterhin enthalten die *Übungscassetten* wichtiges Nachsprech- und Einübungsmaterial; wir weisen im Lehrbuch darauf hin, wann Sie diese Cassetten benutzen sollen (▷ CC).
Mit Hilfe dieser vier Arbeitsmittel können Sie auch einmal den Lernstoff einer Sitzung nachholen, die Sie versäumen mußten.

Viel Vergnügen bei der Arbeit mit *Take Off* und ein erfolgreiches Lernen wünschen Ihnen

der Verlag und die Autoren.

Inhaltsverzeichnis

Unit 0   **My name is . . .**   Page 6

Seinen Namen sagen
Jemanden begrüßen
Sich verabschieden

Grammatik
Persönliche und besitzanzeigende Fürwörter
this/that: *Formen von* be
Fragesätze und Kurzantworten
Mehrzahlbildung

Unit 1   **Nice to meet you**   Page 10

Wo man herkommt
Was man von Beruf ist
Jemanden vorstellen
Text: Opinion

Ländernamen; Alphabet; Can you . . . ?
a/an; the
Fragesätze; (Kurz-)Antworten

Unit 2   **How to get there**   Page 19

Zahlen, Telefonnummern
Wie man sich am Telefon meldet
Adressen; Wegauskünfte
Text: York town walk

Zahlen; Ordnungszahlen
there-*Sätze; Befehlssätze*
Die besitzanzeigende Form des Hauptwortes
Besitzanzeigende und persönliche Fürwörter (Mehrzahl)

Unit 3   **Shopping**   Page 30

Kleider beschreiben: Aussehen,
Größe, wie sie einem gefallen
Kleider und andere Dinge kaufen:
wo man sie bekommt; Preise
Text: London – my favourite shops

Eigenschaftswörter
Unregelmäßige Mehrzahlformen; die besitzanzeigende Form in der Mehrzahl
these/those; can/cannot
Paarwörter

Unit 4   **Time and date**   Page 40

Zeitangaben und Datum
Öffnungszeiten, Fahrpläne
Ein Wochenende in Norwich planen
Geburtstage, Geschenke
Text: Flexitime

Fragen mit Fragewörtern
Shall we . . . ?/Let's . . .; could/couldn't
have got/has got
Ordinalzahlen/Datum; Zeitangaben
Die Objektform der persönlichen Fürwörter

Unit 5   **Invitations**   Page 50

Einladungen: wie man sie ausspricht,
annimmt oder ablehnt, weil man
gerade etwas anderes tut/vorhat
Pläne für die nahe Zukunft
Text: A summer course for you?

Would you like . . . ?
Die Verlaufsform der Gegenwart (present progressive)
if-*Sätze* (I)

Stop over 1   Page 56

Unit 6	**Every day**	Page 58	*Grammatik*
	Gewohnheiten und Tagesläufe schildern Über seinen Beruf und seine Vorlieben sprechen Wie man zur Arbeit fährt Text: Meals on wheels		*Die Gegenwartsform des Verbs* (simple present): *Aussagesätze; Verneinungen und Fragen mit* do/does usually/always/often/sometimes
Unit 7	**Travelling in Britain**	Page 68	
	Verkehrsmittel, Städte (Brighton und Dartmouth) und Hotels (in Brighton) miteinander vergleichen Ein Hotel buchen Text: Regions of Britain		*Die Steigerung von Eigenschaftswörtern* *Vergleichssätze*
Unit 8	**Food and drink**	Page 78	
	Im Hotel ein Frühstück bestellen Im Restaurant ein Essen aussuchen und bestellen In einem 'pub' Getränke bestellen Einkaufen im Supermarkt Text: Fast food – big money		*Redewendungen mit* will some/any
Unit 9	**Talking about the past**	Page 86	
	Über seine Ferien berichten Erzählen, was man gestern getan hat Wie man seinen Partner/seine Partnerin kennenlernte Text: Class reunion		*Die Vergangenheitsform des Verbs* (simple past): *Aussagesätze; Verneinungen und Fragen mit* did
Unit 10	**What's the matter?**	Page 93	
	Sich nach dem Befinden erkundigen Bei Krankheit und Mißgeschick Mitgefühl und gute Wünsche ausdrücken und Ratschläge geben Wetterberichte; Gespräche über das Wetter Text: Mother's little helper		should/shouldn't *Die Befehlsform mit* Don't *Besitzanzeigende Fürwörter bei Kleidung/Körperteilen* *Ausrufe* *Zukunft mit* will
	Stop over 2	Page 102	
Anhang	Grammatikbegriffe	Page 104	
	Grammatik	Page 106	
	Wörterverzeichnis	Page 118	
	Alphabetische Wortliste	Page 140	
	Höraufgaben-Texte	Page 142	
	Erklärung der Lautschrift	Page 145	

Unit 0
My name is ...

Wie man seinen Namen sagt und jemanden nach dem Namen fragt
Wie man jemanden begrüßt und sich nach dem Befinden erkundigt
Wie man sich verabschiedet

1.1 I'm your guide.

Hello, I'm Lucy. I'm your guide.

Hello. I'm Pat Lewis. I'm your English teacher.

Man schreibt

I am ...
What is ...

Man spricht aber sehr oft die Kurzform, vor allem nach Wörtern wie I, what etc., also:
I'm
What's

Die Schreibung in unseren Dialogen soll die gesprochene Sprache widerspiegeln.

Good evening, Mr. Taylor.

Good evening. My name is Taylor.

And what's your name, please?

I'm Alf Berg.

Hello, Alf. Nice to meet you.

▷ CC

Unit 0

1.2 Are you Walter Thompson?

> *Ja/Nein-Fragen beantwortet man nicht nur einfach mit 'Yes' oder 'No', sondern hängt noch einen kurzen Satz an, in dem man das Hilfsverb aus der Frage aufgreift.*
>
> ▷ G 6.1 (a), G 7 (c)

– Excuse me, are you Walter Thompson?
– No, I'm not.
– Oh, sorry.

– Excuse me, are you Walter Thompson?
– Yes, I am.
– My name is Pat Dickens.
– Hello. Nice to meet you.
– Nice to meet you, too.

 (1) Schreiben Sie Ihren Namen auf eine Karte. Wenn die Karten gut gemischt sind, ziehen Sie eine. (2) Gehen Sie dann herum und versuchen Sie, die Kursteilnehmerin/den Kursteilnehmer zu finden, deren/dessen Karte Sie gezogen haben. (3) Wenn Sie die gezogene Karte an den richtigen Teilnehmer zurückgegeben haben, und wenn Sie Ihre eigene Karte wiederhaben, setzen Sie sich hin.

▷ AB1·CC

1.3 Names!

> *Mit THIS weist man auf etwas (jemanden) in der Nähe hin, mit THAT auf etwas (jemanden) weiter weg vom Sprecher.*
>
> ▷ G 1 (d)

– I'm Inge.
– This is Inge. And I'm Fred.
– That's Inge. This is Fred. And I'm Ann.
– That's Inge. That's Fred. This is Ann. And I'm . . . .
– . . . .

Machen Sie reihum weiter.

▷ AB2

2.1 Good morning, Mrs Finch. – Good morning, Miss Miller.

Hören Sie sich die folgenden vier Aufnahmen an.

Welches Bild paßt zu welcher Aufnahme?

Numerieren Sie die Bilder.

Unit 0

2.2 Ziggy

Wie erkundigt sich Ziggy nach dem Befinden der Iris?

_____ ?

Daisy, Rose, Iris, Lily, and Violet are names for flowers

and for _____.

a name – names
a flower – flowers
a girl – girls

▷ G 3 (a)

▷ AB3

2.3 How are you today?

Wenn Blumen sprechen könnten, würde Iris wohl eine der folgenden Antworten geben:

Begrüßen Sie Ihre beiden Nachbarn im Kurs und fragen Sie sie, wie es ihnen geht.

▷ CC

2.4 How are you?

Hören Sie sich die folgenden vier Aufnahmen an und entscheiden Sie:

Woran merken Sie, wie der jeweiligen Person zumute ist?

Die angesprochene Person fühlt sich ...

	1	2	3	4
... gut				
... nicht so gut				

2.5 Fine, thanks.

Begrüßen Sie jetzt noch einmal einige Kursteilnehmer. Fragen Sie sie auch, wie es ihnen geht!

▷ AB4, AB5

3 Goodbye.

▷ CC

nine 9

Unit 1

Nice to meet you

Wie man nach der Herkunft fragt und sagt,
aus welchem Ort/Land man kommt
Buchstabieren (Namen und Ort)
Wie man jemanden um etwas bittet
Wie man seinen Beruf angibt
Wie man jemanden vorstellt (Name, Ort/Land, Beruf)

1 Nice to see you again.

Begrüßen Sie die anderen Kursteilnehmer/innen.

Hello, Inge. Nice to see you again.

Excuse me, are you Bob?

Hello, Tom. How are you?

Fine, thanks.

2.1 Where are you from?

Are you English?

No I'm not. I'm from Scotland, so I'm British.

Where are you from?

I'm from the States.

Sehen Sie sich den Globus an und machen Sie sich mit den Ländernamen vertraut.

Canada
the (United) States/the USA

England
Scotland } Great Britain
Wales

Northern Ireland

Ireland

New Zealand

Australia

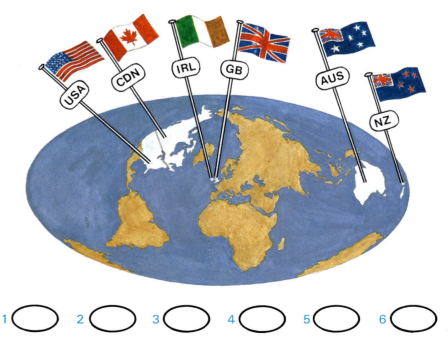

Hören Sie sich jetzt die Aufnahmen an und tragen Sie die Autokennzeichen der Länder ein, aus denen die Sprecher kommen.

1 ◯   2 ◯   3 ◯   4 ◯   5 ◯   6 ◯

2.2 Are you English?

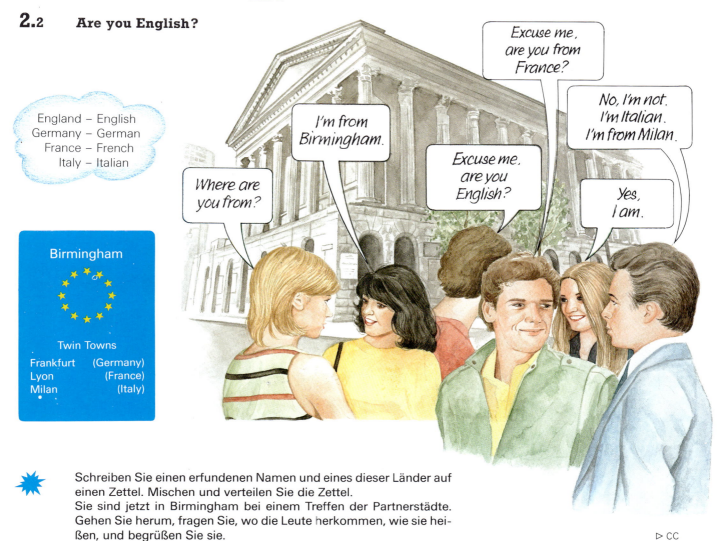

Schreiben Sie einen erfundenen Namen und eines dieser Länder auf einen Zettel. Mischen und verteilen Sie die Zettel.
Sie sind jetzt in Birmingham bei einem Treffen der Partnerstädte. Gehen Sie herum, fragen Sie, wo die Leute herkommen, wie sie heißen, und begrüßen Sie sie.

▷ CC

2.3 I'm from a village near Munich.

▷ AB1·CC

Unit 1

2.4 Is that an English car?

Auf einem Parkplatz in Birmingham fallen Ihnen einige Automarken auf, deren Herkunft Sie nicht kennen.
Fragen Sie Ihren „Gastgeber".

a French car
an old car

Vor Selbstlauten sagt und schreibt man an.

▷ G 2

▷ AB2, AB3

Is that an English car?

Is that an Italian car?

No, it isn't. I think it's an American car.

Yes, it is.

 3.1 Can you spell that, please?

Hören Sie, wie die drei Personen auf der Cassette ihren Namen buchstabieren.
Können Sie die fehlenden Buchstaben ergänzen?

1 _Y_ _A_ _ _ _E_ _ _
2 _W_ _O_ _O_ _ _ _ _
3 _ _ _A_ _ _ _E_ _

3.2 Can you spell your name, please?

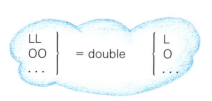

LL
OO } = double { L
...   O
             ...

Can you spell
WILLY WELLWOOD?

– Can you spell your surname, please?
And your first name?

– And where are you from?
Can you spell that, please?   ▷ CC

Unit 1

 3.3 **In a hotel in England**

Listen, please.

What is the guest's name?
Where is he from?
What is his nationality?

3.4 **In a hotel in Frankfurt**

– Good evening. My name is Pierce. I've got a reservation for tonight.
  – Can you spell your name, please?
– P-I-E-R-C-E.
  – Oh, yes, Mr Pierce. What's your first name?
– Robert.
  – And where are you from?
– Vancouver, Canada.
  – Thank you. Here's your key, Mr Pierce.

 Denken Sie sich andere Personen und Orte aus – vielleicht kennen Sie aus dem Fernsehen andere englische oder amerikanische Namen und Orte? Spielen Sie dann die Szene mit Ihrem Nachbarn/Ihrer Nachbarin durch und füllen Sie dabei nach seinen/ihren Angaben den „Meldezettel" aus.

▷ CC

Unit 1

4.1 Jobs

Welches Bild paßt zu welcher Anzeige?

a   b

– I think he's/she's a (secretary).

> He ♂
> She ♀
>
> We write   he is/she is
> We say   he's/she's
>
> ▷ G 1, G 6.1 (a)

c   d   e

▷ CC

4.2 What's your job?

▷ AB 4 · CC

Vor Berufsbezeichnungen benutzt man 'a/an'.

Ihr/e Kursleiter/in hilft Ihnen herauszufinden, wie Ihr Beruf auf englisch heißt.

– I'm	a shop assistant/a student/a housewife/.... an engineer.
I work in	a factory/a supermarket/a flower shop/a hotel/.... an office.

14   fourteen

Unit 1

4.3 I'm an engineer.

– Where are you from?
– I'm from Milan.
– And what's your job?
– I'm an engineer.
– And how do you like Birmingham?
– Oh, very much! It's an interesting city!

 Stellen Sie sich vor, Ihr Kurs ist heute zu Besuch in der englischen Partnerstadt. Zu Gast sind dort auch Gruppen aus anderen Partnerstädten. Sie wollen die Gäste kennenlernen und fragen, wo sie herkommen, was sie beruflich tun, wie es ihnen in England gefällt.
(1) Denken Sie sich eine Person aus; schreiben Sie auf einen Zettel, wo diese Person herkommt (aus welcher Partnerstadt/welchem Land) und was sie von Beruf ist (an engineer, a secretary, ... work in an office/...).
(2) Mischen Sie die Zettel und verteilen Sie sie neu.
(3) Gehen Sie dann herum und sprechen Sie mit den „Gästen".

 5.1 This is Nancy McDonald.

Listen, please.

– Ann, this is Nancy McDonald. She's from ①. She's NBG's ② here in ⑤. Nancy, this is Ann McGregor.
  – How do you do?
    – How do you do? Nice to meet you.
  – Are you from the States?
    – No, I'm not. I'm from Canada, from ③, but my family is from ④.

Nancy's   the guest's
Ann's

Die besitzanzeigende Form schreibt man im Englischen mit Apostroph: 's.
▷ G 3 (b)

① Where is Nancy McDonald from? _____ .
② What is Nancy's job? _____ .
③ Where is Ann McGregor from? _____ .
④ Where is Ann's family from? _____ .
⑤ Where are Nancy and Ann now? _____ .

fifteen   15

Unit 1

5.2 How do you do?

Und das sagt man, wenn man in ungezwungenen bzw. in formellen Situationen jemandem vorgestellt wird.

(1) Stellen Sie Ihre beiden Nachbarn/Nachbarinnen einander vor.
(2) Und jetzt sind Sie bei einem Empfang des ...ischen Botschafters und werden von einem Kursteilnehmer einem anderen vorgestellt.

▷ AB5·CC

5.3 This is Bill Bailey.

I	live in Hamburg.
	work in an office.
He	lives in England.
She	works in a factory.

Suchen Sie aus einer Illustrierten Bilder von Menschen heraus, die Ihnen auffallen, aber nicht unbedingt solche von „Berühmtheiten". Erfinden Sie dann einen Namen/Beruf/Wohnort und stellen Sie Ihre Person/en dem Kurs vor.

▷ AB6, AB7

– This is Bill Bailey.
He's from England, but he lives in the United States now.
He's a cowboy.

– This is Beverley Hill.
She's from Hollywood.
She works in a night club in Las Vegas.

16   sixteen

6 Lesen Sie gern?

Dann versuchen Sie es doch einmal mit diesem englischen Text.

(1) Überfliegen Sie den Text: welche beiden typischen Landestrachten sind erwähnt?

☐ hat ☐ kilt ☐ Lederhosen

(2) In welchem Land (= 'country') erwartet man diese Trachten zu sehen?

(3) Überfliegen Sie den Artikel noch einmal. Worum geht es darin:

☐ um einen Schotten in Afrika?

☐ um einen Afrikaner im Schottenrock?

☐ um einen Schotten in Lederhosen?

(4) '... a tourist who wants to be like us' – „der wie wir sein will": Wie denkt der Verfasser über diesen Mann?

☐ Er findet das gut.

☐ Er findet das unpassend.

(5) Was sagt der Verfasser über die meisten anderen Touristen?

Unit 1

OPINION
by

Alan McFarlane
(Edinburgh)

FASHION is so international today that you normally cannot say where a person is from when you only see his or her clothes.

Some clothes of course, are typical of a country or a region, like the "Lederhosen", or the kilt.

But sometimes you see a person in a national costume, and you know that he or she is not from that country – like the African man in a kilt in a street in Edinburgh last Sunday.

Is he "only a stupid tourist"? **I** think that it is nice to meet a tourist who wants to **be like us**. Most tourists only want to **look at us** – like people in the zoo look at the exotic animals.

Sie haben sicher gemerkt, daß man beim Lesen vieles versteht, wenn man nur ein bißchen Mut zum Raten hat.

Streichen Sie jetzt einmal alle Wörter an, die Sie (a) in den beiden ersten Units schon gelernt haben, oder die (b) im Deutschen und im Englischen ganz ähnlich aussehen, oder die wir im Deutschen als „Fremdwörter" benutzen.

Nur der kleine Rest der Wörter wird Ihnen noch Schwierigkeiten gemacht haben. Diese Wörter finden Sie im Vokabelteil in einem „Kasten": Sie gehören *nicht* zum Lernstoff wie die anderen Vokabeln; Sie können sie der Einfachheit halber hier nachschlagen statt in einem Wörterbuch, brauchen Sie aber nicht zu lernen!

Lesen Sie jetzt den Text noch einmal genauer. Wenn Sie den Sinn verstanden haben, haben Sie diese Aufgabe gut bewältigt!

Unit 1

7 **Who is it?**

Listen, please.

a Jill Brown
Manchester

b Jill Browne
Chester

c Jill Browne
Manchester

8 **Where is it?**

– I think | it's a town in . . . .
that's in . . . .
. . . .

18 eighteen

Unit 2
How to get there

Zahlen

Wie man Telefonnummern und Adressen angibt und erfragt

Wie man nach dem Weg fragt und jemandem den Weg erklärt

Wie man jemanden warnt, und wie man eine Anweisung gibt

1.1 Ten, nine, eight, ...

0 = [əʊ] *Brit. Englisch*
= zero *Am. Englisch und „technische" Zahlen*

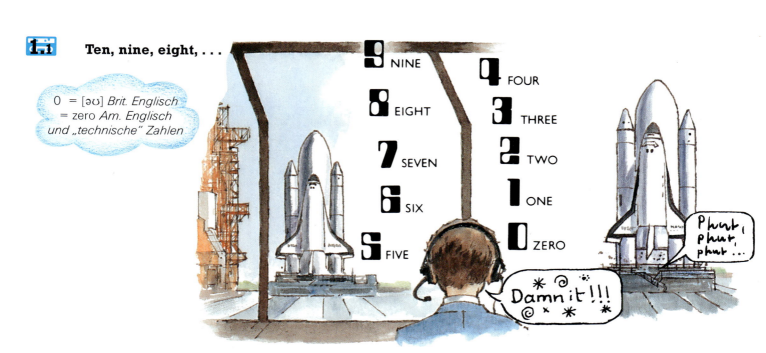

1.2 One, two, three, ...

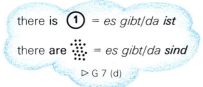

there is ① = *es gibt/da ist*
there are ⋮ = *es gibt/da sind*
▷ G 7 (d)

How many flowers are there in Ziggy's garden?

– There's a lily, there's an iris, there's ..., there are ... flowers.

▷ AB1·CC

 How many are there?
Jeder der drei (oder zwei) Spieler erhält 3 Münzen (oder Knöpfe/Streichhölzer), von denen er 0, 1, 2 oder 3 hinter dem Rücken in eine Hand nimmt; jeder Spieler versucht dann zu erraten, wieviele Münzen (...) insgesamt in den drei Händen sind – und erhält die Münzen, wenn er richtig rät.

Unit 2

1.3 What is his telephone number?

Listen, please.

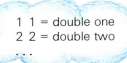
1 1 = double one
2 2 = double two
...

1 What is his telephone number? __ __ __ __ __ __
2 What is his telephone number? _4_ _4_ __ __ _1_ _1_

1.4 What's your telephone number?

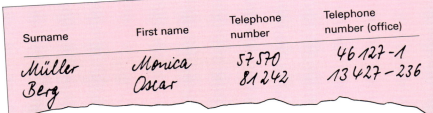

Surname	First name	Telephone number	Telephone number (office)
Müller	Monica	57570	46 127-1
Berg	Oscar	81 242	13 427-236

Legen Sie eine Liste mit den Telefonnummern der anderen Kursteilnehmer an.

Wenn Sie nicht sicher sind, ob Sie alle Nummern richtig mitgeschrieben haben, fragen Sie:

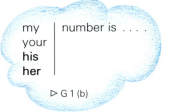
my / your / his / her number is ....
▷ G 1 (b)

What's your telephone number?

My number is...........

It's...........

– What's Monica's / Oscar's number?
– Her / His number is ....

▷ AB2

1.5 Hello, John.

Listen, please.

1
– Hello.
  – Is that 335 3022?
– No, this is

(What is this number?) __ __ __   __ __ __ __

  – Oh, sorry, wrong number.

2
– 335 3022.
  – Hello, is that you, John?
– Yes, speaking.
  – This is

(Who is it?) _____ .

  – Oh, hello, _____ .

Unit 2

1.6 Is that you, Peter?

Setzen Sie sich mit dem Rücken zur Klasse, oder schließen Sie die Augen.

Ein/e Kursteilnehmer/in meldet sich dann mit seiner/ihrer Nummer.

Versuchen Sie, an der Stimme zu erraten, mit wem Sie „verbunden" sind.

▷ AB3·CC

1.7 Directory Inquiries. Which town, please?

Listen, please.

Then find the name of the hotel/person in the telephone directory and write down the number.

1.8 Just a moment!

▷ G 3 (b)

Take a telephone directory of your town (or take the telephone list from 1.4); your neighbour/s can phone you for Inge's/Peter's/...'s telephone number, or for the number of your night school/of a bank/ of a supermarket/of the *XYZ* Hotel/....

▷ AB4

twenty-one 21

2.1 Bingo

Listen, please. What are the last two numbers to complete your Bingo?

Wenn Sie eine der Zahlen auf Ihrem Bingo-Zettel von der Cassette hören, kreuzen Sie sie an. Wenn eine 5er-Reihe komplett ist, rufen Sie „Bingo!"

2.2 Bingo – again

(1) Tragen Sie 9 Zahlen zwischen 1 und 100 in die Felder ein.
(2) Hören Sie gut zu, wenn der Spielleiter in beliebiger Reihenfolge Zahlen aufruft; streichen Sie die Zahlen an, die Sie haben.
(3) Rufen Sie „Bingo", wenn Sie alle Zahlen angestrichen haben!
(4) Spielen Sie Bingo auch in kleineren Gruppen, vielleicht mit weniger Zahlen (20 – 50 oder 70 – 100).

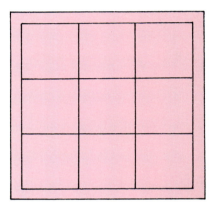

11	eleven	20	twenty	80	**eighty**
12	twelve	21	twenty-one	90	ninety
13	thirteen	22	twenty-two	100	a (one) hundred
14	fourteen	23	twenty-three	200	two hundred
15	**fifteen**	30	thirty	220	two hundred and twenty
16	sixteen	40	**forty**	1.000	a (one) thousand
17	seventeen	50	**fifty**	1.000.000	a (one) million
18	**eighteen**	60	sixty	2.320.000	two million three hundred and twenty thousand
19	nineteen	70	seventy		

▷ AB 5 · CC

2.3 Buzz!

Spielen Sie „Buzz" in Gruppen von 3 bis 5 Teilnehmern und auch mit anderen „Buzz-Zahlen".

* ... because it is **3**!
** ... because it is two times **3**!
*** ... because it is three times **3**!
**** ... because there is a **3** in this number!

Unit 2

3.1 What's his address?

Listen, please.
Then write down . . .

= Their address is . . .
▷ G 1 (a, b)

1 his address: _____ Street, _____
2 her address: _____ Road, Coventry _____
3 their address: _____ Av., _____
4 where the cinema is: It's in _____ Square.

3.2 The Millers, what's their address, please?

Ask your neighbour and write down the post code.

Mr & Mrs D G Miller
13 King Edward Avenue
Blackpool FY2 9TA

Mr & Mrs B Johnson
2 Weston Road
Bath BA1 2XT

And what's your address?

▷ AB6

4 They live on the third floor.

Erfinden Sie 10 Personen/Paare. Sagen Sie Ihrem/Ihrer Partner/in, wo sie wohnen; er/sie muß die Namen korrekt in die Klingelschilder eintragen.

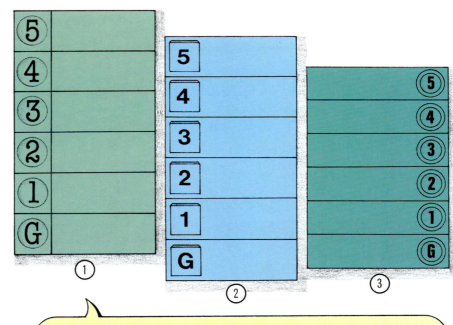

1 one	1st	the **first**
2 two	2nd	the **second**
3 three	3rd	the **third**
4 four	4th	the **fourth**
5 five	5th	the **fifth**

They live . . .
▷ G 1 (a,b)

Jack – he lives in the second building on the third floor.

Jill – she lives in the .... building on the ground floor.

Colin and Mary – they live in the .... on the ....

▷ CC

twenty-three 23

Unit 2

5.1 Turn left!

Turn left!
Listen, please!
= die „Befehls"-Form!
▷ G 6.3 (e)

turn left   (go) straight ahead   turn right

5.2 Be careful!

Stellen Sie einige Hindernisse, z.B. Stühle, den Papierkorb, eine Tasche in Ihrem Klassenzimmer auf. Verbinden Sie einem Kursteilnehmer jetzt die Augen und dirigieren Sie ihn sicher von einer Ecke des Raums um die Hindernisse herum in die andere! Sie können auch mehrere Partner-Paare sich gleichzeitig von verschiedenen Seiten durch die Hindernisse dirigieren lassen.

5.3 Excuse me, can you tell me how to get to the bus station?

Hören Sie sich die drei Aufnahmen an und schreiben Sie die Namen der Gebäude, nach denen gefragt wird, in die jeweils richtigen „Häuser" auf dem Stadtplan.

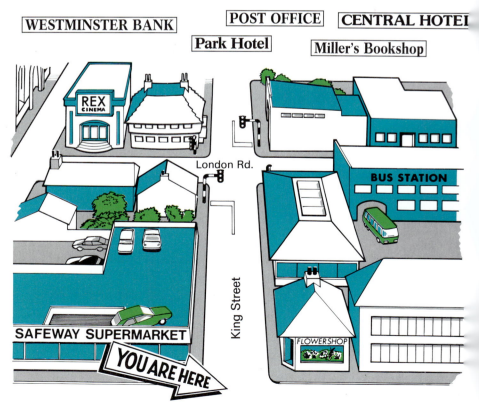

24   twenty-four

Unit 2

5.4 Go straight along here ...

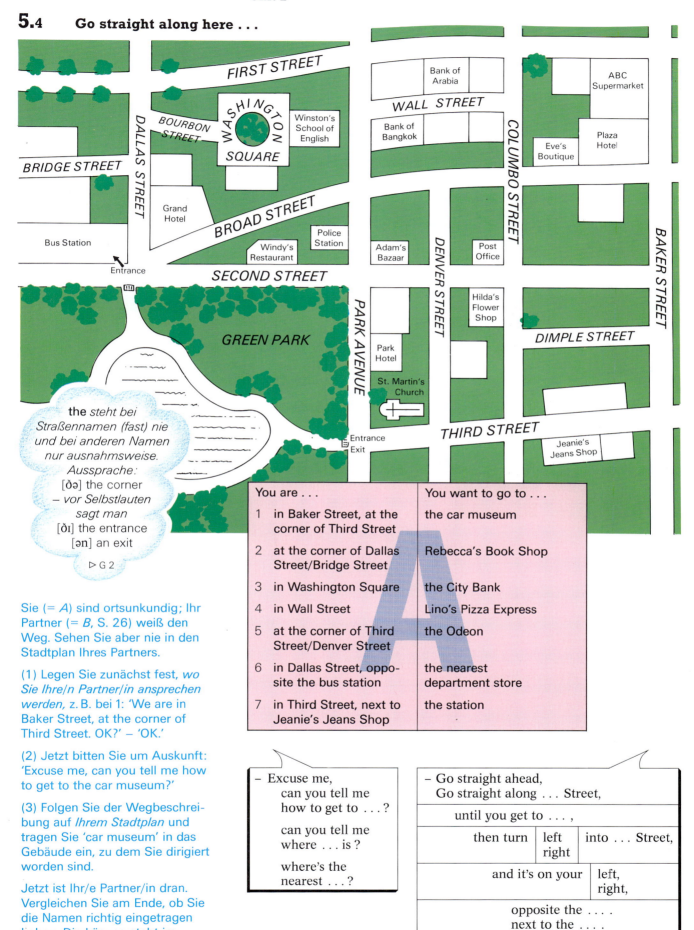

the steht bei Straßennamen (fast) nie und bei anderen Namen nur ausnahmsweise. Aussprache:
[ðə] the corner
– vor Selbstlauten sagt man
[ðɪ] the entrance
[ən] an exit

▷ G 2

	You are ...	You want to go to ...
1	in Baker Street, at the corner of Third Street	the car museum
2	at the corner of Dallas Street/Bridge Street	Rebecca's Book Shop
3	in Washington Square	the City Bank
4	in Wall Street	Lino's Pizza Express
5	at the corner of Third Street/Denver Street	the Odeon
6	in Dallas Street, opposite the bus station	the nearest department store
7	in Third Street, next to Jeanie's Jeans Shop	the station

Sie (= A) sind ortsunkundig; Ihr Partner (= B, S. 26) weiß den Weg. Sehen Sie aber nie in den Stadtplan Ihres Partners.

(1) Legen Sie zunächst fest, *wo Sie Ihre/n Partner/in ansprechen werden,* z.B. bei 1: 'We are in Baker Street, at the corner of Third Street. OK?' – 'OK.'

(2) Jetzt bitten Sie um Auskunft: 'Excuse me, can you tell me how to get to the car museum?'

(3) Folgen Sie der Wegbeschreibung auf *Ihrem Stadtplan* und tragen Sie 'car museum' in das Gebäude ein, zu dem Sie dirigiert worden sind.

Jetzt ist Ihr/e Partner/in dran. Vergleichen Sie am Ende, ob Sie die Namen richtig eingetragen haben. Die Lösung steht im Stadtplan *B*.

– Excuse me,
  can you tell me how to get to ...?
  can you tell me where ... is?
  where's the nearest ...?

– Go straight ahead,
  Go straight along ... Street,
  until you get to ...,
  then turn left / right into ... Street,
  and it's on your left, / right,
  opposite the ....
  next to the ....

Unit 2

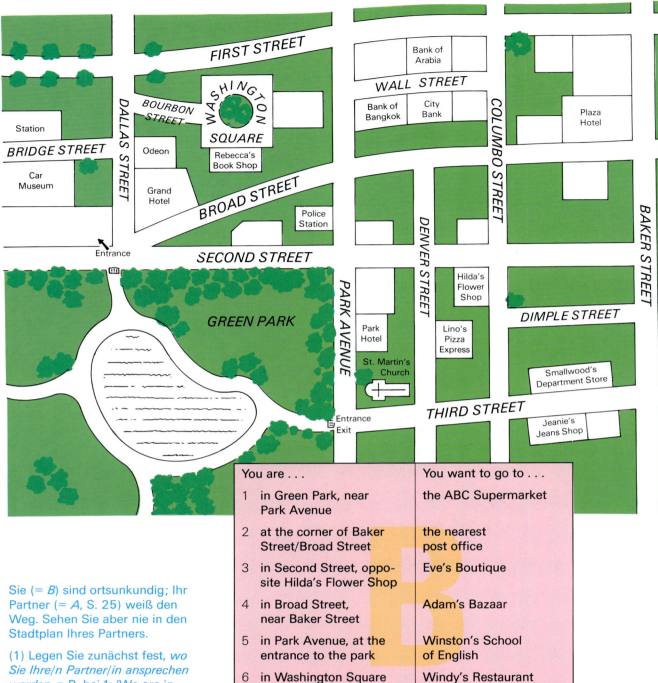

You are . . .	You want to go to . . .
1 in Green Park, near Park Avenue	the ABC Supermarket
2 at the corner of Baker Street/Broad Street	the nearest post office
3 in Second Street, opposite Hilda's Flower Shop	Eve's Boutique
4 in Broad Street, near Baker Street	Adam's Bazaar
5 in Park Avenue, at the entrance to the park	Winston's School of English
6 in Washington Square	Windy's Restaurant
7 in Green Park, near the exit to Park Avenue	the bus station

Sie (= B) sind ortsunkundig; Ihr Partner (= A, S. 25) weiß den Weg. Sehen Sie aber nie in den Stadtplan Ihres Partners.

(1) Legen Sie zunächst fest, *wo Sie Ihre/n Partner/in ansprechen werden,* z. B. bei 1: 'We are in Green Park, near Park Avenue. OK?' – 'OK.'

(2) Jetzt bitten Sie um Auskunft: 'Excuse me, can you tell me how to get to the ABC Supermarket?'

(3) Folgen Sie der Wegbeschreibung auf *Ihrem Stadtplan* und tragen Sie 'ABC Supermarket' in das Gebäude ein, zu dem Sie dirigiert worden sind.

Jetzt ist Ihr/e Partner/in dran. Vergleichen Sie am Ende, ob Sie die Namen richtig eingetragen haben. Die Lösung steht im Stadtplan A.

▷ AB7·CC

– Excuse me,
 can you tell me how to get to . . . ?
 can you tell me where . . . is?
 where's the nearest . . . ?

– Go straight ahead, Go straight along . . . Street,		
until you get to . . . ,		
then turn	left right	into . . . Street,
and it's on your	left, right,	
opposite the . . . . next to the		

Unit 2

6 Is there a supermarket?

Hören Sie sich die Aufnahme an, auf der ein Angestellter eines Reisebüros dem Kunden Auskünfte über ein englisches Feriendorf gibt. Tragen Sie dann die Nummern der Geschäfte usw. an der richtigen Stelle in das Bild ein.

1	SUPERMARKET	5	PUB
2	SELF SERVICE RESTAURANT	6	LADIES' HAIRDRESSER'S
3	NIGHT CLUB	7	TAXI
4	RENDEZVOUS BAR		

7 How to get from the station to ...

Erklären Sie Ihrem Partner den Weg vom Bahnhof/von der Touristeninformation/... zu verschiedenen Orten in Bristol/Bath.
Erklären Sie auch auf einem Stadtplan Ihrer eigenen Stadt einem Fremden den Weg, z. B. vom Bahnhof zum Stadtzentrum/....

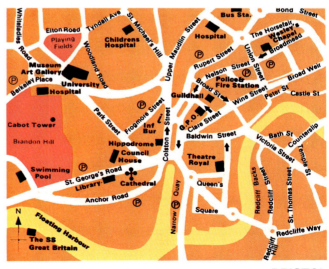

BRISTOL

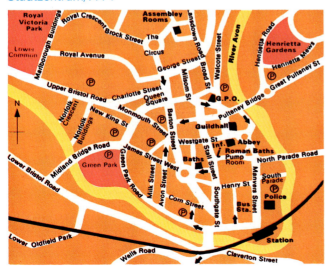

BATH Somerset

i tourist information
➡ one way

twenty-seven 27

Unit 2

8 YORK TOWN WALK

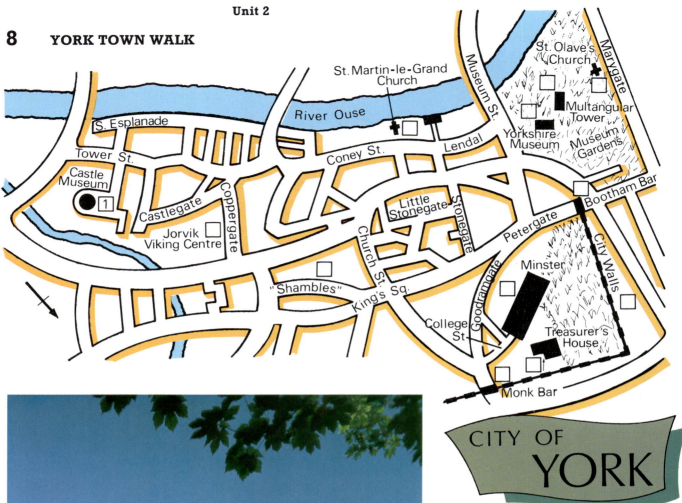

CITY OF YORK

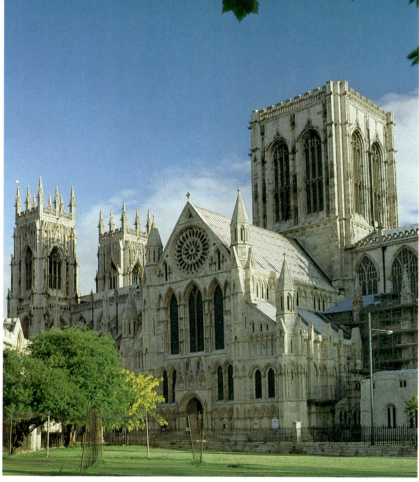

Minster of York

Start the walk at the Castle Museum [1] – **the** Museum of Folklore of Yorkshire.
Turn left, cross Tower Street, and go on to South Esplanade. Turn right and follow the River Ouse. At the bridge, turn right and left again into Coney Street. Pass St. Martin-Le-Grand Church [2] and walk into Lendal. Cross Museum Street and pass through the gates into Museum Gardens. In the Gardens, there are the Yorkshire Museum [3] – which gives a detailed picture of life in York from pre-historic times, the Multangular Tower [4] built in the 4th century, a good example of Roman military architecture, and St. Olave's Church [5].

Unit 2

Castle Museum

Go on through the gates into Marygate. At the end of Marygate turn right for Bootham Bar 6. Go up on to the city walls 7 and walk in a north-east direction to Monk Bar 8. Along Goodramgate to College Street, and then on to the Treasurer's House 9 – built in about 1100, re-built in the 17th and 18th century, with its fine collection of furniture. Go on to the Minster 10 – one of Europe's largest churches, and one of the master works of western architecture; Gothic in design, it was started in about 1200; badly damaged by fire in 1984. From the West Door, cross and turn left into Petergate, then right along Stonegate and left into Little Stonegate.

When you get to Church Street, turn left and go on to King's Square, then right again into the 'Shambles' 11. At the end, turn right and left again, and go along Coppergate, where there is the entrance to the new Jorvik Viking Centre 12 – small electric 'time-cars' take you back to the time of the Vikings; 'Jorvik' is the name of the Viking city that archeologists found in Coppergate.

Turn left into Coppergate and go back to the Castle Museum to end the walk.

Jorvik Viking Centre

Zeichnen Sie den Rundgang auf dem Stadtplan ein und ergänzen Sie die fehlenden Zahlen für die Gebäude.
Wieviele Kirchen, wieviele Museen sind im Text erwähnt?
Welche anderen Sehenswürdigkeiten werden beschrieben?
Worum handelt es sich dabei vermutlich?

Unit 3

Shopping

Wie man ausdrückt, ob einem etwas gefällt
Wie man fragt, wo man etwas bekommt
Wie man beschreibt, was man haben will:
Farbe – Größe – Material
Wie man sagt, ob es paßt oder nicht
Preise
Wie man um etwas bittet

1   **There's a T-shirt in my suitcase.**

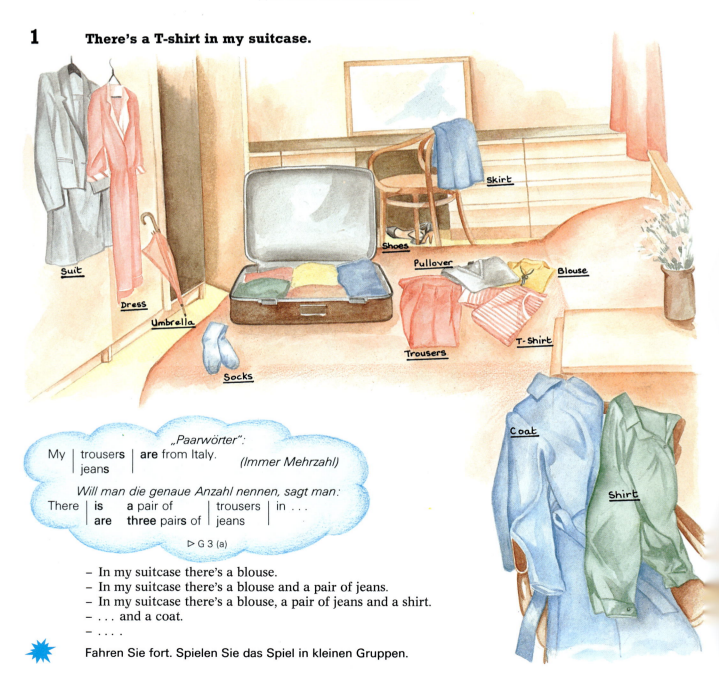

„Paarwörter":
My | trousers / jeans | **are** from Italy.   *(Immer Mehrzahl)*

Will man die genaue Anzahl nennen, sagt man:
There | is   a pair of | trousers | in ...
        | are   three pairs of | jeans

▷ G 3 (a)

– In my suitcase there's a blouse.
– In my suitcase there's a blouse and a pair of jeans.
– In my suitcase there's a blouse, a pair of jeans and a shirt.
– ... and a coat.
– ... .

Fahren Sie fort. Spielen Sie das Spiel in kleinen Gruppen.

Unit 3

2.1 That's a beautiful dress over there!

Hören Sie den beiden Personen auf der Cassette bei einem Schaufensterbummel zu. Finden Sie heraus, was *ihr* und was *ihm* gefällt! Kreuzen Sie die entsprechenden Dinge an.

	She likes	He likes
the dress		
the coat		
the pullover		
the blouse		

2.2 Yes, but it's very expensive.

Jetzt sind Sie und Ihr Partner vor dem gleichen Schaufenster; unterhalten sich über die Dinge, die Sie sehen.

– That's a beautiful	dress.	
That	blouse coat . . .	is	very nice. beautiful. smart.

| – Yes, it is.
Hm. | But it's quite expensive.
And it's not too expensive.
. . . . |

▷ AB1·CC

3.1 She's wearing a beautiful grey blouse . . .

Hören Sie sich die Aufnahme von einer Modenschau an und tragen Sie bei den Sachen, die das erste Modell trägt, in den entsprechenden Kästchen eine 1 ein, beim zweiten eine 2, und beim dritten eine 3.

	white	black	grey	red	green	blue	yellow	brown
blouse				1				
pullover								
skirt								
dress								
coat								
shoes								

3.2 ... by Laura Ashley!

This is Jenny. She's wearing a cotton blouse by Jil Sander, and a pair of jeans by Fiorucci.

And this is Oscar. He's wearing a pullover made of best Irish wool.

It's a beautiful blouse, and it's not very expensive.

It's a very smart pullover.

(1) Schreiben Sie Ihren Namen auf einen Zettel; die Zettel werden gemischt und neu verteilt. Schreiben Sie jetzt auf, was der/die Teilnehmer/in trägt, dessen/deren Namen Sie gezogen haben. Lesen Sie die Beschreibung vor; die Gruppe muß erraten, wer es ist: 'That's Inge.' – 'No, I think it's Karin.' . . .
(2) Bereiten Sie auch selbst eine „Modenschau" vor. Zwei oder drei Teilnehmer aus jeder Gruppe führen ihre eigene Kleidung vor, als wären es Modelle berühmter Modeschöpfer; ein oder zwei andere Teilnehmer kommentieren die Vorführung.

▷ CC

4.1 Where can we get jeans?

(1) Zwei Personen besprechen vor dem Übersichtsplan in einem Kaufhaus, was sie einkaufen wollen. Hören Sie sich die Aufnahme an und ergänzen Sie die folgende Einkaufsliste:

x T-shirt for Billy
x
x socks
x
x

SMALLWOOD'S

4th floor
Radio & TV Department
Records · Cassettes

3rd floor
Sports Wear
Children's Wear

2nd floor
Men's Wear

1st floor
Ladies' Wear

Ground floor
Books · Magazines
Newspapers · Souvenirs
Cameras · Films

(2) Hören Sie die Aufnahme noch einmal.
Auf welchen Etagen werden die beiden einkaufen?

– They do their shopping on the _____ floor,
the _____ floor,
and the _____ floor.

Besitzanzeigende Form

Einzahl	*Mehrzahl*
lady – the lady's dress	ladies – Ladies' Wear
man – the man's shoes	men* – Men's Shoes
child – the child's book	children* – Children's Wear

* Diese Mehrzahlformen sind unregelmäßig!

▷ G 3 (a, b)

Unit 3

4.2 Excuse me, I'm looking for picture postcards.

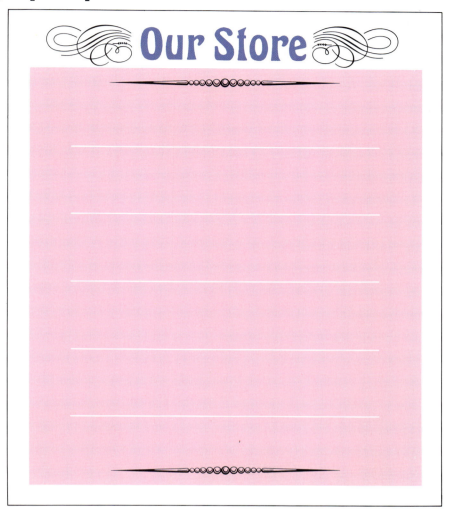

> You **can get** dresses …
> Beachten Sie die Wortfolge in Sätzen mit **can**:
> das Verb steht **nicht** wie im Deutschen am Ende des Satzes!
> ▷ G 6.2 (a); G 7 (a)

(1) Schreiben (oder zeichnen) Sie die Dinge ein, die man in Ihrem 'department store' kaufen kann. Oder rufen Sie Ihrem Kursleiter/Ihrer Kursleiterin zu, was er/sie an der Tafel einzeichnen/hineinschreiben soll:

> we – our
> you – your
> **you** heißt auch „man".
> ▷ G 1 (a, b)

(2) Ein/e Kursteilnehmer/in bekommt jetzt den selbsterstellten Übersichtsplan und „arbeitet" an der Information des Kaufhauses. Fragen Sie ihn/sie, wo es gibt, was Sie suchen.

> blous**es**
> dress**es**
>
> Beachten Sie die **Aussprache** bei Wörtern mit **s**-Laut am Ende. Beachten Sie auch die Schreibung!
> ▷ G 3 (a)

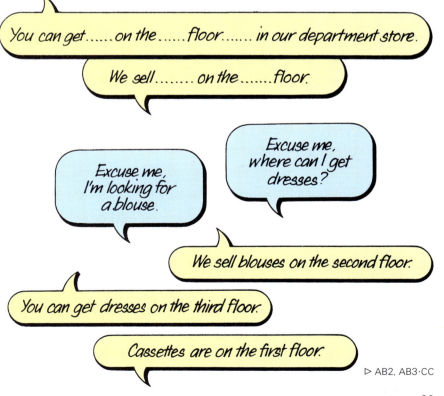

▷ AB2, AB3·CC

Unit 3

5.1 Can I help you?

– What size, please?
  – I'm not quite sure.
– 38?
  – No, that's too small. 40, or 42.

Listen, please.

What is Mrs Franklin looking for? _____ .

What is her size? _____ .

She cannot buy the first one because it's too _____ .

The second one is _____ .

5.2 What's your size?

I'm not quite sure. I think it's five and a half.

Ladies' Wear							
Germany	36	38	40	42	44	46	48	50
GB	8	10	12	14	16	18	20	22
USA	6	8	10	12	14	16	18	20
Men's Wear							
Germany	44	46	48	50	52	54	56	58
GB/USA	34	36	38	40	42	44	46	48

Shoes													
Germany	36		37		38		39		40		41		42	
GB	3	3½	4	4½	5	5½	6	6½	7	7½	8	8½	9	9½
USA	4½	5	5½	6	6½	7	7½	8	8½	9	9½	10	10½	11

5.3 I'm looking for a pair of jeans.

these/those bei Wörtern in der Mehrzahl:

jeans, trousers, socks, shoes, pullovers, . . .s

▷ G 1 (d)

– Can I help you?
  – Yes, please. I'm looking for a pair of jeans.
– What size, please?
  – I'm not quite sure. Twelve, I think.

– What about these?
  – Hm, well – those over there are nice. Can I try them on, please?
– Yes, certainly.

Unit 3

this/that (one) *bei Wörtern in der Einzahl:*

skirt, coat, pullover, . . .

▷ G 1 (d)

– I'm looking for a skirt.
 – What size, please?
– Ten.

– What about this one?
 It's very smart.
 – Oh, I like that one over there.
 Can I try it on, please?
– Yes, certainly.

– I'm afraid	they are	too	big/small.
	it's		long/short.
			not the right colour.

| – Yes, | they're all right. These, please. |
| | it's all right. This one, please. |

(1) Üben Sie diese Kaufgespräche ein.
(2) Zwei Kursteilnehmer/innen spielen als Pantomime eine kurze Verkaufsszene vor. Die anderen müssen erraten, was gekauft wurde; die Szene soll aber *nicht beschrieben* werden!
(3) Die Szene wird dann noch einmal „in Zeitlupe" vorgespielt, und die Zuschauer erfinden den Dialog dazu, legen also den beiden Spielenden „Worte in den Mund". Diese entscheiden, ob der vorgeschlagene Dialog in ihrem Sinne ist.

▷ AB4·CC

Unit 3

6.1 How much is it?

Listen, please.

1 How much is the umbrella? – It's £ _____ .
2 How much is a postcard to Germany? – It's _____ p.
3 How much are the picture postcards? – They are _____ p each.
4 How much is the map of London? – It's £ _____ .

6.2 It's two pounds fifty.

Denken Sie sich Preise aus; Ihr/e Nachbar/in fragt Sie dann danach.

▷ AB 5

6.3 Can you change a £ 50 note, please?

Listen, please.

*Das Hilfsverb **can** hat **immer** die gleiche Form, auch nach he/she/the man/Jim/...*

*In allen Sätzen mit **can** + Vollverb, also auch in Fragen, bleibt das Vollverb „mitten im Satz", vor den Ergänzungen.*

▷ G 7 (a, b, c)

1 The man ☐ can | change the note.
☐ cannot

2 The shop assistant ☐ can | change the note.
☐ cannot

▷ AB6

6.4 Souvenirs, souvenirs!

Unit 3

- I'm looking for a Snoopy T-shirt.
  - What about this one?
- Hm. Can I see another one, please?
  - Yes, certainly.
- Ah yes, that's nice. How much is it?
  - £ 4.99.
- Here you are.
  - Thank you. Here's your change.
- Thank you. Goodbye.

"Oops! Sorry, love – nearly gave you the right change!"

 Sehen Sie sich an, was Kunde (A) und Verkäufer (B) in solchen Situationen sagen könnten, und spielen Sie dann ähnliche Szenen mit Ihren Nachbarn.

- I'm looking for a | poster of London Bridge, please.
  I'd like a | picture postcard of Tower Bridge.
  | pen, please.
  | map of London, please.

Yes, that's nice.
Hm. Can I see another one, please?
I'd like this one/that one.

How much is it?

Oh, that's quite expensive.
Oh no, that's too expensive.
Thank you.

- Posters are over there.

What about this one?
Here's a nice . . . .

Here you are.

£ 5.50.

Thank you. Here's your change.

▷ CC

Unit 3

7 The flea market

(1) Erfinden Sie einen Dialog zwischen ein oder zwei Personen, die hier auf diesem Flohmarkt einkaufen wollen, und dem/den Verkäufer/n.

(2) Wenn Sie möchten, bauen Sie in den Ecken des Klassenzimmers Verkaufsstände auf. „Verkaufen" Sie dort die Mäntel/Jacken/Pullover/Schuhe der anderen Kursteilnehmer oder andere mitgebrachte Dinge (a poster, a vase, a picture of Queen Victoria, an umbrella, a map of Greenland, a pen, etc.). Wer Glück hat, findet seine eigenen Sachen wieder. Die Verkäufer müssen versuchen, die angebotenen Dinge auch anzupreisen und „wirklich" loszuwerden!

8 It's from Macy's.

Listen, please.

Carol's new	☐ blouse	is from Macy's.
	☐ dress	
	☐ coat	

Macy's is a	☐ boutique	in	☐ York.
	☐ supermarket		☐ London.
	☐ department store		☐ New York.

What was the problem?	The right	☐ price.
		☐ size.
		☐ colour.

9 LONDON – my favourite shops

You are shopping in London, and you would like to buy these things; where can you get them? Look at the shops on page 39.

You can get __A__ in shop number ....

38 thirty-eight

LONDON – my favourite shops

The "shop" in London, of course, is Harrods – one of the world's best and biggest department stores. But there are a number of small shops where shopping can be even more interesting, and more personal. These are some of my favourites:

1 **The Reject China Shop**, 33–35 Beauchamp Place, London SW3, nearest Underground Knightsbridge. Big selection of fine English china and porcelain. Not all in perfect condition, but good quality at mini-prices.

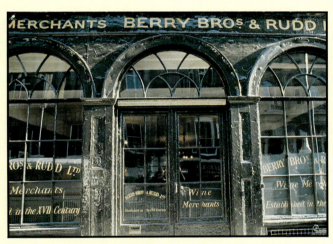

2 **Berry Bros. & Rudd**, 3 St. James's Street, London SW1, nearest Underground Green Park, closed Saturdays. Fine old wine shop, famous for Port and Bordeaux. A very good selection of cognacs.

3 **Charbonnel et Walker**, 31 Old Bond Street, London W1, nearest Underground Piccadilly Circus. Home-made sweets and chocolates. The Queen Mother's favourite shop.

4 **Loon Fung**, 39 Gerrard Street, London W1, nearest Underground Leicester Square. Best Chinese supermarket in the centre of London's China Town.

5 **Paxton & Whitfield**, 93 Jermyn Street, London SW1, nearest Underground Piccadilly Circus. Famous for English cheese, especially Stilton and Cheddar.

6 **J. D. Shah & Co.**, 161 Drummond Street, London NW1, nearest Underground Euston Square. Indian spices and foods, probably the best selection in Europe. Ideal for those who like mixing their own curries.

Unit 4

Time and date

Wie man nach der Zeit fragt und Zeitangaben macht

Wie man das Datum sagt und schreibt:

Wochentage – Monatsnamen

Wie man einen Vorschlag macht, und wie man Vorschläge annimmt oder ablehnt

Wie man fragt und sagt, ob etwas vorhanden ist

 It's six o'clock.

Hören Sie sich die folgenden Rundfunkansagen an und tragen Sie in den Uhren 4 bis 10 die Zeit ein, die angesagt wird.

> 8:30 = 'half **past eight**'
> *oder*
> 'eight – thirty'.

1.2 Have you got the time, please?

Listen, please.
What is the answer?

1 – It's almost _____ o'clock.
2 – It's half past _____ .
3 – It's _____ .

1.3 What's the time, please?

Now ask your neighbour.

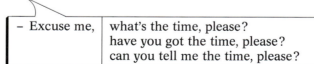

– Excuse me, | what's the time, please?
have you got the time, please?
can you tell me the time, please?

– It's five o'clock.
It's almost six o'clock.
. . . .

▷ CC

40 forty

Unit 4

1.4 When is the museum open?

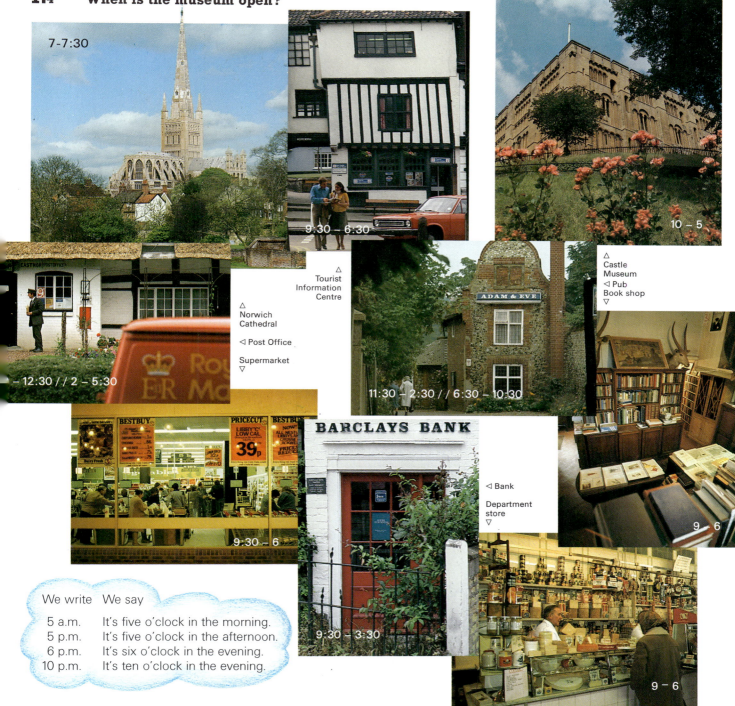

We write	We say
5 a.m.	It's five o'clock in the morning.
5 p.m.	It's five o'clock in the afternoon.
6 p.m.	It's six o'clock in the evening.
10 p.m.	It's ten o'clock in the evening.

Sie machen Ferien in Norwich.
Um Ihren Tag planen zu können,
fragen Sie Ihren englischen Be-
kannten/Ihren Nachbarn:

▷ AB1·CC

– When's the cathedral open?
  What time are the pubs open?
  Is the post office still open after five o'clock?
  Are the pubs still open at midnight?

– It's open from ... to ....
  They're open from ... in the morning
     till ... in the evening.
  No, it isn't.
  No, they aren't. They're open till ....

forty-one 41

Unit 4

2.1 It's a quarter past eight.

It's . . .

five to four
eight minutes to four
(a) quarter to four
twenty-five to four

five past four
eight minutes past four
(a) quarter past four
half past four

So sagt man im Gespräch die Uhrzeit. Bei „ungeraden Zeiten" (= solchen, die nicht durch 5 teilbar sind) fügt man meist 'minutes' hinzu.

Listen, please.

What's the time?

1	☐	5.04	☐	4.50	☐	4.05
2	☐	10.03	☐	9.57	☐	3.10
3	☐	8.45	☐	9.45	☐	9.15
4	☐	8.15	☐	8.50	☐	9.10
5	☐	6.38	☐	6.28	☐	7.22

2.2 What time is it, please?

– What time is it, please?
  – It's twenty past nine.
– Twenty past nine?! Oh, I really have to go now. My bus leaves at twenty to ten.

| – What time | is your | bus | home after night school? |
| When | | train | to work in the morning? |

– It's at . . . .
I go to work by car.
I walk home/to work.

▷ AB2·CC

Unit 4

2.3 When's the next train to Norwich?

Listen, please.

Zeitangaben:
6.05/6:05 = (the) six oh five
(train to London)
DEP 18 00 = departure
at six (o'clock)
ARR 20 30 = arrival
at eight thirty
(in the evening)

It's at ☐ 5.30
☐ 5.25
☐ 5.13

2.4 Is there a train to Norwich in the afternoon?

– Is there a train to ... in the morning/...?
What time are the trains to ...?

– Yes, there's one at ....
There's one at ..., and ....

LONDON — IPSWICH, NORWICH												SO	SX	SX	SO	SX		SX	SO	SX					SX	SO		
											1530	1550	1620	1630	1650	1730	1810	1830	1840	1930	2030	2150	2300	2300			
Mondays to Saturdays											1545	1650	1710	1743	1745	1801	1850	1935	1950	2004	2050	2153	2315	0051	0037		
London Liverpool Street	0715	0830	0930	1030	1130	1230	1330	1430	1530															0201	0137		
Ipswich	0845	0952	1050	1145	1250	1345	1450	1545	1650	1710	1743	1745	1801	1850	1935	1950	2004	2050	2153	2315							
Norwich	0941	1047	1137	1256	1352	1456	1552	1656	1737	1757	1840	1841	1848	1949	2031	2045	2101	2145	2252	—	0201	0137					
														Sundays										1815	1853	1933	—
														Norwich	0724	0927	1017	1217	1417	1527	1625	1730	1815	1853	1933	—
														Ipswich	0825	1025	1122	1322	1522	1625	1731	1824	1915	1944	2024	2200
Sundays		0830	0930	1030	1230	1430	1630	1730	1830	1930	2030	2230		London L'pool St.	1005	1205	1305	1505	1705	1758	1858	1946	2044	2112	2145	2354
London Liverpool Street																											
Ipswich		1014	1107	1211	1411	1611	1759	1855	1959	2052	2159	0001														
Norwich		1118	1203	1315	1515	1715	1858	1945	2058	2142	2258	0100														

LONDON — CAMBRIDGE, ELY, KING'S LYNN																			SX	SO	SX	SO	SX	SO	SX			SX	SX
				SX	SO	SX	SX	SO											1535	1535			1604	1625	1635	1655			
Mondays to Saturdays					0835	0835			0935		1035		1135		1235		1335		1435	1504	1504			1748	1742	1814			
London Liverpool Street				SX	0835							1104		1204		1304		1404	1404	1542	1622	1628	1659	1640	1725	1748	1812	1800		
London King's Cross	0640	0710	0740	0804			0904		1004	1026	1040	1120	1142	1226	1240	1320	1342	1426	1440	1520	1600	1646		1732	1732		1842			
Cambridge	0814	0845	0910	0922	0943	0940	1026	1040	1120	1142	1226	1240	1320	1342	1426	1440	1450	1532	1551	1640										
Ely	0845	0909			1001	1010		1200					1400				1440													
King's Lynn					1041	1050		1240					1440																	

			SX	SX	SO	SX	SO	SX	SX						SX	SO													
Mondays to Saturdays			1715	1735	1735			1805	1835		1935		2035	2035		2205	2335													
London Liverpool Street						1745	1804	1804			1904		2004		2104		2210	0054												
London King's Cross	1703	1741	1845	1852		1915	1922	1931	1930	1951	2029	2052	2124	2142	2152	2228	2329	2348												
Cambridge	1828	1841	1925	1930					1949	2009		2127		2210	2220															
Ely										2049				2250	2300															
King's Lynn																														

Sundays				0935		1035		1235		1435		1635		1735		1835		1935		2035		2135		2305
London Liverpool Street	0700	0806	0906		1006		1106	1206	1306	1406		1506	1606		1706		1806	1906		2006	2106	2155	2246	2256	2346	0017
London King's Cross	0846	0946	1046	1055	1146	1200	1246	1346	1355	1446	1546	1604	1646	1746	1755	1846	1855	1946	2000	2046	2055	2146	2217			
Cambridge	0927			1127					1432			1611			1819		1927		2018				2257			
Ely				1212		1359			1510			1704			1857				2058							
King's Lynn																										

SX Saturdays excepted   SO Saturdays only

▷ AB3·CC

Unit 4

3 Plan a weekend in Norwich.

– On Saturday morning In the afternoon After that	we	could can	go to .... go on a boat trip. ....
Let's	go to ...	in the afternoon.	
Shall we	...	on Sunday evening? ... ?	

The days of the week:

Monday
Tuesday
Wednesday
Thursday
Friday
Saturday
Sunday

could (= könnte) folgt in Form und Satzbau den gleichen Regeln wie **can**.
▷ G 6.2 (a); G 7 (a, b, c)

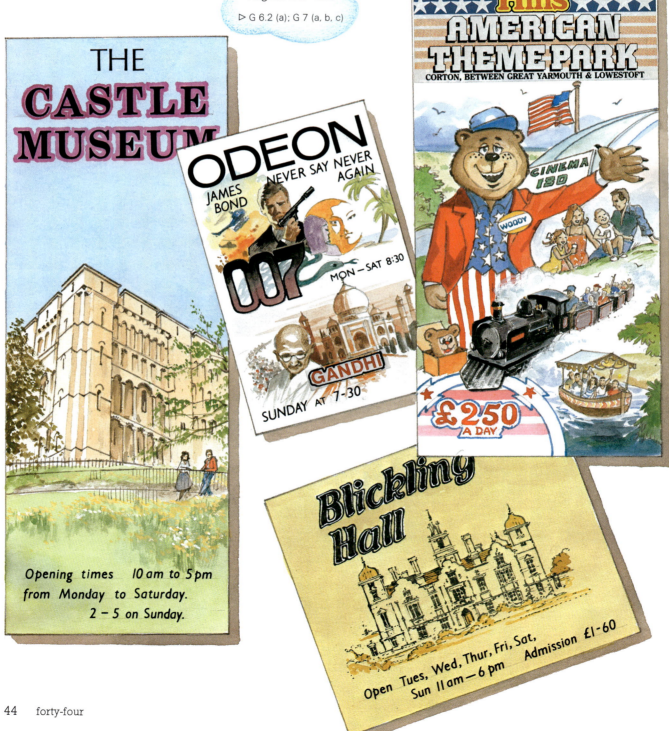

THE CASTLE MUSEUM

Opening times 10 am to 5 pm from Monday to Saturday. 2 – 5 on Sunday.

ODEON
JAMES BOND NEVER SAY NEVER AGAIN
007
MON – SAT 8:30
GANDHI
SUNDAY AT 7-30

Pleasurewood Hills
Open Daily from 10am
AMERICAN THEME PARK
CORTON, BETWEEN GREAT YARMOUTH & LOWESTOFT
£2.50 A DAY

Blickling Hall
Open Tues, Wed, Thur, Fri, Sat, Sun 11am – 6 pm   Admission £1-60

Unit 4

- Yes, that's a good idea.
   Well, I'm not really interested in . . . .
      Could we . . . instead?
   Oh, no, let's . . . instead.

(1) Schreiben Sie Ihren drei Nachbarn je ein Briefchen, in dem Sie einen Vorschlag machen, was Sie wann mit ihnen unternehmen wollen:

Dear Karin, Shall we go to ... on Sunday mor... Yours, Alf

Dear Tom, Let's go to the Cinema on Saturday evening Yours, Elke

(2) Stellen Sie aus den Vorschlägen, die *Sie* erhalten, Ihr Wochenende zusammen:

SAT	
morning	Blickling Hall/Jenny
afternoon	Castle Museum/Fred
evening	cinema/Chris

(3) Berichten Sie dann dem Kurs:
'On Saturday morning I'm going to . . . with . . . .'

(4) Arbeiten Sie jetzt in Gruppen und diskutieren Sie einen gemeinsamen Plan für das Wochenende.

▷ AB4·CC

Unit 4

4.1 When's your birthday?

The names of the months:

January	July
February	August
March	September
April	October
May	November
June	December

Hören Sie sich die Aufnahme an, und kreuzen Sie die Geburtstage im Kalender an.

6th	the sixth	20th	the twentieth
7th	the seventh	21st	the twenty-first
8th	the eighth	22nd	the twenty-second
9th	the ninth	23rd	the twenty-third
10th	the tenth	24th	the twenty-fourth
11th	the eleventh	25th	the twenty-fifth
12th	the twelfth	...	
13th	the thirteenth	...	
14th	the fourteenth	31st	the thirty-first

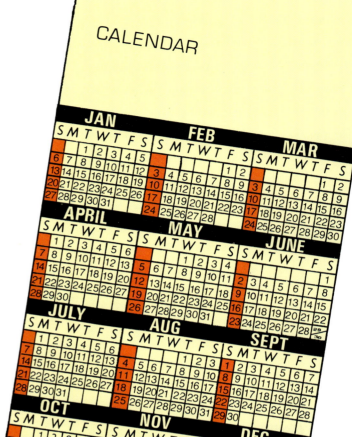

4.2 It's on the twenty-first of June.

Write down when your husband's/wife's/friend's birthday is (but be careful that your neighbour cannot see it). Then your neighbour has to find out when it is:

- Is it in January?
- No, it isn't.
- Is it in June?
- Yes, it is.
- Is it on a Monday?
- No, it isn't.
- Is it on a Friday?
- Yes, it is.
- Is it the twenty-first of June?
- Yes, it is.

▷ AB5·CC

We write	We say
5th April 1986	The fifth of April, nineteen eighty-six.
5 April 1986	April the fifth, ...
(US:) April 5, 1986

Now your neighbour can go on. When is his/her friend's/son's/daughter's/. . .'s birthday?

46 forty-six

Unit 4

5.1 Birthday presents

Listen, please.

> Bei Sätzen mit **have got** (= haben) gleicher Satzbau wie bei solchen mit **can + Verb**: **got** (= das Verb) bleibt immer „mitten im Satz", **vor** der Ergänzung.
>
> ▷ G 7 (a, b, c)

for	me
	you
	him/her
	us
	them

▷ G 1 (a)

What has she got for him?

– It's Jack's birthday on Saturday.
  – Have you got a nice present for him?
– Oh, yes, I have.
  – What have you got?
– I've got _____ for him.

Whose birthday is it next week?

– It's _____ next week, isn't it?
  – Yes, it is.
– What present have you got for her?
– Nothing yet, I'm afraid.

5.2 Has she already got a present for him?

Talk to your neighbour about his wife's/her husband's/his or her children's birthdays/his or her friend's birthday:

When is it? Has he/she already got a present for her/him/them? And what about his or her own birthday? What have they got for her or him?

- a book
- a record
- a camera
- a cassette recorder
- some flowers
- a pair of socks

> We write **He** / **She** has got . . . .
>
> We say **He's** / **She's** got . . . .
>
> ▷ G 6.1 (b)

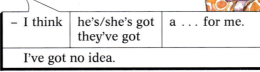

Is that a present for me?

– I think	he's/she's got they've got	a ... for me.
I've got no idea.		

▷ AB6 a+b, AB7, AB8·CC

5.3 Have you got the key?

Die Spielregeln für „Quartett" kennen Sie sicher; Ihr/e Kursleiter/in hat Spielkarten für Sie.

Have you got the 'film'?

Yes, I have. Here you are.

No, I haven't, but have you got the '............' for me?

6 Flexitime

YOU & US

This is the page for YOUR letters to us

Dear Marge,

Flexitime is wonderful! I have to be in the office from 10 to 12, and from 1 to 3, but for the rest of the day, I can come and go when I like. So I have got more time for the shopping in the morning or in the early afternoon, and I have got more time for the children when they come home from school. I love flexitime!

Yours,
Betty M.
(London SE 8)

Dear Marge,

Flexitime is not a good idea for our firm. I often have to talk to my colleagues before I can start work, but they are never there! The other girls in our office never start work before 10. So, who answers the phone for them? Who has to do all the urgent things early in the morning? I do! Because I start work at 8.30 so that I can be back home when the children come back from school.

Yours,
Frustrated,
Pangbourne

FLEXITIME

Today, most office workers in Britain work 37 or 40 hours a week, from Monday to Friday, and many of them can start and finish work when they want – they work "flexitime", they have got flexible working hours.

What are the pros and cons of "flexitime"? This is what our readers say:

Dear Marge,

There is one bad thing about flexitime – you have to get up early! If you get up late, the work in the office never ends . . .
After a late night at the disco, if you start work at 10 . . . it's murder!

Yours,
Penny R.,
Brighton

Dear Marge,

I think that flexitime is a really good idea. I like to finish work so early that I can do the shopping and make dinner before Jack comes home. I start work at 8 or 8.30 in the morning, so I can leave the office at 3 or 3.30, and sometimes I can take an afternoon off, too, I think it is a wonderful system!

Yours,
Brenda L.,
Sussex.

Dear Marge,

Flexitime? No, thank you, not for me! Try to phone an office in the morning before 10, or at 12.30, or after 3! There is only a 50:50 chance that there is someone there to answer the phone. In Japan, people still work 10 or 12 hours a day, but in England our effective working time is down to 4 hours "core time" – and this is really tea time and talking about last night's TV in most offices, I'm afraid.

Yours,
Chris C.D.,
Potter's Bar

---

(1)

	is for flexitime,	is against flexitime,
Betty M.		
Penny R.		
'Frustrated'		
Brenda L.		
Chris C.D.		

(2)

	Betty M.	Penny R.	'Frustrated'	Brenda L.	Chris C.D.
. . . because he/she can go shopping in the early afternoon.					
. . . because he/she has got more time for his wife/her husband.					
. . . because he/she has got more time for the children in the afternoon.					
. . . because he/she has to do extra work for his/her colleagues.					
. . . because he/she cannot speak to people in other firms when he/she wants to.					

Unit 4

 7 What's on?

Hören Sie sich die folgende Programmvorschau an und ergänzen Sie rechts die fehlenden Zeiten.

8 Can you listen to a story?

Wenn Sie einem Text eine Information entnehmen wollen, brauchen Sie ihn oft nur zu überfliegen.

Versuchen Sie, so schnell wie möglich aus dem vollständigen Programm für Nachmittag und Abend Antworten auf folgende Fragen zu finden:

(1) How many music programmes can you listen to?

Music: _____

(2) You are in your hotel room from 1 to 3, and from 6 to 8;

	Yes	No
• can you listen to a story?	☐	☐
• is there a programme with pop or jazz?	☐	☐
• is there an interview?	☐	☐

WEDNESDAY Radio

Jerry Mike Channel's having 'fun' when fellow Radio Active 'jocks' Mike Stand, Nigel Pry, Mike Flex and Anna Daptor 'drop in' on his morning show – tonight at 30 minutes after the big hour

1.0 The World at One: News
Presenter Sir Robin Day

1.40 The Archers

2.0 Woman's Hour
with Sue McGregor
Guest of the Week:
actress Vanessa Redgrave

3.0 Afternoon Theatre
Snapshots by JO GILL

3.47 Time for Verse

4.0 Piano Portrait
PATRICIA CARROLL plays Victorian music

4.40 Story Time
Tulku (4)
Adventures during the Boxer rebellion

5.0 PM News
with Susannah Simons and Peter Ruff

6.0 The Six O'Clock News
with BRYAN MARTIN including **Financial Report**

Stereo
Music from America
BBC PHILHARMONIC ORCHESTRA conducted by GUNTHER SCHULLER

Letter from America
by Alistair Cooke

8.0 News

8.10 *Stereo*
Jazz Today
The best of present-day jazz on records presented by CHARLES FOX

Series
Checkpoint
A weekly series about listeners' problems by Roger Cook

9.0 *Stereo*
Vienna Philharmonic Orchestra
conducted by EUGEN JOCHUM
Bruckner Symphony No 7 in E (given in March 1982 in the Royal Festival Hall, a BBC digital recording)

10.0 The World Today: News
John Morgan reporting

Stereo
Radio Active
Music and entertainment

A Book at Bedtime
Anne of Geierstein (14) by Sir Walter Scott

Today in Parliament

12.0 News and Weather

Unit 5

Invitations

Wie man jemanden einlädt

Wie man eine Einladung dankend annimmt
oder mit Bedauern ablehnt

Wie man eine Ablehnung begründet
oder eine Entschuldigung vorbringt

Wie man Interesse bekundet

Wie man sagt, was man gerade eben oder in naher Zukunft tut

Wie man sich verabschiedet

1.1 Would you like to come over for a drink?

Listen, please.

What is the first, second, third,
fourth invitation?
Fill in the right number.

50 fifty

Unit 5

1.2 What are you doing on Saturday?

– Hello, Andrea. What are you doing on Saturday?
– Well, nothing, really.
– Would you like to come and have dinner with us?
– Yes, thank you. I'd love to. What time?
– Eight o'clock.
– Yes, that's fine. See you then. Oh, there's my bus. Bye.
– Bye. See you on Saturday!

Plan what you want to do, and when.
Then 'phone' 5 or 6 other students and invite them.

When?	Your invitation:			
• this evening • tonight • on Sunday/Monday/... • tomorrow • at the weekend	• come	over for a drink and meet some friends to my birthday party ...	• go to	the cinema with me a concert with us a pub with Jack and me Peter's/...'s party with me ...

▷ AB1·CC

2.1 Why can't they come?

Listen, please.
Then fill in what they say.

*Wenn etwas **gerade im Augenblick** oder **in naher Zukunft** geschieht, drückt man durch die Verlaufsform aus, gebildet aus **am/are/is** und der Grundform des Verbs, an die man **ing** anhängt:*
I **am** work**ing** tonight.
What **are** you do**ing** ...?

▷ G 6.3 (d)

Betty   – I'm helping _____ _____ _____ homework.
Raymond – I'm _____ tonight.
Sandra   – I'm just leaving for _____ _____ .
Kate   – I'm having _____ _____ _____ _____ .

2.2 I'm sorry, but I'm painting the bathroom.

Schreibregeln:
1 *Stummes **e** am Ende der Grundform entfällt:*
   leav**e** – I'm leaving
2 *Mitlaute (**t, n,** etc.) werden nach einem kurzen, betonten Selbstlaut verdoppelt:*
   ge**t** – ge**tt**ing
   pla**n** – pla**nn**ing

▷ G 6.3 (d)

Now invite your neighbour; why can't he/she come?

– Hello, Jennifer.
  We're having a party.
  Would you like to come over?
– I'm sorry, but I'm washing the car.
– Oh, that's a pity.

• watch an interesting film on TV
• play with the children
• drink a glass of wine with ...
• ...

▷ AB 2 · CC

Unit 5

2.3 How many guests can you invite to your party?

A

You want to have a party on Saturday/Sunday/... at ... o'clock.

Ask the other students if they can come.

If an answer is 'Yes', you can say:

'Oh, good.'/'Fine.'
'I'm glad you can come.'

If an answer is 'No', you can say:

'Oh, that's a pity.'
'Well, never mind.'

('Goodbye.')

Ask as many people as you can.

B

Your friend wants to invite you to his/her party.

If you want to go, you can say:

'Yes, thank you, I'd love to come.'
'Thank you for the invitation.'

If you can't go, tell him/her why not:

'I'm sorry, but .... '
- meet a friend
- go to a concert with ...
- go on holiday ...
- work late on ...
- ...
- already go to Inge's party

('Goodbye.')

Now tell the class how many guests are coming to your party. Who is coming?

2.4 We're having a party.

Some invitations are very pleasant, and it is a pity if you have to say 'no':

– Hello, Harry. What are you doing at the moment?
– I'm just leaving for night school.
– Oh, we're having a party. It's a pity you can't come over.

- watch an interesting video
- sit in the garden with a bottle of wine
  ⇨ come over
- go to the theatre/the cinema/a concert and we've got one extra ticket.
  ⇨ come along

But sometimes people phone you because they need you:

– Hello, Jo. What are you doing tonight?
– Oh, nothing, really.
– Oh, good. Could you perhaps come over for an hour or two and look after the baby?

- help me in the garden/ with the car/...
- play tennis with Amanda instead of me
- help me with my English homework
- take me to the station/ the airport
- ...

▷ AB 3 · CC

Unit 5

2.5 I'd love to, but I can't.

(1) Schreiben Sie 5 bis 6 Dinge auf, zu denen Sie Ihre/n Partner/in einladen wollen, oder die er/sie für Sie tun soll.
(2) Verraten Sie es aber nicht vorher, sondern „rufen Sie ihn/sie an" und fragen, was er/sie gerade tut.
Er/Sie ist entweder vorsichtig (und will nicht schon wieder Ihr Baby hüten!) und sagt, womit er/sie beschäftigt ist; vielleicht erwartet er/sie aber auch eine nette Einladung und sagt, daß er/sie nichts Besonderes tut.

– Hi, Mary. What are you doing at the moment?
– I'm washing my hair. Why?
– Oh, that's a pity.
So you can't look after the baby for an hour or two?
– No, I'm sorry, I'd love to, but I can't.
– Well, never mind. See you at the office tomorrow, then. Bye.
– Bye. See you tomorrow.

▷ AB4

3.1 What's Jack doing?

(1) Say hello to your neighbours and ask them where Dick/Harry/Liz/... is and what he/she is doing.

– Hello, Nancy. Hello, Dick.
– Hello, Samantha. Thanks for the invitation. Where's Jack?
– He's talking to our neighbour.

I am	reading
you are	
he/she/it is	
we/they are	

Welche Form von **be** *gewählt wird, richtet sich danach, über wen gesprochen wird.*

▷ G 6.3 (d)

Fragen bildet man durch Umstellung von **is/are/am**:

She is reading.
→ Is she reading?

Peter is reading a book.
→ What is Peter doing?

▷ G 7 (c)

– Is he/she reading a book?
Well, what *is* he/she doing then?

– No, he/she isn't.
Yes, I think he/she is.
Oh, I think he/she's ...ing ....

- wash the car
- play with the children
- paint a picture
- learn to use his/her home computer
- write a letter
- read a book
- listen to a record
- phone a friend
- watch TV
- ...

(2) Tell your neighbour the names of three persons (your husband/wife/friend/children/...); your neighbour has to find out what they are doing at the moment:

▷ AB5, AB6, AB7·CC

3.2 Pictures from a summer course

Ron and Sheila like going on 'hobby holidays' where they can learn something new, or where they have got time for their hobbies.
Here Sheila is talking to friends about their pictures from a summer course at a college in the United States.

(1) Fill in the verb.

– This is our College. Here we . . . (sit) in front of the main building.

– This is Ron's Creative Writing group. Can you see Ron? He . . . (write) a story for children.

– And this is his course in Modern American Literature. They . . . (read) Micky Mouse comics!

– And here I am in my Painting Workshop. I . . . (paint) a picture of my teacher's wife.

– And this is Charles. He's an engineer from Kansas. Here he . . . (play) the piano.

– Oh – and here I . . . (learn) to use a home computer.

– And this is Jim. He's a teacher from Ohio. He was in my Photography Workshop. Here he . . . (take) a picture of me, while I . . . (take) a picture of him.

(2) Now Ron is talking about the pictures!
('. . . This is my Creative Writing Group. Can you see me? I . . . .')

(3) Bring along some pictures of your own holidays next week!

Unit 5

54 fifty-four

Unit 5

4 A summer course for you?

A lot of American colleges offer summer courses for people who do not just want to spend their holidays on the beach. Here are some of the typical courses at an American summer school.

Southampton College

(72102) ART 235
(72103) ART 335
(72154) ART 535
Lab Fee $40.00
Connie Evans
Monday – Friday
July 12 – July 30
9.00 a.m. – 12.20 p.m.

This course helps students to develop a personal style: still life, portraits, people and landscapes with oils and acrylics. Demonstrations of different techniques and critiques.

(72106) ART 271
(72154) ART 571
Lab Fee $40.00
Staff
Monday – Friday
July 12 – July 30
9.00 a.m. – 12.20 p.m.

This course teaches beginning students technical and creative use of the camera, film development and printing. Students must have a 35 mm camera.

(72302) MUS 171
Lab Fee $20.00
Colonius Davis
Monday – Friday
July 12 – July 30
1.00 p.m. – 4.20 p.m.

Group and individual lessons at beginning level.

(72303) MUS 245
(72351) MUS 545
Judith Alstader
August 1 – August 15

This music workshop, under the direction of Judith Alstader with the artists of the Minnewaska Music Society, offers an intensive program of chamber music and singing, chorus, orchestra, master classes, seminars and concerts. Professionals, pre-professionals, college music students and amateur instrumentalists and singers are all welcome. For further information, please call 516-282-4000 for special brochure.

(63403) ENG 240
R.B. Weber
Monday – Thursday
1.00 p.m. – 3.15 p.m.

A study of the literature of Science Fiction from 19th century writers such as Poe and Jules Verne to 20th century writers, like George Orwell, and to moderns such as Isaac Asimov, Ray Bradbury, and Kurt Vonnegut.

(64802) SOC 111
Joseph Sacco
Monday and Wednesday
6.00 p.m. – to 9.50 p.m.

The nature and origin of conflicts with the value system of our society: alcoholism, family problems, social and psychological pressures of society, discrimination, crime and young people.

(NSSR-AS104A)
David Levine
Monday, July 18 to
Wednesday, July 28
2.00 p.m. – 4.00 p.m.

An introduction for the beginner into the world of personal computers. Students learn enough BASIC to operate computers and solve problems. Some hands-on work in class.

(1) Ordnen Sie die Kurstitel den Kursbeschreibungen zu!

PIANO WORKSHOP

SOCIAL PROBLEMS

PAINTING WORKSHOP

SCIENCE FICTION

PHOTOGRAPHY: BLACK AND WHITE

INTRODUCTION TO MICROCOMPUTERS

CHAMBER MUSIC WORKSHOP

(2) Finden die folgenden Personen einen für sie geeigneten Kurs?

a Peter sucht einen Kurs in technischem Zeichnen.
b Jean fotografiert gut, möchte aber kreativer mit Farbe umgehen können.
c Dorothy spielt seit ein paar Monaten Klavier und möchte intensiv üben.
d Charles hat einen kleinen Computer gekauft und sucht eine Einführung in das Programmieren.
e Amanda interessiert sich für Zukunftsromane.
f Thomas will in den Ferien etwas über soziale Probleme der 3. Welt und über Entwicklungshilfe lernen.

fifty-five 55

Stop over 1

S 1 Can you stop me?

S 2 A town walk

Can you write a 'town walk' for your town or village?
Work in groups.

S 3 Who is it?

Talk about another student:
What is he or she wearing?
The others have to find out who you are talking about.

Stop over 1

S 4 How to get there – or not!

Can you write down what these people say?

Nach einer Idee von Viktor Augustin und Klaus Haase: <u>Blasengeschichten</u> Deutsch als Fremdsprache. PAS/DVV: Bonn/Frankfurt 1980, 2. Aufl. (Bildgeschichte 10)

S 5 What are they doing?

Are you a good actor?
Here are some things you can 'do' – and the others have to find out *what* you are doing!

say goodbye to (your husband/... ?)

buy/sell (what?)

have dinner (with a friend/with your boss?/... ?)

phone (who?)

read/write (what?)

take a picture (of what? or of a friend?)

try on (what?)

listen to (a record?/jazz music?/... ?)

play (the piano?/with the children?/Skat?/... ?)

talk to (a neighbour/your teacher?/... ?)

work (in the garden?/in the office?/... ?)

drink (what? where? with Peter/... ?)

paint (what?)

meet (a friend?/your wife?/... ?)

look for (what?)

sit (where?)

watch (TV?/a film?)

fifty-seven 57

Unit 6

Every day...

Wie man sagt, was man täglich oder regelmäßig tut
Wie man Fragen nach dem Alltag
oder nach den Gewohnheiten von Menschen stellt
Wie man sagt, was man mag oder nicht mag
Wie man Bedauern und Mitgefühl ausdrückt
oder daß man sich mit jemandem freut

1.1 A usual morning for an unusual person

Listen, please.

(1) What does he do first, and what is the last thing he does in the morning?
Fill in 1, 2, 3 etc.
(2) What is his job?
(You can answer in German.)

1.2 What is the first thing you do in the morning?

- have breakfast (a)
- listen to some music/the news (b)
- make a cup of tea (c)
- go for a run (d)
- have a shower (e)
- go to the bathroom (f)
- ...

| – I | always
usually
often
sometimes | go for a run.
.... |

*Diese Form, die einfache Gegenwart, zeigt, daß etwas **regelmäßig, immer wieder** geschieht.*
▷ G 6.3 (a)

*Die Wörter **always usually, often** und **sometimes** stehen **direkt vor dem Verb**.*
▷ G 5 (a)

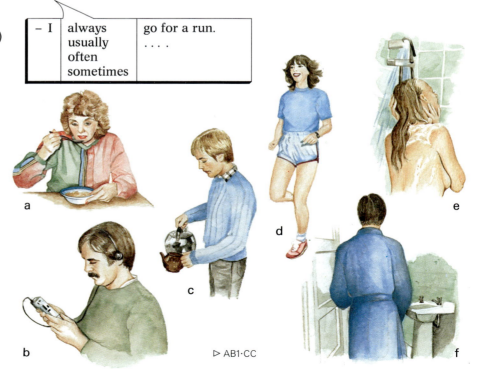

▷ AB1·CC

Unit 6

1.3 Day in, day out

What Helen does every day.

- She gets up at seven.
- She . . . (have) breakfast with the family.
- She . . . (drive) to town.
- She . . . (work) at a computer.
- She does the shopping.
- She . . . (play) with the children.
- She . . . (learn) German at night school.
- She watches TV with her husband.

(1) Tell the class about your day.
(2) Tell them about your partner's day, or a friend's/neighbour's day.

> Wenn das Verb sich auf **he/she/it**, einen Namen oder auf ein Wort in der Einzahl (**my teacher/ the man/. . .**) bezieht, wird ein **s** angefügt.
>
> Schreibregeln
>
> G 6.3 (a)

(3) Schreiben Sie jetzt eine Kurzfassung Ihres Tagesablaufs auf einen Zettel. Die Zettel werden gemischt und neu verteilt. Lesen Sie den Tagesablauf des Teilnehmers vor, den Sie gezogen haben.
Die Gruppe rät, um wen es sich handelt.

1 – I usually get up at . . . .
   In the afternoon I go . . . .
   . . . .

2 – He/She always gets up at . . . .
   In the evening he/she goes . . . .
   . . . .

▷ AB2·CC

fifty-nine 59

Unit 6

1.4 A day in the life of . . .

In British magazines you can often read about a day in the life of typical or interesting people.

(1) Can you write about the day of one or two of these people? You can use
- in the morning/afternoon/. . . ,
- first/then/after that,
- always/. . . ,

to make your story interesting.

● taxi driver

● night school teacher

● milkman

● shop assistant in a duty-free shop at Gatwick airport

● doctor in a hospital

(2) Now tell the other students about your person's day; they have to find out who it is.

– He / She	gets up at . . . . goes to work/starts work at . . . . works till . . . . gets home at . . ./goes to bed at . . . . does the shopping/meets friends/plays with the children/ sees the family/watches TV/goes out/. . . .

Unit 6

1.5 What do you and your friend do in the evening?

1
| – What do you and your | friend
wife
husband | usually do in the evening? |

| – We | usually
often | go to a pub/the cinema/. . . .
read a book.
drink . . . .
go and see friends.
. . . . |

2

And what's your........ doing at the moment?

I think .... sleeping now.

And why do you think so?

Because........ always sleeps when I'm here.

▷ AB3·CC

2.1 Do you like working with people?

Holiday and work at Neptune's

	Yes	No
Have you got a friendly, open personality?	☐	☐
Are you good at sports?	☐	☐
Can you drive a car?	☐	☐
Can you play tennis?	☐	☐
Do you speak foreign languages?	☐	☐
Do you like working with people?	☐	☐
Do you want to work where other people go on holiday?	☐	☐

If all your answers are 'yes', and you are between 21 and 30, you are the person we are looking for!

Please phone Henry at **NEPTUNE HOLIDAY CLUB** – 01-467 2121.

Am Anfang einer Ja/Nein-Frage steht immer ein Hilfsverb:
Can you drive a car?

Der Aussagesatz, mit dem diese Frage „verwandt" ist –
I **can drive** a car –
enthält auch schon dieses Hilfsverb.

*Wenn ein solcher Aussagesatz **kein Hilfsverb** enthält –*
I speak foreign languages –
so muß man die Frage mit **do** *beginnen:*
Do you **speak** foreign languages?

▷ G 7 (c)

Yes, I have.
No, I haven't.
Yes, I am.
No, I'm not.
Yes, I can.
No, I can't.
Yes, I do.
No, I don't.

Answer the questions.
Are you a good 'animateur'?
Is this a job for you?

▷ AB4, AB5

Unit 6

2.2 Do you like music?

(1) Find out what your neighbour likes.

- pop music/jazz/classical music
- going to the cinema/the theatre
- Jane Fonda/Dustin Hoffman/...
- going for long walks
- doing sports
- fast cars
- flowers/roses/...
- animals
- children
- the colour red/blue/...
- reading books
- working in the garden
- ...

*In Antworten auf Ja/Nein-Fragen greift man das **Hilfs**verb der Frage wieder auf, hier also: **do**.*
▷ G 7 (c)

(2) Now tell the group about your neighbour:

– He/She likes ... and ....

▷ AB6·CC

2.3 Find your group!

 You are on holiday with NEPTUNE's, and on the first day, among thousands of people in Venice, you can't find your guide and your group!
Your teacher has got a card for you. The card tells you who you are and who to look for. When you find him/her, go with him/her and look for the other people from your group. Ask *all* the questions on your card: there are three or four groups, and they are all *very* similar!

You are PAT.	You have to look for TERRY.	have to look for PAT.
"I live in Manchester."	S/he lives in Manchester.	lives in Lancaster.
"I work at Manchester airport."	S/he works for ICC.	works at the post office.
"I play squash."	S/he plays volleyball.	
"I like working in the garden."	S/he likes driving sports cars.	likes painting. plays football.

62 sixty-two

Unit 6

2.4 Your dream partner...

He	lives in Hollywood.
She	works for MGM.
	drives a Chevrolet.
	likes animals.
	plays tennis.
	drinks cocktails.
	looks like (your favourite film star).

(1) Ask your neighbour. He/She knows everything about these people*. But you can only ask questions where the answer is 'Yes' or 'No', and you cannot ask 'Is it Alec/... ?'.
And: **you have only got twenty questions to** find out his/her name.
(2) If you cannot find him/her with 20 questions, try again***. Here is another 'dream partner':

He	lives in Australia.
She	works on a kangaroo farm.
	drives a Land Rover.
	likes sports.
	plays rugby.
	drinks Scotch whisky.
	looks like (your favourite film star).

Remember: There are again five people who could be your 'partner' – but they are not the same people as in the first game.

Does Alec live in Hollywood?
Yes, he does.

Does Chloe like animals?
No, she doesn't.

		Alec Annabel	Burt Belinda	Chris Chloe	Dennis Denise	Elmer Elaine
lives in...						
1	Hollywood	+				
2	Australia					
works...						
1	for MGM					
2	on a kangaroo farm					
drives a...						
1	Chevrolet					
2	Land Rover					
likes...						
1	animals					
2	sports					
plays...						
1	tennis					
2	rugby					
drinks...						
1	cocktails					
2	Scotch					
looks like...						
1	**					
2	**					

* There is a key for your neighbour on page 145.
** Fill in the name of your favourite film star.
*** Or let your neighbour ask the questions now.

▷ AB 7

2.5 The 'ideal' boss, husband, wife,...

(1) Write down five things an 'ideal' boss/husband/wife/... does, or what he/she is like.

Bei Fragen nach einer „dritten" Person wird das Do am Anfang der Frage verändert zu Does; das Verb bleibt aber unverändert:
Does he/she/your wife help you?
▷ G7 (c)

(2) Now ask your neighbours:

(3) Write down the answers, then tell the other students:

He	buys... flowers.
She	helps... with the housework.
	makes... a cup of tea in the morning.
	takes... out.
	says something nice about... work.
	is always friendly.
	has got an open personality.

– Does your... Does he/she	buy you flowers? help you with the work? ... ?	– Yes, he/she does. No, he/she doesn't. Well, sometimes he/she does. ....
	Is he/she always friendly? Has he/she got an open personality?	

– Inge has/hasn't got an ideal boss. He always/never ...s ....

▷ CC

Unit 6

3.1 **What do you think about the present train and bus services?**

		every day	from time to time	never
1	How often do you travel by ... bus?			
	train?			

2	When do you usually start your journey?	☐ before 8 ☐ between 8 – 9 ☐ after 9	☐ between 4 – 5 ☐ between 5 – 6 ☐ after 6	

		10 ...	20 ...	30 minutes	1 hour	more
3	How long does each journey take?	☐	☐	☐	☐	☐

		never	once	twice	three times	more
4	How often do you change trains/buses?	☐	☐	☐	☐	☐

5	What do you think about the present services?	☐ very good ☐ not very good	☐ good ☐ bad	

The City of Liverpool wants to find out what people think about the present bus and train services.
Please listen to this interview with a bus passenger and fill in her answers.

3.2 **How do you travel to the town centre?**

In Fragesätzen mit einem Fragewort gilt die gleiche Regel über den Einsatz von do/does wie bei den Ja/Nein-Fragen:

Ist in dem verwandten Aussagesatz kein Hilfsverb vorhanden, wird die Frage mit do/does gebildet, z. B.
*I **get** back home at 6. – When **do** you **get** back home?*

Aber:
*I **can come** at 7. – When **can** you **come**?*

▷ G 7 (c)

1 How do you travel to work/to the town centre/to the nearest town? How does your husband/wife/friend/... travel ... ?
2 When do you leave the house in the morning? When does your ... leave ... ?
3 What time do you arrive at work/in the town centre/in ... ?
4 When do you leave again?
5 When do you get back home?
6 How often do you change trains/buses?
7 What do you think about the present services?

 Ask (1) your neighbour, and then (2) some of the other students and find out how many hours they (or their husbands/wives/other people they know) spend on the train/bus/underground or in the car every day. Then ask the other students about their children and how they travel to school/work.

▷ AB8·CC

Unit 6

4.1 I'm sorry to hear that.

4.2 How nice for you!

(1) Write down on a small card what you like and what you do not like about your job (or a job you would like to have).

(2) Mix the cards and take some of them. Now work in groups:
Tell the others about 'your job'. They have to say what they feel for you.

Vollverben wie like, meet, go aber auch have to werden mit **do** oder **does** und **not** verneint:
I like – I **do not** like *(Kurzform:* don't*)*
he likes – he **does not** like *(Kurzform:* doesn't*)*

Das Vollverb bleibt in der verneinten Form stets unverändert.

▷ G 7 (b)

▷ AB9, AB10·CC

5 Meals on wheels

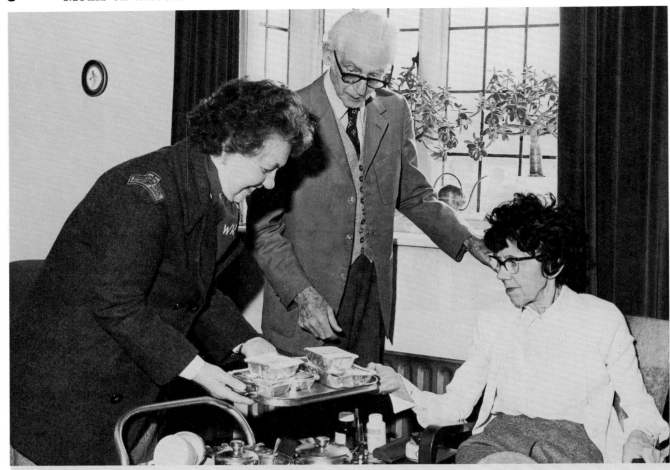

MEALS ON WHEELS

Marjory Stiles, a 45-year-old housewife, works for 'Meals on Wheels' every Tuesday and Friday. She and another helper take out 22 meals to old people. She picks up the meals at her local church, where other helpers cook them. Here she tells us about her day as a 'Meals on Wheels' helper.

My day starts at 11 o'clock when I pick up my partner and drive to the church. We get the list of names and addresses, put the meals into the car and start on our round. The list is usually the same, but sometimes one of our 'customers' has died.

The meals cost 60p, and the old people say that this is not very expensive, because our meals are the best of all the 'Meals on Wheels' they get. For their 60p our customers get a main course – meat or fish – with two vegetables and a pudding. There is not usually enough time to talk to the old people because, if we talk for too long with one person, the other meals get cold. It is a pity, really, because I know how much the old people like to have the chance to talk to us.

There is *Mrs Pendleton*, for example. The only person she sees from one day to the next is the 'Meals on Wheels' helper. I am worried about her because she never goes out of the house. She says she is ill, but she also says that the doctor never comes: he just sends her some pills.

George Woodford is still more difficult. He is 84. He was born in the house next door and only knows his own village and his place of work. He never washes, and smokes one cigarette after another. He is not very careful about how he dresses, so he is not very popular with the 'Meals on Wheels' helpers. He has got six radios in his house and plays with them non-stop all day long.

The last customer on my round, and the one I feel most sorry for, is *Mrs Grosvenor-Holmes*. She lives in a very big house. The house is very old and needs a lot of repairs. She dresses carefully and wears a lot of make-up. Like George she smokes non-stop, and talks non-stop, too, if she has the chance. When her husband died, he left her the house, but no children, she says, and no money for the repairs . . . .

Our work ends at 12.30. Then I drive home quickly and make my husband's meal. Half an hour later we sit down to lunch and talk about our day, he about the office, I about my dear old people.

Unit 6

(1) Lesen Sie den Text zügig durch, ohne sich mit Einzelheiten aufzuhalten. Ordnen Sie dann die Aussagen in der Reihenfolge des Textes!

Mrs Stiles writes about:

☐ an old man; the helpers do not like him very much.

☐ what the old people get to eat, and what their main problem is.

☐ what she does when she starts work.

☐ an old lady who is very ill.

☐ what she and her husband talk about over lunch.

☐ an old lady who has problems with her house.

(2) Mrs Stiles works from ... to ..., on ... and ....
What does she do? Make a list!
    She picks up her partner.
    She drives ....
        ....
Does Mrs Stiles like her work?
What do the old people need – often more than the meals?

(3) What does Mrs Stiles tell us about the old people?

(Kreuzen Sie an:)	Mrs P.	G.W.	Mrs G.-H.
smokes a lot of cigarettes			
dresses carefully			
does not dress carefully			
talks a lot			
is at home most of the time			

Does the doctor always look after Mrs Pendleton when she needs him?
Why is George Woodford not very popular?
What is Mrs Grosvenor-Holmes' main problem?

6 Twenty questions

Listen to this quiz.
What is the man's job?

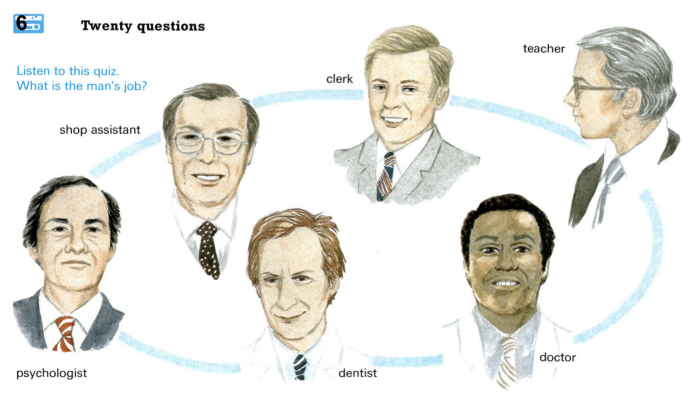

shop assistant — clerk — teacher — psychologist — dentist — doctor

sixty-seven 67

Unit 7
Travelling in Britain

Wie man Vergleiche anstellt

Wie man Gefallen und Vorlieben ausdrückt

Wie man Ratschläge und Empfehlungen gibt

Wie man Zustimmung und Widerspruch ausdrückt

Wie man seine Meinung begründet

1.1 What's the best way of getting to Heathrow?

Listen, please.

What does the lady at the hotel reception recommend?

☐ the bus
☐ the tube
☐ a taxi

– Excuse me, what's the best way of getting to Heathrow airport from here?
 – You can take the . . . .
– Is the . . . faster?
 – No, not really. And from here you have to change twice. So I think you should take the . . .

1.2 How do I get to Frankfurt airport from here?

A British/An American tourist wants to get to the nearest airport from your town.
Tell him/her how to get there.

– The best way of getting there is . . . .
You can take the . . . to . . . .
You have to change at . . . .
It's about an hour from here.

▷ CC

Unit 7

2.1 Cheaper, faster, more comfortable

Do you always fly to Glasgow?

Well, I often go by plane, because it's faster, but when I've got the time I travel by train. It's more comfortable.

Listen, please.

1 The first person travels by _____ because it is _____ and _____ _____ .

2 The second person travels by _____ because it is _____ .

3 The travel agent recommends a flight because it is much _____ _____ and much _____ .

2.2 How do you prefer to travel?

Bei der Steigerungsform wird an kurze Eigenschaftswörter (wie im Deutschen) er angehängt.

Mitlaute nach kurzen, betonten Selbstlauten werden bei der Schreibung verdoppelt; stummes e entfällt:
big – bigger
safe – safer

Lange Eigenschaftswörter werden durch vorangestelltes more gesteigert.

▷ G 4 (a)

How do you prefer to travel when you are on holiday in Germany/Austria/Switzerland, by car or by train?

– I prefer to travel by	car, train, coach, plane,	because it's	cheaper. faster. safer.
			more convenient. more comfortable.

And when you travel to Italy/Spain/Denmark/... ?
And when you travel with the family?
And when you go on a sight-seeing trip?

▷ AB1·CC

sixty-nine 69

Unit 7

2.3 ... by car, by coach, by plane or by train?

(1) You want to travel from London to Edinburgh/Newcastle/York on a weekday (and one way only, so that there are no special fares for you).
How would you travel?

(2) You are at a travel agent's in London. Your partner works there. You want to go to Edinburgh/ . . . . Ask him/her:

– What's the cheapest/fastest way of getting to . . . ?
– How much is a single/return ticket?
– How long does it take?
– What time are the trains/flights?

Come to Britain!

Travelling by Car

BTA Fact Sheet 2

Travelling by Car

The best thing about it: you can go where and when you want to, travel from door to door – without a lot of planning before you start your journey.

Driving in Britain can still be very cheap: at 35 miles per gallon during out-of-town driving, a journey from London to Newcastle-upon-Tyne does not cost more than £12 (with petrol at about £1.50 per gallon).*

Some distances between towns in Britain

Aberdeen													
419	Birmingham												
577	176	Brighton											
499	84	150	Bristol										
465	110	125	164	Cambridge									
591	198	81	201	124	Dover								
124	291	452	371	341	467	Edinburgh							
141	289	460	370	352	482	43	Glasgow						
350	99	270	179	202	292	222	220	Liverpool					
514	121	54	125	58	75	390	405	215	LONDON	283 miles			
343	86	257	166	174	279	215	213	36	202	Manchester			
232	199	338	283	227	360	108	149	180	283	152	Newcastle		
493	160	177	222	61	171	369	380	229	111	201	255	Norwich	
484	63	99	69	78	152	361	354	164	58	151	247	136	Oxford
322	128	268	221	157	284	195	208	101	209	71	83	185	185	York

1 mile ≈ 1.6 km
1 gallon ≈ 4.5 litres

*1984

NATIONAL EXPRESS Rapide

Rapide
London Vic   9.00 am   2.00 pm   4.00 pm
Newcastle   2.35 pm   7.00 pm   9.00 pm
£18.00 return   £12.00 single

London Vic   9.00 am   9.30 pm
Edinburgh   6.00 pm   6.30 am
£18.00 return   £9.50 single

Rapide
London Vic   8.30 am   4.00 pm
York   1.00 pm   8.45 pm
£15.50 return   £10.00 single

British airways Super Shuttle
LONDON-EDINBURGH-LONDON
One way £60
Return £96*
* special fare

London – Edinburgh

Depart London	Arrive Edinburgh	
0710	0820	Daily ex Su
0810	0920	Daily ex Sat
0910	1020	Daily
1110	1220	Daily
1310	1420	Daily ex S
1510	1620	Daily
1710	1820	Daily
1810	1920	Daily ex Sat
2010	2120	Daily

Lon-Newcastle (1h)
7.30   9.30   15.00
17.30 20.00
single £57
return £74
(special fare)

Unit 7

This is InterCity...

- **Fast** City-centre to city-centre at 100 mph on many journeys - and even faster by InterCity 125.

  London to Birmingham in 1 hour 34 minutes

  London to Newcastle in 2 hours 55 minutes

- **Comfortable**
- **Safe**

Some example fares (2nd class):

From London to...

	Single	Return
Edinburgh	£35	£38*
Newcastle	£32	£37*
York	£20	£25*

*IC-Savers, not Fri!

InterCity from London

⇌ InterCity

LONDON – YORK, DURHAM, NEWCASTLE, EDINBURGH, DUNDEE, ABERDEEN

Mondays to Saturdays										SO																		
London King's Cross	0005	—	—	0532	0730	0800	—	0900	0930	0950	1000	1035	1100	1200	1235	1300	1400	1500	1535	1600	1637	1700	1726	1800	1900	2000
York	0413	0647	0757	0825	0945	1012	1030	1110	1140	1201	—	1245	1259	1359	1445	—	1559	1710	1745	1759	1845	—	1935	2004	2115	2210
Durham	0524	0737	0847	—	1036	1140	1140	1214	1231	—	—	1336	1406	1507	1536	1608	1650	—	1836	1901	—	—	2026	2100	2206	2312
Newcastle	0543	0757	0904	—	1054	1107	1200	1209	1249	1306	1253	1354	1404	1504	1554	1609	1708	1815	1854	1904	—	2004	2044	2109	2224	2330
Edinburgh	0900	0954	1044	—	1234	1247	—	1346	—	1447	1430	1534	1541	1647	—	1746	1848	1952	—	2045	2145	—	2252	—	—	—
Dundee	—	1108	—	—	—	1405	—	—	—	1643	1545	—	1751	1855	—	1852	2048	—	—	2204	—	2351	—	—	—	—
Aberdeen	—	1221	—	—	—	1518	—	—	—	1810	1659	—	1940	—	—	2021	2210	—	—	2316	—	—	—	—	—	—

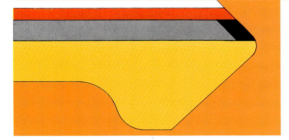

"Is it cheaper to fill up with litres or gallons?"

2.4 I think you should go by train.

A British or an American tourist in your town wants to get to Heidelberg (or other famous places). Tell him or her what you think is the best way of getting there.

How do I get to .... from here?

There are good train services from here to ....

There are regular buses, too.

Well, I think it's .... er/more .... to go by ....

▷ AB2

seventy-one 71

Unit 7

3.1 Brighton or Dartmouth?

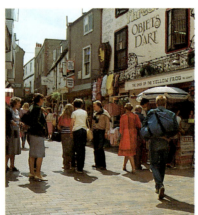

BRIGHTON
One of the most elegant seaside towns in England!
Royal Pavilion (1) Built for the Prince Regent (George IV) between 1790 and 1822.
Palace Pier (2) One third of a mile long, England's oldest pleasure pier (opened in 1901).
The Lanes (3) In the 17th century the centre of a fishing village, today ideal for shopping, with lots of interesting boutiques, antique shops, pubs and cafés.
Aquarium and Dolphinarium Britain's largest aquarium, opened in 1872. 1,000 seat dolphinarium with 6 dolphin shows every day.

DARTMOUTH
A quiet fishing port, and one of Britain's most pleasant holiday resorts for those who like a quiet and peaceful holiday (4).

Compare the two towns.

– I think Brighton/Dartmouth is Brighton/Dartmouth seems to be	bigger/smaller nicer/quieter more interesting more attractive better for children/families cheaper/more expensive	than Dartmouth/Brighton.
I think ... has got better/more hotels/shops. I think there's more entertainment in ... than in .... is nearer to London than		

– I'm sorry, I don't agree.	I think ... is just as nice as .... I don't think ... is as interesting as ....

Vergleichssätze:

A is (not) **as** ... **as** B.
A is ...**er** than B.
A is **more** ... than B.

▷ G 4 (b)

Where would you prefer to spend a two week holidays, in Brighton or in Dartmouth?
Compare two places in Germany and tell a foreign guest which one you think is better for him/her as a holiday resort.
Do you know two places in Italy/Spain/France/Denmark/... where German tourists like spending their holidays? Compare them: which of them do you find nicer/more attractive/... ?

▷ AB3·CC

Unit 7

3.2 Which hotel is better for you?

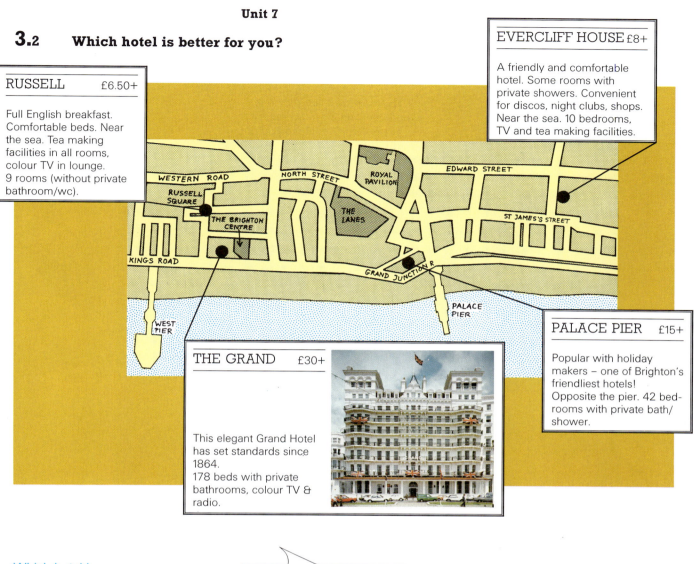

RUSSELL £6.50+

Full English breakfast. Comfortable beds. Near the sea. Tea making facilities in all rooms, colour TV in lounge. 9 rooms (without private bathroom/wc).

EVERCLIFF HOUSE £8+

A friendly and comfortable hotel. Some rooms with private showers. Convenient for discos, night clubs, shops. Near the sea. 10 bedrooms, TV and tea making facilities.

PALACE PIER £15+

Popular with holiday makers – one of Brighton's friendliest hotels! Opposite the pier. 42 bedrooms with private bath/shower.

THE GRAND £30+

This elegant Grand Hotel has set standards since 1864.
178 beds with private bathrooms, colour TV & radio.

Which hotel is
- cheaper?
- more expensive?
- quieter?
- more comfortable?
- nicer/bigger?
- better?
- nearer to the shopping centre/ the Pier/the beach?

– The . . . is	more comfortable nicer	than the . . . .

– I'm afraid I don't agree.	I think the . . . is just as comfortable as the . . . . I don't think the . . . is as nice as the . . . .

▷ AB4·CC

3.3 I think the Plaza is the best hotel in town.

Which hotel/restaurant in your town can you recommend?

– I think the . . . is the	best quietest most comfortable	hotel restaurant	in . . . .

*Die 2. Steigerungsstufe wird durch Anhängen von **est** gebildet, bei langen Eigenschaftswörtern durch vorangestelltes **most**.*

▷ G 4 (a)

Sonderformen haben:

good – better – best
a lot of – more – most

▷ AB5·CC

Unit 7

4.1 I'm looking for a single room.

Listen, please.

– Park Hotel, good evening.
  – Good evening. I'm looking for a . . . room for . . . . Have you got anything free?
– With private bathroom or shower?
  – With . . . , if possible.
– Yes, that's possible.
  – How much does it cost?
– . . . per night.
  – Hm. Haven't you got anything cheaper?
– Only without bath or shower.
  – All right. I'll take one . . . .

The lady takes ☐ a single room   ☐ without bath   for ☐ two nights.
                ☐ a double room   ☐ with shower   ☐ tonight.

4.2 Dear Sir, . . .

```
The Manager,                          Marktstraße 12
King's Head Hotel,                    6460 Kleinstadt
Market Street,                        W.-Germany
Looe, Cornwall PL13 1BH
                                      14 July 1986

Dear Sir,

     Please reserve a double room with private bathroom
or shower and WC from August 2 - 14 (12 nights) in my name.
     I would prefer a quiet room at the back of the hotel,
if possible.
     Please confirm my booking as soon as possible.

          Yours sincerely,

          Peter Braun
```

Write a letter to one of the hotels on page 73 and ask them to reserve a room for your holidays.

4.3 Booking a hotel room

Unit 7

You are on holiday in Devon. A train from London has just arrived, and a lot of tourists are looking for hotel rooms. These rooms are still free:

- single room
- double room
- private bathroom/WC
- shower
- very quiet
- nice view

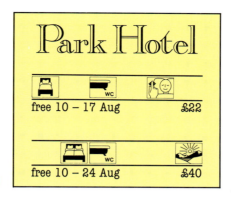

1

2

3

4

And this is what you (and the other tourists) are looking for:

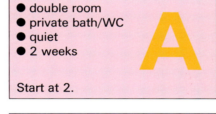

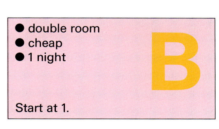

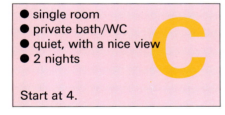

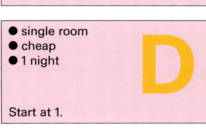

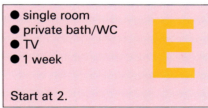

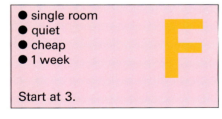

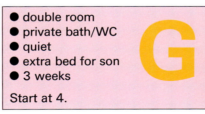

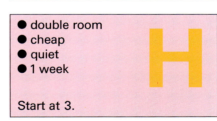

(1) One or two students work at the reception of each hotel; put up signs with the names of the hotels in each corner of the classroom.
(2) The others are the tourists A, B, C, . . . ; work in pairs if there are more students than there are cards for tourists.
(3) Walk round and try to book a room. Be careful: there are so many tourists that not everybody can find the ideal room!

▷ CC

seventy-five 75

5 Regions of Britain

Please fill in:

Main holiday areas: _____

Industrial areas: _____

Poor areas/areas with
economic problems: _____

An area with a lot of
English language schools: _____

Regions where a lot of people
want independence from England: _____

Regions where people speak
English and their own language: _____

Northern Ireland

"God made Ireland one island, so why make it two countries?" ask the Roman Catholics in Ireland. The Protestants, on the other hand, think that Northern Ireland is a legitimate part of the United Kingdom. It is one of the most problematic regions of the United Kingdom – politically and economically – and there is no reason to think that the situation will change in the next few years.

Wales...

... is not only an ideal country for holidays, it is also a highly industrialised part of Britain. Cardiff (Welsh: Caerdydd) with its docks and metal industry is the main centre on the south coast. Many Welsh people prefer Welsh to English, and want more political independence for Wales.

The South...

... is very popular with tourists from the Continent, with a lot of English language schools for foreigners along the coast. Cornwall and Devon with their picturesque coastlines are among the most attractive holiday areas in England. But it is not only a tourist area, it is also a rich agricultural region.

Scotland

The main export article is still whisky, but the area around Glasgow is one of Britain's most important industrial areas. Scotland, too, has got old and unprofitable industries, but North Sea oil – Scotland's black gold – is helping the Scottish economy to overcome these problems. The biggest tourist attractions are, of course, the Highlands and the many lakes ("Lochs") – like Loch Ness. The Scots, with their own school and legal systems, have a long tradition of political independence, but for some it is not enough...

The North

The Lake District and the Yorkshire Dales and Moors are very popular with British holidaymakers. They are among the most beautiful parts of England, but there are a lot of problems, too: the area around Newcastle is one of the poorest regions in Britain today, with more people out of work than anywhere else in England or Wales. Its old and unprofitable industries find it more and more difficult to sell their products on the world market.

The Midlands ...

... still the industrial centre of England: Birmingham, Sheffield, Coventry and other Midlands cities and towns were "the workshop of the world" a hundred years ago. The textile, coal and steel industries of the Midlands were second to none in the world at that time, but today's factories are no longer as modern as those in Germany or Japan, and a lot of people in this region are out of work and very poor.

East Anglia

A pleasant, mainly agricultural region, ideal for a quiet holiday on the coast of the North Sea. Colchester, built 2000 years ago by the Romans and the oldest town in England, and Norwich are typical for smaller towns in England today.

London

For most foreigners, London *is* England. One of the biggest cities in the world, it is certainly an interesting place to visit: there are the sights of London – The Tower, Buckingham Palace, Westminster – there are the museums, the West End theatres and cinemas, and, of course, the shops. But London is also one of the most important international banking and trade centres in the world.

seventy-seven

Unit 8
Food and drink

Wie man im Restaurant ein Essen bestellt
Wie man um etwas bittet
Wie man etwas anbietet
Wie man sagt, ob etwas gut oder schlecht ist
Wie man fragt, ob etwas vorhanden ist

 What would you like for breakfast?

Look at the breakfast menu and listen, please.
What does the man order?

BREAKFAST MENU
FRUIT JUICE
TOMATO JUICE
CORNFLAKES
BACON AND EGGS
OR
SAUSAGE, TOMATOES
TOAST OR BROWN BREAD
BUTTER, JAM, MARMALADE
TEA OR COFFEE

1.2

£10 LETTER

MY daughter's American friends were visiting us.
At breakfast, one of them said: "Isn't it lovely – a real British breakfast!"
I looked at the table. There was Danish bacon, there were Italian tomatoes, Belgian eggs and marmalade made from foreign oranges...
Then I looked at the milk and thought: "Ah! That **IS** British – the good old pinta!"
— Mrs LILIAN MORRIS
Leominster,
Herefordshire.

★ ★ ★

How a home brew halted an inva...

Waiter!... Waiter!... Waiter!

Unit 8

1.3 Can I have cornflakes, please?

Work in groups of 3 or 4; one of you is the waiter/waitress and takes the orders.

– Good morning. What would you like for breakfast?
  – Orange juice, bacon and eggs, and toast, please.
– Coffee or tea?
  – Tea, please.

– Can I have cornflakes, please?
  – Yes, madam. And what else would you like?
– A boiled egg, if that's possible.
  – Yes, certainly.
– And coffee, please. ▷ AB 1 · CC

2.1 Blondie

seventy-nine 79

Unit 8

2.2 What do they order?

Listen to these people, as they order their lunch. Which table are they sitting at, 5, 7 or 9?

2.3 Can I have the menu, please?

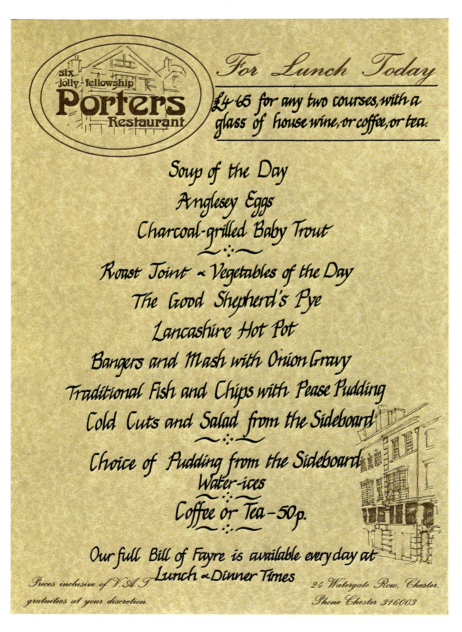

Six Jolly Fellowship Porters Restaurant

For Lunch Today

£4·65 for any two courses, with a glass of house wine, or coffee, or tea.

Soup of the Day
Anglesey Eggs
Charcoal-grilled Baby Trout

Roast Joint & Vegetables of the Day
The Good Shepherd's Pye
Lancashire Hot Pot
Bangers and Mash with Onion Gravy
Traditional Fish and Chips with Pease Pudding
Cold Cuts and Salad from the Sideboard

Choice of Pudding from the Sideboard
Water-ices
Coffee or Tea – 50p.

Our full Bill of Fayre is available every day at Lunch & Dinner Times

Prices inclusive of V.A.T.
gratuities at your discretion.

24 Watergate Row, Chester
Phone Chester 316003

Waiter! Can I have the menu, please?

Just a moment, sir.

Excuse me, Miss, I'd like to order.

Yes, madam.

Are there any good Restaurants near here?

Unit 8

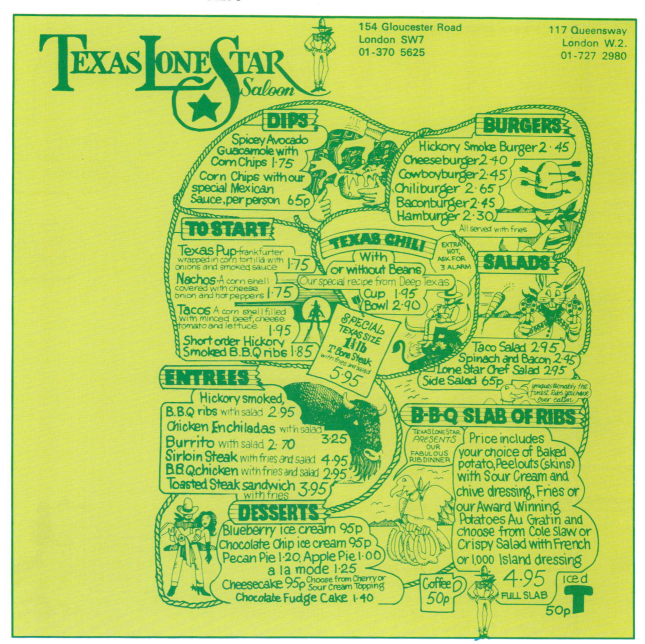

I'll / She'll have / take ...

Zukunftsform, gebildet aus 'll (= will) und der Grundform des Verbs.

▷ G 6.3 (c)

Work in groups of 3 or 4; one of you is the waiter/waitress and takes the orders.

– What would you like to start with?
  – I'd like a salad, please.

– And what about you, sir?
  – I'll have the same.

– And what would you like to follow?
  – Roast chicken, please.
– And as a vegetable?
  – Peas. Peas and chips, please.
– Yes, madam, one roast chicken with peas and chips. And you, sir?
  – Can I have the chicken with boiled potatoes, please?
– Yes, certainly. And what would you like to drink?

  – Have you got a dry white wine?
– Yes, sir. What about a Liebfraumilch?
  – *Erm* – well, I think I'll have a pint of lager.
  – And I'll take a mineral water, please.
– Thank you.

▷ AB2·CC

Unit 8

2.4 Here's your roast chicken, sir.

* Who is the best waiter in your group?
  Four or five of you order their meal from this (or another) menu; the 'waiter/waitress' has nothing to write on, and has to try to remember what you order. He/She has to come back to the group after one minute and 'serve' the meals/drinks (– he/she can write them on small cards in that minute!).

3.1 Have a drink!

Listen, please.
What do they order?

Unit 8

3.2 I'd like a sherry.

some steht in **bejahenden** Aussagesätzen; es heißt „etwas, ein wenig/ein paar" oder hat im Deutschen gar keine Entsprechung. Man benutzt some auch in Fragen, mit denen man etwas **anbietet**: 'Would you like some . . . ?'

▷ G 1 (e)

– What would you like?
  – I'd like a sherry.
– Dry or sweet?
  – Medium, please.

– And what about you?
  – Half a pint of lager, please.

– And you, Peter?
  – *Erm* – well, I think I'll have a Scotch.
– Would you like some ice in it?
  – No, thanks.

 You want to buy your neighbours a drink. Ask them what they would like.

▷ AB3·CC

4.1 Can I have the bill, please?

 Listen, please.

	🐟	🍷
The man liked		
did not like		

4.2 And how did you like your meal?

Work together with your neighbour. Tell him/her (= the waiter/waitress) what you liked/did not like.

cold   very good   not very fresh

warm   very good   good

I'm afraid the meat wasn't cooked.

But the fish was very good.

▷ CC

Unit 8

5.1 What do we need?

More and more people go on camping holidays, because it is cheaper to cook your own meals than to eat in a restaurant.

Listen to these two people in a supermarket.
What do they want to buy?

5.2 Is there any sugar on our shopping list?

> **any** steht in **verneinenden** Aussagesätzen und in **Informationsfragen** ('Have you got any sugar/apples?'). Zusammen mit **not** heißt es „kein(e)"; in Fragesätzen hat es keine deutsche Entsprechung.
>
> ▷ G 1 (e)

You are spending a one-week camping holiday with English friends in Scotland.

(1) Work in groups. Talk about what you would like to eat. Then make a shopping list.
(2) Tell the other groups what you have got on your list. They should ask questions.

Who has got the most interesting menu for the week?

▷ AB4·CC

Unit 8

6 Fast food – big money

(1) Before you read the text:
– Is there a McDonald's/ Wendy's/Burger King/... in your town?
– Who eats there regularly?
– Do you (often) go there?
– What do(n't) you like about it?

(2) Now read the text and try to understand the main ideas.

FAST FOOD – BIG MONEY

McDonald's is certainly the biggest name in the fast food business, and, more than that, it is a new way of eating, a new way of life for millions of people, not only in America. For most people "fast food" is typically American, but it only started in America in 1954 when Ray Kroc, the real "ideas man" and owner of McDonald's, first met the McDonald brothers at their hamburger stand in San Bernardino, California.

What makes fast food places like McDonald's so popular? In the first place they are what their name says they are – fast. At McDonald's, they say, you never have to wait longer than 60 seconds for your order. Secondly, they are cheaper than restaurants – even a father of four can usually afford to take his family out for a meal if he goes to a fast food shop. And for teenagers it is a popular meeting (and eating) place before the disco or after the cinema. Thirdly, they are all almost clinically clean. And – you can get not only hamburgers there, as in the early days, but also chicken, sea food, pizza, tacos and pancakes.

The fast food idea was not McDonald's, but it was McDonald's that helped to make it an American institution with their typical buildings, with their aggressive television advertising, and with their well-loved clown, Ronald McDonald. McDonald's motto is: "Quality, service, cleanliness and value"; a customer should get the same quality and service in New York, in Singapore, Munich, Paris or in a small town in the mid-west. Eleven million people per day eat at one of the almost 8,000 McDonald's fast food shops worldwide. In 1982, McDonald's sold almost eight billion dollars' worth of Big Macs, Quarter Pounders and other "delicacies". The whole of the fast food industry makes more than 40 billion dollars per year in sales and employs almost two million people.

This is certainly big business for the people who own the fast food shops, but what about the people who work there? Most of them are students or housewives who like the flexible working hours: the shops are open from early in the morning (sometimes 5.30 a.m.) until late at night (often 1 a.m. at weekends). But the pay is not very good; often the wives and children of unemployed factory workers have to accept the working conditions (night work, stress, no social security) when they want to help the family budget.

And there is not much time to talk to the customers, who usually leave after no longer than 15 minutes, anyway. There are no cigarette machines, no public telephones, no jukeboxes, no fruit machines; the atmosphere is as "aseptic" as the food: no quiet corners, no comfortable seats, no wine list, nothing to make the place interesting <u>after</u> your meal. But this is not what the typical fast food customer is looking for, it seems. "The food is good, and it's fast," says a young father who is enjoying a meal with his daughter. "It was her idea to come here." And a 21-year-old student, who is enjoying two Quarter Pounders, says "You know what you're getting when you come to McDonald's." And this is perhaps the most important thing for McDonald's customers in more than 30 countries today.

(3) Put the following sentences in the right order. (Bitte bringen Sie die folgenden Sätze, die den Inhalt der einzelnen Absätze des Textes zusammenfassen, in die richtige Reihenfolge.)

☐ ... is about when fast food shops started to become popular, and who made them popular.
☐ ... tells us about McDonald's.
☐ ... is about the people who work for McDonald's.
☐ ... says why fast food shops are so popular.
☐ ... is about the people who eat at fast food shops.

7 What's number 8, please?

Frau Klein is in an Indian restaurant in London. She orders number 8 on the menu. What is in number 8? Listen, please.

☐ meat
☐ fish
☐ vegetables
☐ salad
☐ chutney
☐ rice
☐ potatoes

eighty-five 85

Unit 9
Talking about the past

Wie man über etwas Vergangenes berichtet

Wie man eine Geschichte erzählt

Wie man nach Ereignissen in der Vergangenheit fragt

Wie man ausdrückt, daß man einer Sache nicht ganz sicher ist, oder daß man etwas nicht weiß

Wie man Äußerungen eines anderen kommentiert; wie man zum Beispiel Erstaunen, Interesse, aber auch Zweifel ausdrückt und dadurch ein Gespräch in Gang hält

1.1 From Florida – with love

Dear Sally,
Daphne and I are spending a wonderful holiday over here! First, we went to New York, and from there to Florida. We spent a day at Disney World last week, and Mickey Mouse gave Daphne a big kiss. Yesterday we went to the Everglades. An alligator almost ate my shoe!!! The weather is very good, and the people over here are very friendly.
Love,
Paul

go – went
spend – spent
give – gave
eat – ate

Viele Verben haben „unregelmäßige" Formen zum Ausdruck der Vergangenheit, die man auswendig lernen muß.

▷ G 6.3 (b)

Diese Formen bleiben jedoch immer gleich, auch wenn sie sich auf eine „3. Person" beziehen. (he/she/it/Jim/...).

learn – learn**ed**
start – start**ed**

*Die meisten Verben bilden die Vergangenheitsform durch Anhängen von **ed** an die Grundform bzw. durch **d**, wenn das Verb schon auf ein **e** endet:*
phon**e** – phon**ed**

▷ G 6.3 (b)

Besonderheiten in der Schreibung:
travel – trave**ll**ed
prefer – prefe**rr**ed

Artist Concept of NASA Space Center, Cape Kennedy neighboring cities.

POST CARD

Address

Dear Jonathan,
This is our third week over here in the States. We started our trip in New York and travelled by car to Florida. There are so many interesting things to see! Last week we visited Disney World but did not like it, although we learned a lot about America there. We preferred the Kennedy Space Center, where they showed us the place where all the flights to the moon started from.
Best wishes from Helen and me,
Norman

KSC Tours, Visitor Center, TWA - 810, Kennedy Space Center, Fl. 32899
83739

*Fragen und Verneinungen in der Vergangenheit werden nach den gleichen Regeln gebildet wie solche in der Gegenwart; bei Vollverben benutzt man dabei stets **did**:*

I **did** not **like** it.
Did Norman **like** Disney World?
Where **did** he **start** his trip?

*Beachten Sie, daß das Vollverb immer in der (unveränderten) Grundform steht, und daß sich **did** nie verändert.*

▷ G 7 (b, c)

- Where did Norman/Paul start his trip?
- Where did they travel to?
- Did Paul/Norman like Disney World?
- What did Norman prefer?
- Where else did Paul go?   ▷ AB1

 Where did you spend your holidays?

Listen to these two men. Which of the maps show where they spent their holidays?

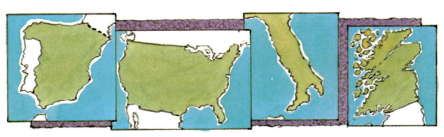

Unit 9

1.3 What did you do on holiday?

– Last summer we went to . . . .
Two years ago I spent my holidays in . . . .

I	did a lot of sight-seeing.
We	spent all day at the beach.
	visited . . . .
	swam a lot.
	played tennis.
	. . . .

– Did you | go to . . . , too?
          | see the . . . ?
          | like the . . . ?
          | . . . ?

– Yes, I did.
  No, I didn't.

didn't = *Kurzform von* did not
▷ G 6.1 (c), G 7 (c)

▷ AB2·CC

2.1 I took Joan Collins out to dinner.

Listen, please.

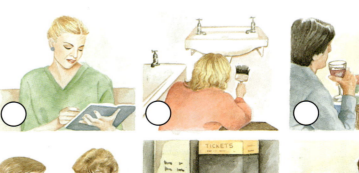

What did these people do? Fill in number 1, 2 or 3 in the picture that shows what the person did.

2.2 What did you do last night?

Unit 9

(1) Here are some usual and unusual things people do in the evening.

- went to a pub
- spent the evening with Brigitte Bardot at a night club
- visited a friend in hospital
- looked after Pat's baby
- took Jane Fonda out to dinner
- had dinner at a restaurant
- robbed a bank
- watched TV
- painted the bathroom
- played with the children
- planned my next holiday in Nepal
- phoned my friend in Tokyo
- played bingo and won £25
- read a book
- had a drink with Humphrey Bogart
- spent a quiet evening at home
- made a dress
- met friends at the station
- went out with Dan
- washed the car
- drove Jim to the airport
- played tennis with John McEnroe
- worked with my home computer
- answered a letter

Schreibregel:
plan – pla**nn**ed
rob – ro**bb**ed

Nach kurzem, betontem Selbstlaut wird der Mitlaut verdoppelt.

(2) Now write each one of these on one card. Mix them carefully; each of you has to take 3 (4 or 5) cards.

(3) Walk round and talk to the others:

Oh, hello, Jane. I tried to phone you last night, but you weren't in. Where were you?

Me? I was at home. I watched TV all evening.

Oh, I spent a wonderful evening with .... at ....

Oh, really?
Oh, did you?
Come on!
You did what?

was/were:
nur bei diesem Hilfsverb gibt es 2 Vergangenheitsformen
I, he/she/it – **was**
we, you, they – **were**

▷ G 6.1 (a)

Schreibregel:
try – tried : Grundform endet auf Mitlaut + y

play – played : Grundform endet auf Selbstlaut + y

▷ G 6.3 (b)

(4) And what did you really do?

▷ AB3·CC

Unit 9

3.1 Where I met my partner

(1) Listen to the cassette first; do not read the text on this page while listening.

(2) Now read the stories.

(3) Make two lists, one of the 'fillers' the <u>speakers</u> use, and one of the things the <u>listeners</u> say to show that they are interested in the story.

speaker   listener

(4) Then try to write them down as stories for a magazine. What do you have to leave out?

▷ AB4, AB5

1

– We worked in the same office, you see.
– Oh, really?
– Yes, he was sort of quiet. I mean, he didn't speak very much. And – erm – he didn't flirt with the girls. But then, one day he asked me to baby-sit for him.
– Did he?
– Yes, he wanted to go out with a girl, you see. His wife was dead, by the way, . . .
– Oh, dear.
– . . . and he lived with his 3-year-old son all alone. So I went over to his house, and – erm – I spent the evening there.
– Mhm.
– His house was all in a mess.
– Oh, dear.
– Yes. D'you know what I did? I cleaned the bathroom and washed his shirts and did some other things in the house, you know, and, well, when he came back, he was even quieter than before. He looked round and said: 'Why did you do that?'
– And what did you say?
– Well, I smiled and answered: 'The next time – why don't you go out with <u>me</u> and ask the other girl to look after the baby?'

2

– I met him in Italy, actually.
– Did you?
– Yes, he was in the same hotel, and we often sat at the same table for dinner. I was – I was alone on holiday, you see.
– Mhm.
– Well, then, when I was ill for almost a week, he kind of looked after me, bought me newspapers, and sweets, and flowers, you know.
– That's nice.
– Yes, he was very nice, actually, but he never said that he liked me, and, well, when we got back to England, I thought everything was over, you know.
– Mhm.
– But he wrote, and phoned me, and invited me out, and we actually met again.

3

– You see, I was 28 actually when I took driving lessons, and – erm – she was my instructor, and I felt really terrible.
– Mhm.
– I mean, she was really nice, she helped me a lot, but I was kind of nervous and I made one mistake after another.
– Oh, dear.
– Yes, one day she stopped me and asked: 'What's the matter?' D'you know what I did?
– No, what?
– I told her that perhaps a male instructor would have been better for me.
– Oh, no, you didn't.
– Yes. But she kind of smiled and said: 'What is it that really makes you nervous, the driving – or me?'
– Hmm.
– Well, after that we went out together, and – er – by the way, I passed the test, and – erm – guess how the story went on.

Unit 9

3.2 And where did you meet your partner?

- at work/in the office
- on holiday
- in a club/at my tennis club/...
- at a dance
- at (night) school
- ...

Have you got any good ideas for a 'boy meets girl' love story? Write them down; work in groups.
Then *tell* the story to the others.

▷ AB6·CC

4 Things to remember

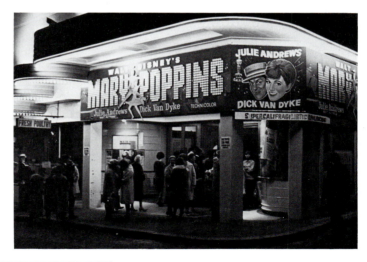

– When did	you	get a TV? get a radio? get your first bike/car? smoke your first cigarette? get your first kiss? see your first film?

– About ... years ago.
I think it was in 1950.
I'm not sure, but I think ....
I'm afraid I don't know.

When did your parents ... a/their ... ?

▷ AB7, AB8·CC

Unit 9

5 Class reunion

Class Reunion

① The text is about . . .

② One group of people . . .
   (a)   (b)   (c)
   and their 'problems':
   . . .

③ Other people . . .
   (d)   (e)
   and what they are like:
   . . .

④ The author sees that he
   is like ( ) and ( )
   What does he think
   about this?

What are your old schoolfriends like today?
When was the class reunion?

Last Saturday we met again for the first time in twenty years. I don't know why, but when I arrived at the old pub I was very nervous. There was already a noisy, cheerful group there: "Hello"; "How are you?"; "What are you doing now?"; "Isn't that Chris Dodson, who brought a white mouse into music class once?"; "Look, there's Tom Bream, who . . . ."; "Well, well, well, we're not quite as slim as we were 20 years ago . . . ."; "Is that really your own hair?"

I stopped and listened to these voices of the past.

There was Anthony H., a most charming young man – charming, that is, when he was young. A great success with all the girls in town. After he left school he went to Australia, married a farmer's daughter, started a small business and went bankrupt twice. His wife left him and he came back to England. He now works as a bank clerk and seems to have a drink problem. He talked about his family back in Australia non-stop all evening.

And there was Bruce F., perhaps the most intelligent boy in the class. He went on to university, studied mathematics, became an engineer and worked for an American computer company. Three years ago he left the company because he was not sure that he was really doing what he wanted to. He now lives on the money he earns from odd jobs, but he says that he is happy and that he has now got time to think, and to do the things that are really important to him.

Leslie D. has got time, too – too much time. He is out of work. He was an engineer, too, in a factory in Yorkshire, but it closed down two years ago. At forty, he says, it is almost impossible to find another job.

A lot of the other "old boys" had the same kind of problem: something unexpected had changed their lives.

But there were the others, too: noisy, cheerful, optimistic. John B., for example, is now a biology and sports teacher at our old school. For him nothing had changed in life; he is still as conservative as ever. He could not understand Bruce: what was wrong with computers? We all need them for a better way of life.

Howard G., once a quiet boy who loved flowers, was now a doctor. A pompous little man who wanted to "send the Pakistanis back where they came from". He seemed to forget that a lot of them come from Birmingham, Bradford and Sheffield.

Suddenly I saw myself as in a mirror. What was I doing? A happily married man with three children and a comfortable house in a respectable neighbourhood. And then I thought of the articles I wrote for a large popular daily newspaper. Bruce certainly did not read my articles, and, if he did, he certainly did not like them. I realized that I was more like John and Howard, and I suddenly found this an unpleasant idea . . . .

Unit 10
What's the matter?

Wie man sich nach dem Befinden erkundigt,
und wie man darauf reagiert
Wie man Bedauern und Mitgefühl ausdrückt
Wie man jemandem alles Gute wünscht
Wie man jemandem einen Rat gibt
Wie man über das Wetter spricht

  1.1 How are you?

Listen, please.

Can you tell what these people feel like?

	a	b	c
1	☐	☐	☐
2	☐	☐	☐
3	☐	☐	☐

1.2 Quite well, can't complain.

 Walk round, say 'Hello' to the other students, and ask them how they are.

▷ AB1·CC

Unit 10

2.1 I've got a headache.

Listen, please.

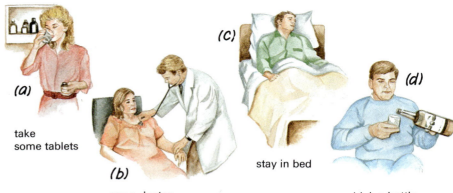

(a) take some tablets
(b) see a doctor
(c) stay in bed
(d) drink a bottle of whisky

These three people are ill, or do not feel very well today.
What does the other person recommend?

1 ___ 2 ___ 3 ___

2.2 Take two tablets every four hours.

ASPRIA
20 Tablets
Contains Aspirin
Keep out of the reach of children

ASPRIA
for headache pain
rheumatic pains – colds
flu

Adult Dose
2 to 3 tablets every 4 hours, if needed. Do not take more than 15 tablets in 24 hours, unless so directed by a doctor.

Children's Dose
Do not give to children under 3 years, except on medical advice. 3-5 years, 1/2 tablet, 6-12 years, 1 tablet. If needed, repeat the dose at intervals of 4 hours, but do not give more than 4 doses in 24 hours. If the child is no better in 24 hours, consult your doctor.

Each tablet contains 320 mg Aspirin.

If symptoms persist, consult your doctor.

ASPRIA
Keep out of the reach of children

Ratschläge, Verpflichtungen und Aufforderungen, etwas zu tun oder nicht zu tun, drückt man mit **should/should not** *(shouldn't) und der Grundform des Verbs aus.*

▷ G 6.2 (d)

▷ AB2

		Right	Wrong
1	ASPRIA helps when you have got a headache.	☐	☐
2	You should take this medicine until you feel better.	☐	☐
3	You should not take more than 15 tablets a day without asking your doctor.	☐	☐
4	Children under 6 should take 1 tablet every 4 hours.	☐	☐
5	Children of 6-12 should not take more than 8 tablets per day.	☐	☐

Unit 10

2.3 I hope you'll get better soon.

(1) Can you show that you are ill without saying what the matter is?

You have got
 . . . a headache. (1)
 . . . a cold. (2)
 . . . the flu. (3)

You have hurt your
 . . . foot. (4)
 . . . leg. (5)
 . . . back. (6)

Körperteile (und Kleidungsstücke) stehen in der Regel mit einem besitzanzeigenden Fürwort:

I've hurt **my foot**.
He took **his coat** and left the house.

▷ G 1 (b)

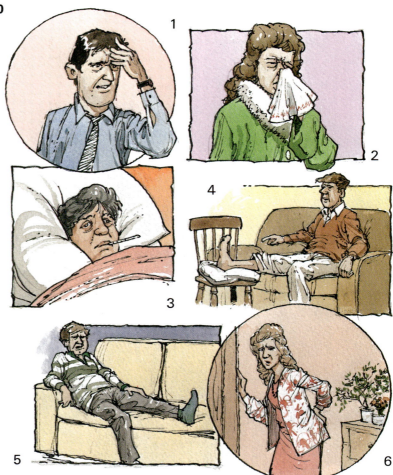

(2) This is what people usually say to somebody who does not feel well:

- You should see a doctor.
- Is it serious?
- Have you got a temperature?
- Would you like some tablets?
- I'm sorry to hear that.
- I hope you'll get better soon.

(3) Now walk round so that the others can see that you are ill. Talk to the people you meet. ▷ CC

– Hello, Susan.
– Hello, Mildred. You don't look very well today. How are you?
– Oh, so-so.
– What's the matter?
– I've got a terrible cold.
– Oh, you should see a doctor.

3.1 Tips for tourists

Can you complete these 'tips . . .', please?

> *Einen Befehl, etwas **nicht** zu tun, drückt man durch **don't** (= do not) vor der Grundform des **Voll**verbs aus.*
>
> ▷ G 7 (e)

Unit 10

A holiday in the south of Europe can be wonderful, but there are some things to remember, if you want it to be a happy one!

- DON'T drink water from the tap.
- DON'T eat fruit without washing it.
- DON'T stay in the sun too long on e first day.
- 'T leave your baggage where cannot see it.
- leave money, traveller's cheques, amera or other valuable things hotel room.
- ve things in the car where body can see them.
- carry too much cash round with you.
- wear swim wear when you visit thedral or a church.
- ke photos of people without asking m.
- 'T think that everybody can speak LISH!

▷ AB3

3.2 You shouldn't leave things in the car.

An English friend, who wants to travel in Germany, shows you these 'Tips for Tourists': does he/she have to be so careful in Germany, too?
Tell him/her what you think.

▷ CC

Unit 10

3.3 What's the matter with you?

On holiday you sometimes meet people who do not look happy:

The hotel is	noisy.
	dirty.
	terrible.

Somebody stole my	camera.
	passport.
	money.

(1) Write these things on one card each, mix them and give everybody one card.

(2) This is what you can say if somebody has got a problem like these:

Oh, I'm sorry to hear that.
That's a pity.
Oh dear, how could that happen?
What a pity!

– Well, I think you should	tell the travel agent about it.
	write a letter to the travel agent.
	complain to the hotel manager.
	speak to her/him.
	go to the police.
	....

▷ CC

(3) Now walk round and ask all the people you meet how they are.
If they are not happy, ask them what the matter is.
If somebody asks you, look at your card and tell him/her what your problem is.

Unit 10

4.1 The weather today

(1) You are going to Brighton tomorrow. You will need

☐ an extra pullover
☐ an umbrella
☐ a T-shirt
☐ your swim wear

(2) What was the weather like in Berlin yesterday?

☐ warm
☐ cool
☐ cloudy
☐ sunny
☐ rainy
☐ foggy

4.2 There will be snow in the north...

Listen, please, and fill in where the weather forecast says these will be.

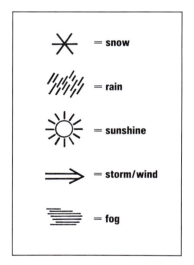

The temperature in London will be _____ °C.

4.3 What do you think next summer will be like?

– I think it will be as cold/warm/nice/bad/... as last year's summer.
I think there will be a lot of rain/sunshine again.
....

▷ AB4

Unit 10

4.4 Talking about the weather

Listen, please.

(1) What is the weather like in number . . .

(2) Listen again; how do these people 'find' something to talk about?

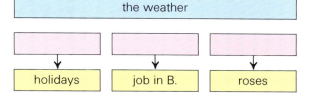

4.5 Nice day today, isn't it?

Write down what these people say about the weather.

– What a	lovely beautiful fine terrible	morning. day.	
It's a	nice . . .	morning, day,	isn't it?
What	lovely . . .	weather!	

– It's (a bit) too	hot warm cool cold wet dry	for this time of the year.
There's too much	rain snow	

   Find some pictures of good/bad weather in magazines. Bring them along; mix them and put them in front of you.
Take one of the pictures and talk to your partner about the weather in the picture. Then go on with the next picture.

▷ AB 5·CC

Unit 10

5   **Mother's Little Helper**

Mother's Little Helper

What a drag it is getting old
'Kids are different today'
I hear ev'ry mother say
Mother needs something today to calm her down
And though she's not really ill
There's a little yellow pill
She goes running for the shelter of a mother's little helper
And it helps her on her way
Gets her through her busy day

'Things are different today'
I hear ev'ry mother say
Cooking fresh food for a husband's just a drag
So she buys an instant cake
And she burns her frozen steak
And goes running for the shelter of a mother's little helper
And two help her on her way
Get her through her busy day

Doctor please
Some more of these
Outside the door
She took four more
What a drag it is getting old

'Life's just much too hard today'
I hear ev'ry mother say
The pursuit of happiness just seems a bore
And if you take more of those
You will get an overdose
No more running to the shelter of a mother's little helper
They just helped you on your way
Through your busy dying day

(1) Mother's 'little helpers' are . . .
(2) Why does she need these 'helpers'?

	Yes	No
● The children make her nervous.	☐	☐
● She is ill.	☐	☐
● The housework is too much for her.	☐	☐
● She is afraid of getting older.	☐	☐
● Her life is not very interesting.	☐	☐

(3) Do these 'helpers' really help her?
(4) What does the word 'overdose' mean?
(5) What could happen to this woman if she does not stop taking pills?
(6) What should she do instead, do you think?

Stop over 2

S 1 How often do you do it?

- eat at a restaurant
- go to the cinema
- drink a glass of wine
- drink a beer
- read a newspaper
- read a book
- buy a blouse/shirt
- buy flowers
- see your best friend
- watch football on TV
- give a present to your partner
- wash your car
- stay in a hotel
- go on holiday
- eat fish
- do sports

Walk round and interview two or three other students. Then tell the class about them.

S 2 Who is the youngest student in your class?

Walk round and find out as fast as possible:

Who ist the youngest student in your class?
Who has to travel the longest to night school?
Who has got the fastest/oldest car?

S 3 What's the best way of getting there?

Work in groups of 5, 6 or 7. Each of you says where she or he lives (In Germany/England/America/. . . ? What town? – or, if you all live in a big city, what part of it do you live in?).

Your teacher wants to visit you. Plan the journey for him/her, but make sure that you find the shortest way, so that he or she can visit you all in one week.

Then tell him/her where to go first, and how to get there (by plane/car/underground/. . . ?), and where to go next, and so on.

Stop over 2

S 4 I like fish, but I don't like hamburgers.

Interview one or two students from your group. Find out what they like or don't like from the following list.

The class then has to guess what your interview partner likes. If they find 10 correct answers, your interview partner has to buy a drink for everyone!

tomatoes
ice-cream
coffee
Chinese food
pizza
fish
tea
whisky
McDonald's fast food
calamari

S 5 What did you do last weekend?

First interview your neighbour. Write down what he or she tells you about last weekend.

Then work together in groups of 4 or 6. Now *you* are Inge/Peter. Tell the group what you did:
'I am Inge/Peter. Last weekend I . . .'

S 6 Next week I'll . . .

What do you think the future will bring?
What will you do, where will you be 2 days/2 weeks/2 months after this English course?

*In January / September / ....
I'll be back and start the next course, I hope.*

Grammatik

G	1	Fürwörter (pronouns)
G	2	Artikel (articles)
G	3	Hauptwörter (nouns)
G	4	Eigenschaftswörter (adjectives)
G	5	Umstandswörter (adverbs)
G	6	Verben (verbs)
G	6.1	Hilfsverben (auxiliaries)
G	6.2	Modale Hilfsverben (modal auxiliaries)
G	6.3	Vollverben (full verbs)
G	7	Satzmuster (sentence structures)
G	8	Grundform/-ing Form (infinitive/-ing form)
G	9	Passiv (passive voice) – erst Bd. 2
G	10	Nebensätze (subordinate clauses)
G	11	Indirekte Rede (reported speech) – erst Bd. 2
G	12	Nebengeordnete Sätze (tags etc.) – erst Bd. 2
G	13	Präpositionen (prepositions)
G	14	Satzmelodie (intonation)

Einige im Grammatik-Teil benutzte Begriffe

deutsch	englisch	Beispiel/Erklärung	behandelt in
Artikel	article		
bestimmter ~	definite ~	the *(der/die/das)*	G 2
unbestimmter ~	indefinite ~	a, an *(ein, eine)*	G 2
Aussagesätze	statements		
bejahende ~	positive ~	'I like New York.'	G 7 (a)
verneinende ~	negative ~	'I don't like New York.'	G 7 (b)
Befehlsform	imperative	'Go!'/'Don't go!'	G 6.3 (e)
besitzanzeigende Form (Genitiv)	possessive case	Peter's car, the number of your house	G 3 (b)
dritte Person Einzahl	3rd person singular	nicht **ich** (1. Person), nicht **du** (2. Person), sondern eine andere Person (3. Person), er/sie/es – he/she/it	G 1 (a) G 6.3 (a)
Einzahl	singular	a/one car	G 3 (a)
Eigenschaftswörter	adjectives	nice, happy, green, quiet	G 4
Fragesätze	questions	'Are you German?'	G 7 (c)
Fragewörter	questions words	What/When/Why/...	G 1 (c)
Fürwörter (Pronomen)	pronouns	*Sie stehen **für** ein anderes Wort: der Mann → er; Karin → sie; usw.* (→ he, she, ...)	
persönliche ~	personal ~	I, you, he, she, it, ...	G 1 (a)
besitzanzeigende ~	possessive adjectives	my, your, his, ...	G 1 (b)
hinweisende ~	demonstrative ~	this/that *(diese, jene)*	G 1 (d)
unbestimmte ~	indefinite ~	some, any, a lot of: *man weiß nicht ganz bestimmt, wieviele ...*	G 1 (e)
Gegenwart (Präsens)	present (tense)		
einfache ~	simple present	Peter lives in London. (= immer)	G 6.3 (a)
Verlaufsform der ~	present progressive (present continuous)	Peter is reading a book. *(= gerade eben! Er ist „am lesen".)*	G 6.3 (d)
Grundform (des Verbs)	infinitive	*Die Form, die man z.B. im Wörterbuch findet; ohne Endungen, z.B.* go, take; *oft davor* 'to': to go, to take.	G 8

German	English	Example/Explanation	Reference
Hauptwörter (Substantive, Nomen)	nouns	house, friend, weather	G 3
Hilfsverben	auxiliaries	be (am/is/are), do, have (→ „helfen" Verben beim Bilden der Zeit- und Frageformen)	G 6.1
modale ~	modal auxiliaries (modal verbs/modals)	can/could, should, would, ... (→ „modifizieren" [= verändern] eine Aussage)	G 6.2
Informationsfragen		„echte" Fragen, mit denen man um eine Information/Auskunft bittet	G 1 (e)
-ing Form (des Verbs)	-ing form	I work – I like working	G 8
Ja/Nein-Fragen (Entscheidungsfragen)	Yes/No-Questions	'Is she here?' – 'Yes, she is./ No, she isn't.' Fragen, die man mit Ja oder Nein beantworten kann.	G 7 (c)
Kurzantworten	short answers	Antworten auf Ja/Nein-Fragen, in denen man auch das Hilfsverb aufgreift: 'Is he ...?' – 'Yes, he is.' 'Can you ...?' – 'No, I can't.'	G 7 (c)
Kurzform	short form	I'm, he's etc. (Langform: I am, he is etc.)	G 6.1, G 6.2
Mehrzahl	plural	2 cars, 6 men	G 3 (a)
Mitlaut	consonant	[m, n, l, r]	G 2, G 3
Objekt	object	(s. „Subjekt")	G 1, (G 7)
Paarwörter (Mehrzahlwörter)	pair words	jeans, trousers (ein Stück, Wortform trotzdem Mehrzahl)	G 3 (a)
Prädikat (Satzaussage)	predicate	Das Prädikat enthält alles, was über das Subjekt (s. u.) des Satzes ausgesagt wird: Peter (= Subj.) likes flowers (= Prä.: Verb + Obj.)	G 7
Satzmuster/Satzstrukturen	sentence structures	Stellung der Wörter im Satz	(G 5), G 7, (G 8, G 10)
Satzbau	word order		
Selbstlaut (Vokal)	vowel	[a, e, ɪ, ...]	G 2
Steigerung, Vergleichssätze	comparison(s)		G 4
Grundstufe		nice (schön) ...	
1. Steigerungsstufe	comparative	nicer (schöner) ...	
2. Steigerungsstufe	superlative	nicest (schönste)	
stimmhaft/stimmlos	voiced/voiceless	(z.B. das 's' der Biene: „Zzzzzz!", aber: das 's' der Schlange: „Sssssss!" Ähnlich bei b – p, d – t und anderen Mitlauten.)	G 3 (a)
Subjekt (Satzgegenstand)	subject	Es gibt an, wer etwas getan hat; das Objekt, wem etwas geschehen ist/für wen etwas getan wurde. I have got a present for her. (I = Subjekt, a present/her = Objekte)	G 1, G 7
Umstandswörter	adverbs	Sie geben die Umstände an, unter denen etwas geschieht,	G 5
~ der Zeit/des Ortes	~ of time/place	... z.B. wann/wo ...	
~ der Häufigkeit	~ of frequency	... wie oft etwas geschieht.	
Verben (Zeitwörter, Tätigkeitswörter)	verbs		G 6
Hilfsverben		(s. o.)	G 6.1
Vollverben	full verbs	to go, to take, ...: „vollständig", weil sie alle Zeitformen bilden; oft auch nur „Verben" genannt.	G 6.3
(un)regelmäßige Verben	(ir)regular verbs	Die unregelmäßigen Verben haben besondere Formen für die Vergangenheit (go – went)	G 6.3 (b)
Vergangenheit	simple past (past tense)	answer – answered, go – went	G 6.3 (b)
Vergleichssätze		(s. „Steigerung")	
Verlaufsform		(s. „Gegenwart")	
Verneinung	negation	It isn't ...; He doesn't ...	G 7 (b)
Vollverben	full verbs	go, take, ... (im Gegensatz zu „Hilfsverben"; meist nur „Verben" genannt)	G 6.3
Zukunft	future (future tense)	I'll take it./I'm going to the cinema on Sunday.	G 6.3 (c, d)

Die Hinweise neben den Überschriften in der Grammatik (z.B. § 127) beziehen sich auf:
Werner Hüllen: Englische Grammatik für Erwachsene. Berlin: Cornelsen & Oxford University Press 1983. Best.-Nr. 5259.

Grammatik

G 1 Fürwörter (pronouns)

(a) *Persönliche Fürwörter* (personal pronouns) § 153 **(b)** *Besitzanzeigende Fürwörter* (possessive adjectives) § 151

● als **Subjekt** des Satzes ● als **Objekt** des Satzes ● vor einem Hauptwort***

I	*(ich)**	me	*(mir/mich)*	my	*(mein)*
you	*(du/Sie)***	you	*(dir/dich/Ihnen/Sie)*	your	*(dein/Ihr)*
he	*(er)*	him	*(ihm/ihn)*	his	*(sein)*
she	*(sie)*	her	*(ihr/sie)*	her	*(ihr)*
it	*(es)*	it	*(ihm/es)*	its	*(sein)*
we	*(wir)*	us	*(uns)*	our	*(unser)*
you	*(ihr/Sie)*	you	*(euch/Ihnen/Sie)*	your	*(euer/Ihr)*
they	*(sie)*	them	*(ihnen/sie)*	their	*(ihr)*

I'm your guide. | Can you help **me**? | This is **my** coat.
Are **you** English? | I can't see **you**. | Is this **your** car?
He lives in London. | It's a present for **him**. | Jim and Tom are **my** best friends.

* „ich" heißt in einigen umgangssprachlichen Wendungen me: 'It's **me**.' (= „Ich bin's."); '**Me**, too.' (= „Ich auch.")
** you heißt auch „man": 'You can't get stamps in that shop.'
*** Körperteile und Kleidungsstücke stehen im Englischen immer mit einem besitzanzeigenden Fürwort.
   'I **hurt** my foot.'/'Somebody stole **my** coat.'

(c) *Fragewörter* (question words) §§ 162–169

Who	**Who** is it? *(Wer . . . ?)*
Whose	**Whose** birthday is it? *(Wessen . . . ?)*
What	**What**'s your name, please? *(Wie . . . ?)* **What** time is it? *(Wieviel Uhr . . . ?)*
	What's Mrs Franklin looking for? *(Was . . . ?)*
Which	**Which** town, please? *(Welche . . . ?)*
When	**When** is the next train to Norwich? *(Wann . . . ?)*
Where	**Where** is she? *(Wo . . . ?)* **Where** is she **from**? *(Woher . . . ?)* **Where** did you go? *(Wohin . . . ?)*
How	**How** do you like London? *(Wie . . . ?)*
	How many flowers are there? *(Wieviele . . . ?)* **How much** is it? *(Wieviel . . . ?)*
	How long does each journey take? *(Wie lange . . . ?)* **How often** do you change trains? *(Wie oft . . . ?)*
Why	**Why** do you think so? – Because . . . . *(Warum . . . ?)*

(d) *Hinweisende Fürwörter* (demonstrative pronouns) § 135

Einzahl	Mehrzahl	Weist hin auf etwas . . .	
this	these	● *Nahes*	I'd like **this** one. / **These** jeans are nice.
that	those	● *Ferneres*	What about **that** one over there? / I'd like **those** shoes over there.

(e) *Unbestimmte Fürwörter* (indefinite pronouns) §§ 136, 138, 140–142, 144, 145, 148, 149

● every – each – all

I get up at 6 **every** morning.	*jede,r,s (überhaupt)*
They are 10 p **each**.	*jede,r,s (aus einer kleineren Zahl, deren Größe bekannt ist.)*
All (the) students in my class	*alle (meistens **mit** Artikel 'the')*

⇨ Von every abgeleitet und wie ein Hauptwort gebraucht sind **everybody** *(jeder)* und **everything** *(alles)*:
   'Everybody likes her.' – 'She knows everything.'

● a lot of (many/much) – more – most

A lot of tourists go to Italy. *(viele)*   – There's **a lot of** work in the office. *(viel)*
There are **more** tourists than last year. – He spends **more** time on the train than I. *(mehr)*
Most tourists come in summer. *(die meisten*)*

* most steht meist ohne Artikel.

Grammatik

⇨ Den genauen Unterschied zwischen many und much behandeln wir erst in Band 2.
Merken Sie sich vorerst diese Wörter nur in größerem Zusammenhang, z. B.:
'There is **too much** work.'/'How **much** is it?' *(zu viel/Wieviel . . .?)* und: How **many** . . .? *(Wieviele . . .?)*

● some – any

in bejahenden Aussagesätzen	in verneinenden Aussagesätzen	in (Informations-)Fragen**
Jack wants to buy **some** postcards. *(ein paar)**	There aren't **any** apples. *(keine)*	Are there **any** pears?*
I'd like **some** ice in my whisky. *(etwas)**	There isn't **any** tea. *(kein)*	Is there **any** sugar?*
What you say to **somebody** who does not feel well. *(jemandem)*	There wasn't **anybody** in the room. *(niemand)*	Is there **anybody** there? *(irgend jemand)*
You can learn **something** from her. *(etwas)*	We haven't got **anything** cheaper. *(nichts)*	Have you got **anything** cheaper? *(irgend etwas)*

* some und any haben sehr oft im Deutschen keine direkten Entsprechungen.
** In Fragen, mit denen man etwas anbietet oder um etwas (Vorhandenes) bittet, benutzt man some:
'Would you like **some** ice in your whisky?'/'Can I have **some** ice, please?'

● no – nothing – none

| I've got **no** idea. | kein(e) *(steht vor einem Hauptwort)* |
| What have you got for him? – **Nothing**, yet. There are **none**. | nichts *(wird benutzt wie ein Hauptwort)* keine *(wird benutzt wie ein Hauptwort)* |

(f) one §160

| Not the red blouse, the white **one**, please. This blouse? – No, that **one**, please. |

⇨ Im Textzusammenhang wird die Wiederholung von Hauptwörtern gern vermieden.

G 2 Bestimmter und unbestimmter Artikel (definite and indefinite article) §§ 122–125

| Vor Konsonanten (Mitlauten) | the flower
the guest | – a flower
– a guest | [ðə] – [ə] |
| Vor Vokalen (Selbstlauten) | the assistant
the engineer
the Irish car
the office
the umbrella | – an assistant
– an engineer
– an Irish car
– an office
– an umbrella | [ðɪ] – [ən] *Beachten Sie: diese Regel bezieht sich auf die* **Aussprache**, *nicht auf die Schreibung der Wörter! Folglich heißt es auch* [ðə] United States, *da 'United' mit dem Mitlaut* [j] *beginnt, und* [ðɪ] hour *(= Stunde), da dieses Wort mit einem Selbstlaut* [aʊ] *beginnt.* |

Besonderheiten im Gebrauch des Artikels

⇨ Den unbestimmten Artikel benutzt man im Gegensatz zum Deutschen bei Berufsangaben: I'm **an** engineer.

⇨ kein bestimmter Artikel in folgenden Wendungen:
by car/train/bus/plane
in summer/winter
on Monday/Tuesday/. . .
to go to school/work

aber:
in the evening/morning/afternoon
to listen to the radio
the school in Green Street *(weil ein bestimmtes Gebäude gemeint ist)*

⇨ *Straßennamen stehen* **ohne** *Artikel:*
I live in Brown Street.
It's in 52nd Street, on the corner of 5th Avenue.

aber:
The High Street *(und ganz wenige andere).*

Grammatik

G 3 Hauptwörter (nouns)

(a) *Einzahl – Mehrzahl* (singular – plural) §§ 107–109

● *Regelmäßige Formen*

Einzahl	Mehrzahl (Schreibung)	(Aussprache)	
book street month	books streets months	[s]	nach „stimmlosen" Mitlauten wie [p, t, k, f, θ]
girl town umbrella key city	girls towns umbrellas keys cities*	[z]	nach „stimmhaften" Mitlauten [b, d, g, l, m, n, ŋ, ð, r, v] und nach Selbstlauten
blouse village dress	blouses villages dresses**	[ɪz]	nach „Zischlauten" [s, z, ʃ, tʃ, dʒ, ʒ]

* y *wird zu* ie + s, *wenn es nach einem Mitlaut steht, vgl.* lady – ladies.
y *bleibt erhalten, wenn es nach einem Selbstlaut steht, vgl.* cowboy – cowboys.
** *Beachten Sie die Schreibung: wenn die Grundform des Wortes auf* -s, -sh *oder* -tch *endet, wird* -es *angehängt, vgl. auch* bus – buses.

● *Unregelmäßige Mehrzahlformen* § 109–110

man – men woman – women ['wɪmən] child [aɪ] – children [ɪ] (house)wife – (house)wives half – halves potato – potatoes tomato – tomatoes (*aber:* radio – radios photo – photos)

⇨ *Die Mehrzahlform von* house [haʊs] *spricht man* ['haʊzɪz] *aus.*

● *Mehrzahlwörter/Paarwörter* § 117

(a pair of)	trousers jeans shoes socks

⇨ trousers *und* jeans *stehen immer mit einem Mehrzahl-*s, *bezeichnen aber nur* ein *Stück; will man eine bestimmte Anzahl hervorheben, setzt man* 'a pair of' *oder* 'two/three pairs of' *davor.*
(Vgl. dt.: Meine Hosen sind dreckig./
Drei Paar Hosen.)

(b) *Die besitzanzeigende Form des Hauptworts* (possessive case/genitive) §§ 119–121

Bei Personen – Einzahl:	**-'s**	
Nancy's dress Ann's car Frank's pullover the guest's name		[z]* [s]

Bei Sachen:	**of**
the number of our house the telephone directory of these towns a map of London the 1st of May	

– Mehrzahl:	**-s'**
ladies' wear – aber bei unregelmäßigen Mehrzahlformen: men's wear the children's birthdays	

* *Die Ausspracheregeln entsprechen denen für die Mehrzahl.*

● *Mengenangaben* (quantifiers)

a glass of wine	a bottle of milk	a pint of lager	a cup of tea

Grammatik

G 4 Eigenschaftswörter (adjectives)

(a) *Steigerung* § 172–175

Grundstufe	1. Steigerungsstufe	2. Steigerungsstufe	
cheap big	cheap**er** big**ger***	cheap**est** big**gest***	*Kurze (einsilbige) Eigenschaftswörter werden durch Anhängen von* **-er/-est** *gesteigert.*
happy	happ**ier***	happ**iest***	*Zweisilbige Eigenschaftswörter, die auf* **y** *enden, werden mit* **-er** *gesteigert; in* Take Off 1 *kamen u.a. vor:* dirty, early, friendly, happy, noisy *sowie* cloudy, foggy, *etc.* *Auch* **quiet** *wird mit* **-er** *gesteigert:* quieter – quietest.
comfortable	**more** comfortable	**most** comfortable	*Lange (zwei-/dreisilbige) Eigenschaftswörter werden durch vorangestelltes* **more/most** *gesteigert.*

* *Mitlaute werden nach einem kurzen, betonten Selbstlaut verdoppelt;* -y *nach einem Mitlaut wird zu* -i.

● *Besondere Formen*

```
good     – better   – best
near     – nearer   – nearest (= nächst[gelegen]e)
                      next (= [örtl. od. zeitl. in der Reihenfolge] nächste)
a lot of – more     – most
```

(b) *Vergleichssätze* (comparisons) § 177

	Grundstufe
Peter is **as** old **as** Jim. Jim is **not as** old **as** Frank. Blackpool is **not as** attractive **as** Brighton.	. . . **as** + *Eigenschaftswort* + **as** . . . . . . **not as** + *Eigenschaftswort* + **as** . . .
	1. Steigerungsstufe
Frank is old**er than** Peter. Brighton is **more** attractive **than** Blackpool.	. . . *kurzes Eigenschaftswort auf* **-er** + **than** . . . . . . **more** + *langes Eigenschaftswort* + **than** . . .
	2. Steigerungsstufe
Frank is **the** old**est** student in our class. London is **the most** interesting city in Europe.	. . . **the** + *kurzes Eigenschaftswort auf* **-est** . . . . . . **the most** + *langes Eigenschaftswort* . . .

G 5 Umstandswörter (adverbs) § 187

(a) *Umstandswörter, die Häufigkeit bezeichnen* (adverbs of frequency) § 201

I	always often usually sometimes never	get up at six.

⇨ *Diese Umstandswörter stehen vor dem Vollverb.*
 Usually, sometimes *und* often *können aber auch am Satzanfang stehen, wenn sie betont werden sollen:*
 Sometimes I get up at seven.

(b) *Umstandswörter der Zeit und des Ortes* (adverbs of time and place) §§ 202, 203

Stellung im Satz:			
Zeit/Ort		*Zuerst immer ORT,*	*. . . dann ZEIT.*
In the afternoon In England	Alex goes Peter works most shops are closed	to Italy in the garden.	every summer. on Sunday.

⇨ *Im Gegensatz zum Deutschen steht die Ortsangabe* **vor** *der Zeitangabe, wenn zwei solcher Angaben aufeinander folgen.*

Grammatik

G 6 Verben (verbs)

G 6.1 Hilfsverben (auxiliaries)

⇨ *Hilfsverben „helfen" Vollverben (wie* go, take, meet *usw.) bei der Bildung der meisten Frageformen und der Zeitformen (außer der einfachen Vergangenheit).*

(a) be   *in der* Gegenwart (present tense) ... § 28

	bejahend (positive)		verneinend (negative)	
	Langform	*Kurzform*	*Langform*	*Kurzform*
I you he, she, it	am are is	'm 're 's	am not are not is not	'm not aren't/'re not* isn't/'s not*
we, you, they	are	're	are not	aren't/'re not*

* *diese Form ist besonders nachdrücklich; man benutzt sie z.B. bei Widerspruch:*
'He's English.' – 'No, he's not.'

... *in der* Vergangenheit (past tense)

	bejahend (positive)	verneinend (negative)	
	Langform	*Langform*	*Kurzform*
I, he/she/it we, you*, they	was were	was not were not	wasn't weren't

* *Einzahl und Mehrzahl*

⇨ *Von allen Verben hat nur* be *2 Formen für die Vergangenheit, nämlich* was *und* were.

(b) have   *in der* Gegenwart (present tense) ... § 33

	bejahend (positive)		verneinend (negative)	
	Langform	*Kurzform*	*Langform*	*Kurzform*
I, you he, she, it we, you, they	have has have	've 's 've	have not has not have not	haven't/'ve not* hasn't/'s not* haven't/'ve not*

* *besonders nachdrückliche Form (s. o.)*

... *in der* Vergangenheit (past tense)

	bejahend (positive)		verneinend (negative)	
	Langform	*Kurzform*	*Langform*	*Kurzform*
I, you, he, she, it, we, you, they	had	'd	had not	hadn't

* *Diese Formen gelten auch für* have got *und* have to.

(c) do/did   *Gegenwarts- und Vergangenheitsformen* § 38

	bejahend (positive) *Langform*		verneinend (negative) *Langform/Kurzform*	*Langform/Kurzform*
	Gegenwart	Vergangenheit	Gegenwart	Vergangenheit
I, you he, she, it we, you, they	do does do	did did did	do not/don't does not/doesn't do not/don't	did not/didn't did not/didn't did not/didn't

⇨ *Aussprache:* do [duː] – does [dʌz]

Grammatik

G 6.2 Modale Hilfsverben (modal auxiliaries)

⇨ *Modale Hilfsverben helfen, die Aussagekraft von Vollverben zu „modifizieren" (= zu verändern); mit ihnen drückt man z. B. „Möglichkeit/Unmöglichkeit", „Höflichkeit" u. a. aus:*
'You **can/can't** get stamps in that shop.' – '**Could** you do that for me, please?'
Modale Hilfsverben stehen immer zusammen mit einem Vollverb in der Grundform. Sie haben keine -s-Endung, keine -ing Form und keine -ed Form.

(a) can – could
§§ 42–44, (48), 61–63, 66

bejahend	verneinend (Lang-/Kurzform)		kann ausdrücken:
can	cannot/can't [ˈkænɒt/kɑːnt]	I can (cannot/can't) read it. You can (cannot/can't) get stamps there. Can you spell that, please?	(Un-)Fähigkeit (Un-)Möglichkeit eine Bitte
could		Could you do that for me? We could go to a pub.	eine höfliche Bitte einen Vorschlag, eine Möglichkeit

(b) would
§§ 42–44, (48), 78–79

bejahend (Lang-/Kurzform)		kann ausdrücken:
would/'d	I'd like to . . ./I'd love to . . . Would you like a drink? Would you like to come to my party?	einen Wunsch ein Angebot eine Einladung

(c) shall
§§ 42–44, (48), 80

in Fragen		kann ausdrücken:
Shall . . .?	Shall we go to the cinema?	einen Vorschlag

(d) should
§§ 42–44, (48), 82

bejahend	verneinend (Lang-/Kurzform)		kann ausdrücken:
should	should not/shouldn't	You should tell the police. You shouldn't eat so much. You should take 3 tablets.	einen Ratschlag eine Aufforderung eine Verpflichtung

(e) have to
§§ (48), 75

bejahend	verneinend	in Fragen
I/you **have to** he/she/it **has to** we/you/they **have to**	I/you **don't have to** he/she/it **doesn't have to** we/you/they **don't have to**	Do you **have to** . . .? Does he/she/it **have to** . . .? Do we/you/they **have to** . . .?

⇨ have to *wird in Fragen und verneinenden Aussagesätzen behandelt wie ein* **Vollverb**.

● *Gebrauch*

	kann ausdrücken:
I have to get up at six every morning. Do you have to work on Sunday?	eine Verpflichtung eine unausweichliche Notwendigkeit

Grammatik

G 6.3 Vollverben (full verbs)

(a) *Formen in der einfachen Gegenwart* (simple present)

I live in New York. You work too much. He plays the piano. She works in a supermarket. It takes an hour to get there.	We watch TV every evening. You get everything at Harrod's. They sell alligators there, too.

⇨ *Mit Ausnahme der 3. Person Einzahl lauten alle Formen wie die Grundform. Die 3. Person Einzahl wird durch ein angehängtes -s gebildet.*

⇨ *Besonderheiten bei der Schreibung:*
-es *wird an die Grundform angehängt, wenn das Verb auf* -sh, -tch *oder* -ss *endet:* washes, watches, guesses.
-ies *ist die Endung, wenn das Verb auf Mitlaut +* -y *endet:* try – tries.
Bei Wörtern auf Selbstlaut + -y *bleibt das* -y *aber erhalten:* play – plays.

⇨ *Besonderheiten in der Aussprache* (vgl. „Mehrzahl der Hauptwörter", → G 3 (a))
Nach Selbstlauten und stimmhaften Mitlauten [b, d, g, l, m, n, ŋ, ð, r, v] *wird das Endungs-*s *stimmhaft gesprochen.*
Nach „Zischlauten" [s, z, ʃ, tʃ, dʒ] *wird noch ein* [ɪ] *eingeschoben:* washes [-ɪz].
Nach stimmlosen Mitlauten [p, t, k, f, θ] *wird das Endungs-*s *stimmlos gesprochen.*

⇨ *Besonderheiten in Aussprache und Schreibung:*
go [gəʊ] – goes [gəʊz]   *aber:*   do [duː] – does [dʌz]
pay [peɪ] – pays [peɪz]   *aber:*   say [seɪ] – says [sez]

● *Gebrauch*

	Das simple present *bezeichnet* ...
I get up at six every morning. I like flowers.	regelmäßige Handlungen und Gewohnheiten etwas, was immer gilt

(b) *Formen der Vergangenheit* (simple past) §§ 54–56

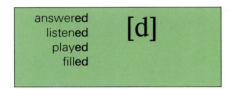
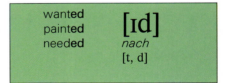

⇨ *Besonderheiten der Schreibung:* (Besonderheiten der Aussprache sind in den Übersichtskästen vermerkt.)
In den allermeisten Fällen wird -ed *an die Grundform des Verbs angehängt.*

-ied *lautet die Endung, wenn das Verb auf Mitlaut +* -y *endet;* y *wird dabei zu* i: try – tried.

Nach kurzem, betontem Selbstlaut wird der Mitlaut am Ende verdoppelt: stop – stopped; plan – planned

Endet die Grundform auf einem „stummen" -e, *so wird nur* -d *angehängt:* like – liked; use – used
Besondere Schreibweise bei prefer – preferred; travel – travelled.

● *Unregelmäßige Verben* (irregular verbs)

In Band 1 von TAKE OFF gehören folgende unregelmäßigen Verben zum Lernstoff:

bring	brought [brɔːt]	get	got [gɒt]	mean	meant [ment]	spend	spent [spent]
buy	bought [bɔːt]	give	gave [geɪv]	meet	met [met]	steal	stole [stəʊl]
come	came [keɪm]	go	went [went]	put	put [pʊt]	swim	swam [swæm]
cost	cost [kɒst]	hear	heard [hɜːd]	read [riːd]	read [red]	take	took [tʊk]
drink	drank [dræŋk]	hurt	hurt [hɜːt]	say [seɪ]	said [sed]	tell	told [təʊld]
drive	drove [drəʊv]	know	knew [njuː]	see	saw [sɔː]	think	thought [θɔːt]
eat	ate [et, eɪt]	learn	learnt, learned [lɜːnt, lɜːnd]	sell	sold [səʊld]	wear	wore [wɔː]
feel	felt [felt]			send	sent [sent]	win	won [wʌn]
find	found [faʊnd]	leave	left [left]	sit	sat [sæt]	write	wrote [rəʊt]
fly	flew [fluː]	let	let [let]	speak	spoke [spəʊk]		
forget	forgot [fəˈgɒt]	make	made [meɪd]	spell	spelt [spelt]		

Grammatik

(c) Zukunft mit 'will' (future with 'will')

	bejahend (positive)	
	Langform/Kurzform	
I, you, he/she/it we, you, they	will/'ll	take go visit

● **Gebrauch**

I think next summer will be as nice as this one.	Mit will und der Grundform des Verbs drückt man **Vorhersagen** und **Annahmen** über die **Zukunft** aus.
I'll take the tomato soup.	Diese Form dient aber auch zum Ausdruck eines **spontanen Entschlusses**.

(d) Die Verlaufsform der Gegenwart (present progressive) §§ (60), 89

I	am	watching	TV at the moment.
You	are	working	again tonight.
He	is	talking	to Jane.
She	is	going	to the cinema.
It	is	raining.	
We	are	sitting	in the garden.
You	are	drinking	my whisky.
They	are	leaving	the cinema.

Schreibregeln

Stummes e am Ende der Grundform entfällt:
leave – leaving

Mitlaute (t, n, etc.) werden nach einem kurzen, betonten Selbstlaut verdoppelt:
sit – si**tt**ing
win – wi**nn**ing

⇨ Die Verlaufsform wird aus einer Form des Hilfsverbs be und der Grundform des Vollverbs gebildet, an die man ing anhängt (wobei die o.a. Schreibregeln beachtet werden müssen).

● **Gebrauch**

	Das present progressive drückt aus, daß etwas ...
'What's Tom doing at the moment?' – 'He's washing the car.'	**zum gegenwärtigen Zeitpunkt** geschieht; wenn man dies im Deutschen hervorheben will, muß man Ausdrücke wie „gerade eben" oder „ist dabei, etwas zu tun" benutzen.
'What are you doing on Saturday?' – 'I'm going to the cinema with Jane.'	**für die nahe Zukunft geplant ist.**

(e) Die Befehlsform (imperative) § 21

Turn left. **Listen**, please.	Die **positive** Befehlsform entspricht der Grundform des Verbs.
Do not stay in the sun too long. **Don't drink** water from the tap.	Die **negative** Befehlsform wird aus do not (= don't) und der Grundform des Verbs gebildet.

Grammatik

G 7 Satzmuster (sentence structures)

(a) *Bejahende Aussagesätze* (positive statements) § 5

Subjekt (Satzgegenstand)	Prädikat (Satzaussage)		Ergänzungen/Objekte
	(Hilfsverb +)	Verb	
My name I	is am		Pierce. an engineer.
I Peter They		live works sell	in Canada. in a factory. radios on the 3rd floor.
She Jill and Peter I We You The children You	is are 'd have can could should	wearing watching like got get* go* see*	a red dress. TV at the moment. some ice in my whisky. two suitcases. blouses on the 2nd floor. to the cinema. a doctor.

* *Im Gegensatz zum Deutschen behält das Vollverb immer seinen Platz **vor den Ergänzungen**:*
*Sie **können** Blusen im 2. Stock **bekommen**./Die Kinder **könnten** ins Kino **gehen**./Sie **sollten** einen Arzt **aufsuchen**.*

(b) *Verneinende Aussagesätze* (negative statements) § 11–12

Subjekt (Satzgegenstand)	Prädikat (Satzaussage)		Ergänzungen
	Hilfsverb mit Verneinung not/n't	Verb	
I It This	'm not 's not isn't		from Australia. very expensive. my pen.
You We You Myra	can't haven't shouldn't isn't	get got drive working	stamps there. a present for him. so fast. tonight.
I Bond We	don't doesn't didn't	like work go	my job. for us. to Spain last year.

⇨ *Wenn in dem verwandten bejahenden Satz bereits ein Hilfsverb vorhanden ist, so wird bei der Verneinung not/n't mit diesem Hilfsverb verbunden:* Myra **is** working tonight. – Myra **isn't** working tonight.

⇨ *Fehlt ein solches Hilfsverb, übernimmt ein hinzugefügtes* **do/does/did** *diese Funktion:*
Bond works for us. – Bond **doesn't** work for us.   We went to Spain. – We **didn't** go to Spain.

⇨ *Nur an diesen Formen von* do *kann man dann sehen, ob es ein Satz in der Gegenwart* (do/does) *oder in der Vergangenheit* (did) *ist, oder ob über eine 3. Person Einzahl* (does) *gesprochen wird;* **die folgende Grundform des Verbs bleibt immer unverändert.**

(c) *Fragesätze* (questions)

● *Ja/Nein-Fragen* (Yes/No-questions) § 7
mit Hilfsverben/modalen Hilfsverben

● *Kurzantworten*** § 18
(short answers)

Hilfsverb	Subjekt	Verb	Ergänzungen
Are Is Is	you this Bob	 reading	Peter Brown? your car? a book?
Can Have Should	you they we	help got answer	me?* posters of London Bridge? this letter?

Yes, I am.***/No, I'm not. Yes, it is.***/No, it isn't. Yes, he is./No, he isn't.
Yes, I can./No, I can't. Yes, they have./No, they haven't. Yes, we should./No, we shouldn't.

Grammatik

* *Die Wortfolge in diesen Sätzen weicht vom Deutschen teilweise ab; vgl. 'Can you **help** me?' und „Können Sie mir **helfen**?"*
** *In Kurzantworten nimmt man das **Hilfsverb** der Frage wieder auf.*
*** *Bei **bejahenden Kurzantworten** wird immer die **Langform** (→ G 6.1 (a)) benutzt.*

● *Ja/Nein-Fragen* (Yes/No-questions) § 7
  mit do/does/did

Hilfsverb	Subjekt	Verb	Ergänzungen
Do	you	watch	TV every night?
Does	Peter	drink	red wine?
Did	Susan	tell	you about it?

● *Kurzantworten* § 18
  (short answers)

Yes, I do./No, I don't.
Yes, he does./No, he doesn't.
Yes, she did./No, she didn't.

⇨ *Am Anfang einer Ja/Nein-Frage steht **immer** ein Hilfsverb. Wenn der mit dieser Frage „verwandte" Aussagesatz kein Hilfsverb enthält, so muß die Frage mit do/does/did beginnen, z.B.:*
I watch TV every night. – **Do** you watch TV . . . ?

Wenn die Frage sich auf eine 3. Person bezieht, beginnt sie mit Does *(he/she/Jack/your teacher/. . .?) – das Verb bleibt dann in der Grundform.*

*Bei Fragen nach etwas Vergangenem steht **immer*** Did *am Anfang einer solchen Frage.*

⇨ *In Kurzantworten greift man das **Hilfsverb** des Fragesatzes wieder auf.*

● *Fragen mit einleitendem Fragewort* (W-questions) *und* be, have (got), can § 9

Fragewort	Hilfsverb	Subjekt	Verb	Ergänzungen
Where	are	you		from?
Where	can	you	get	stamps in this department store?
What	is	Mrs Franklin	looking	for?
When	is	your bus		home after work?
What	have	you	got	for me?

● *Fragen mit einleitendem Fragewort* (W-questions) *und mit* do/does/did § 9

Fragewort	Hilfsverb	Subjekt	Verb	Ergänzungen
When	do	you	get up	in the morning?
Where	does	your wife	work?	
What	did	he	say	to her?

⇨ *Für die Benutzung von* do/does/did *in solchen Fragesätzen gilt das gleiche wie bei den Ja/Nein-Fragen: ist im verwandten Aussagesatz kein Hilfsverb vorhanden, tritt eine Form von* do *ein.*

● *Fragen nach dem Subjekt des Satzes* § 6

Fragewort = Subjekt	Hilfsverb (oder Verb)	Ergänzungen
Who	is	that man over there?
Who	lives	in London?

⇨ *Fragen, die mit* who *(= wer) beginnen, sind Fragen nach dem Subjekt eines Satzes. Sie werden wie deutsche Fragen gebildet („Wer lebt in London?"); auch bei Vollverben (hier:* lives*) steht kein* do/does/did.

Alle anderen Fragen mit Fragewort, die wir in G 7 (c) behandelt haben, sind Fragen nach anderen Satzteilen als dem Subjekt.

Ebenso verhalten sich Fragen nach dem Subjekt mit dem Fragewort what, *z.B.* 'What comes next?' *(Aber:* 'What do you like?'*).*

Grammatik

(d) *Sätze mit* there §20

There **is a** blouse in my suitcase. There **are three** socks in my suitcase.	= dt. „Es gibt/Da sind . . .", there is/are *wird in der Regel zusammen mit einer Ortsbestimmung benutzt.*
Is there a bus stop near the hotel? How many hotels are there in Clacton?	*In Fragen wird* is/are *und* there *vertauscht.*

G 8 Satzmuster mit der Grundform/-ing Form (infinitive/-ing form)

(a) *Manche Verben können als Ergänzung eine Konstruktion mit einem anderen Verb haben; hier steht dann, oft im Unterschied zur entsprechenden Struktur im Deutschen,* to *zusammen mit der Grundform:*

I **want to invite** Carl, too. I'd **love to come**.	*Ich möchte Karl auch einladen.* *Ich würde gern kommen.*

(b) *Bei anderen Verben entspricht der Gebrauch von* to *dem deutschen „zu":*

Brighton **seems to be** nicer. I **prefer to travel** by train when I've got the time.	*Brighton scheint schöner zu sein.* *Ich ziehe es vor, mit dem Zug zu fahren, wenn . . .*

(c) *In wieder anderen Fällen steht das zweite Verb in der -ing Form:*

I **like** garden**ing**. Peter **likes** driv**ing** fast cars.	*Ich liebe es, im Garten zu arbeiten./. . . „das Gärtnern".* *Peter fährt gern schnelle Autos./Peter liebt es, schnelle Autos zu fahren.*

⇨ *Am besten prägen Sie sich solche Strukturen einzeln ein, wenn Sie sie im Lehrbuch finden. Einige Regeln werden Sie später lernen, wenn Sie noch mehr solcher Verben kennen.*

(d) *Die -ing Form kann auch den Platz eines Hauptworts übernehmen, z. B.:*
. . . without ask**ing** your doctor. – Talk**ing** about the weather.

G 10 Nebensätze (subordinate clauses)

Das Deutsche verwendet in Nebensätzen eine andere Wortstellung:

Go straight ahead,	until	**you get**	to the traffic-lights.		. . . because	**it is**	'3'.
Immer geradeaus,	*bis*	***Sie***	*zur Ampel*	***kommen**.*	*. . . weil*	***es***	*eine „3" ist.*

⇨ *Im Englischen entspricht die Wortstellung in Nebensätzen der in Hauptsätzen.*

● *Relativsätze* (relative clauses) §§ 238, 242, 244

An English friend, **who** wants to travel in Germany, . . .	*(. . . Freund, der . . ./. . . eine Freundin, die . . .)*
the first thing ☐ you do in the morning the last thing ☐ he does the person ☐ we are looking for five things ☐ an ideal boss does things ☐ people do in the evening the people ☐ you meet	*In diesen und anderen Beispielen steht im entsprechenden deutschen Satz ein Fürwort (z. B. „die", „welche").* *Im Englischen fallen solche* relative pronouns *häufig weg (Regeln im 2. Band).*

● *Andere Nebensätze*

⇨ *Beachten Sie die Wortfolge im Nebensatz, der im Englischen stets die gleiche Wortfolge wie ein Hauptsatz hat (s. o.!).*

until while when before	Go on, **until** you get to the traffic-lights. . . ., **while** I am taking a photo of him. **When** we went back, everything was over. Don't wear swim wear **when** you visit a church. They always talk about the weather **before** they talk about other things.	*(bis)* *(während)* *(als)* *(wenn)* *(bevor)*

Grammatik

where	Don't leave things in the car, **where** everybody can see them.	*(wo)*
that	I can see **that** you are ill.	*(daß)*
so that	I was **so** nervous **that** I made a lot of mistakes.	*(so..., daß)*
if	Your partner wins, **if** the answer is 'no'.	*(wenn; unter der Bedingung, daß...)*
	He wants to know **if** your answer is 'yes'.	*(ob)*
to	... what they say **to** make their story more interesting.	*(um ... zu)*
	... nothing **to** write on	
although	..., **although** we learned a lot about America.	*(obwohl; obgleich)*

G 13 Präpositionen (prepositions) §210

(a) *Präpositionen mit einem Hauptwort. Sie bezeichnen:*

- *Ort und Richtung*

at Brighton; **at** the bar	*(in, an)*	**in** London; **in** the glass	*(in)*
near London	*(nahe bei)*	**next to** Harrod's	*(direkt neben)*
in front of the house	*(vor)*		
on the table	*(auf)*	**under** the table	*(unter)*
into the house	*(in ... hinein)*		
from London	*(aus, von ... her)*	**to** London	*(nach)*
among hundreds of tourists	*(mitten unter)*	**between** X and Y	*(zwischen [zweien])*

- *Zeit*

at six o'clock	*(um)*	**in** 1940	*(in/–)*	**on** Monday; **on** (the) 3rd of May	*(am)*
from nine **to** five	*(von ... bis)*			**till/until** six	*(bis)*
before six o'clock	*(vor)*	**after** lunch	*(nach)*		

- *andere Verhältnisse, z. B. Mittel, Zweck, ...*

with my friends	*(mit)*	**without** money	*(ohne)*
by car/train	*(mit [Verkehrsmittel])*	**for** Jim	*(für)*
talk **about** him	*(über)*		

(b) *Präpositionen im Satz* §211

Where are you **from**?
I've got nothing to write **on**.
... something to talk **about**.
It tells you who to look **for**.
What are you looking **for**?

⇨ *Präpositionen stehen oft **am Ende eines Satzes**, vor allem in Fragen und verkürzten Nebensätzen.*

G 14 Die Satzmelodie (intonation) §§ 23–24

- *Aussagesätze und Fragen mit einem einleitenden Fragewort, aber auch Befehle und Ausrufe beginnen mit einem stimmlichen Höhepunkt auf der ersten betonten Silbe; die Satzmelodie fällt langsam, auf der letzten betonten Silbe dann stark ab:*

    The children could go to the cinema.   What have you got for Peter?

- *Bei Ja/Nein-Fragen steigt die Stimme auf der letzten betonten Silbe deutlich an:*

    Have you got a car?   Are you German?

- *Wie im Deutschen ist die Satzmelodie aber auch ein Mittel, um einzelne Teile des Satzes hervorzuheben, und sie zeigt auch starke gefühlsmäßige Beteiligung an.*

Wörterverzeichnis

Dieses Wörterverzeichnis ist als „Lernwörterbuch" angelegt: in der mittleren Spalte werden einsprachige Lernhilfen gegeben, die das Erschließen und Behalten der Wortbedeutungen erleichtern sollen.

Und so arbeiten Sie mit diesem Wörterverzeichnis am besten:

(1) „Von links nach rechts": Prägen Sie sich Wörter, mittlere Spalte und deutsche Übersetzung ein. Decken Sie dann die deutsche Übersetzung ab und stellen Sie fest, ob Sie alle Wörter im Gedächtnis haben.

(2) „Von rechts nach links": Decken Sie die linke Spalte ab und versuchen Sie, in der mittleren Spalte das richtige englische Wort dort einzusetzen, wo die Tilde (~) steht. (Achtung: bei Verben, die links mit 'to' stehen, nur ihre Grundform einsetzen.)
Steht ein Wort am Anfang eines Satzes in der mittleren Spalte, so findet sich vor der Tilde der erste Buchstabe groß geschrieben: E~ are you Pat Lewis?)
Wenn in der mittleren Spalte einmal nichts steht: nur das deutsche Wort auf Englisch wiedergeben.

≈	in der mittleren Spalte steht ein *bedeutungsähnliches* Wort
≠	das Wort hat eine abweichende Bedeutung (Zeichen für „ungleich")
→	Verweis auf ein früher vorgekommenes Wort
opposite	Gegenteil/Gegensatz
[!]	Achtung! Wort wird von Deutschen oft falsch ausgesprochen
	Hinweise auf schwierige Betonungen:
O o o oder O o	= Betonung auf der 1. Silbe
o O o oder o O	= Betonung auf der 2. Silbe
o o O	= Betonung auf der 3. Silbe; weitere Betonungen nach dem gleichen System
Fettdruck	Wörter, die in den Prüfungen des Volkshochschulverbandes verlangt werden – wichtiger Lernstoff
normaler Druck	Wörter und Redewendungen, die aus solchem verbindlichen Lernstoff abgeleitet sind
kursive Wörter	lehrwerkeigener Wortschatz – muß man nicht so gründlich lernen

Wörter in Blau sind nur zum Verständnis dieses einen Textes wichtig; sie brauchen nicht gelernt zu werden: tauchen sie später noch einmal auf, werden sie wieder erklärt.

Unit 0

1.1
I [aɪ]		ich
am [æm]	I'm [aɪm] = I am	bin
your [jɔː]	[!]	Ihr(e); dein(e)
guide [gaɪd]		*(Fremden-)Führer/in*
hello [həˈləʊ]	H~, Alf. H~, Pat.	Hallo; Guten Tag
good [gʊd]		gut
evening [ˈiːvnɪŋ]	O o	Abend
Good evening.	G~, Mr Taylor. I am John Smith, your guide.	Guten Abend.
my [maɪ]		mein(e)
name [neɪm]		Name
is [ɪz]		ist
My name is . . .	I am John. ≈ M~ John.	Ich heiße . . .; mein Name ist . . .
Mr [ˈmɪstə]		Herr *(vor Namen)*
English [ˈɪŋglɪʃ]		englisch; Englisch-
teacher [ˈtiːtʃə]	Pat Lewis is your ~.	Lehrer/in
and [ænd, ənd]	Pat is your teacher ~ Lucy is your guide.	und
what [wɒt]		was; wie
What's your name?	W~? – I'm Alf Berg.	Wie heißen Sie?; Wie ist Ihr Name?
please [pliːz]	And what's your name, ~? – Pat Lewis.	bitte
nice [naɪs]		nett; schön; angenehm
to [tʊ, tə]		*hier:* zu
to meet [miːt]		*(jemanden)* treffen; kennenlernen
you [juː]		dich; Sie
Nice to meet you.	I – ~	*Begrüßungsformel, etwa:* Sehr erfreut.
	I'm Alf Berg. – N~, Alf.	

1.2
are [ɑː]	I am Tarzan, you ~ Jane.	bist; sind
you [juː]		du; Sie
Are you . . .?		Sind Sie . . .?/Bist Du . . .?
to excuse [ɪkˈskjuːz]		entschuldigen
me [miː]	I – my – ~	mir; mich
Excuse me, . . .	E~, are you Pat Lewis?	*jemanden ansprechen:* Entschuldigen Sie bitte, . . .
no [nəʊ]		nein
not [nɒt]	I'm ~ a teacher. I'm a guide.	nicht
No, I'm not.		Nein. (Das bin ich nicht.)
sorry [ˈsɒrɪ]		es tut mir leid
yes [jes]	*opposite:* no	Ja.
Yes, I am.	Are you my guide? – Y~.	Ja. (Das bin ich.)
. . ., too [tuː]	Pat is nice and Lucy is nice, ~.	auch
Nice to meet you, too.		*Formel als Antwort auf Begrüßung, etwa:* Freut mich auch.

1.3	names [neɪmz] **this** [ðɪs] This is . . . **that** [ðæt]	'Vanessa' and 'Charly' are English ~. Bob, ~ Pat, my English teacher. Is ~ your guide? – No, ~ is Mr Taylor.	Namen *(Mehrzahl)* diese(r, s); dies, das *(bei Vorstellungen:)* Dies ist . . . . jene(r, s); der, die, das (da)
2.1	**morning** ['mɔ:nɪŋ] **Good morning.** **Mrs** ['mɪsɪz] **Miss** [mɪs]	*opposite:* evening G~, Jim. – G~. Mr Brown – ~ Miller Mr – Mrs – ~	Morgen Guten Morgen. Frau *(vor Namen)* Fräulein *(meist vor Namen)*
2.2	*Hi!* [haɪ] **how** [haʊ] **today** [tə'deɪ] How are you (today)? **some** [sʌm] some **of** my . . . [əv] **best** [best] **friend** [frend] **are** [ɑ:] **flower** ['flaʊə] **for** [fɔ:, fə] **girl** [gɜ:l]	H~, Peter. – Hello, Mr Taylor. Hello, Pat. H~? **[!]**: o O o Peter, this is my ~, John. 'Iris' and 'Rose' are names for ~s. This is a flower ~ you. 'Iris' is a name for a ~ and for a flower.	*(umgangssprachlich:)* Hallo! wie *(Fragewort)* heute Wie geht es dir/Ihnen (heute)? einige einige meiner . . . beste(r, s) Freund/in sind Blume für Mädchen

2.3	**fine** [faɪn]
	I'm fine.
	thanks [θæŋks]
	thank you ['θæŋk jʊ]
	so [səʊ]
	bad [bæd]
	Not so bad.
	
	so-so
		
		How are you? – I'm fine, ~.
		= thanks
		
		opposite: good
			fein; gut
			Mit geht's gut.
			danke
			danke (schön)
			so
			schlecht
			je nach Tonfall: Recht gut;
			  oder: Nicht so besonders.
			etwa: Na ja, es geht; *auch:*
			  Nicht schlecht.

3	**goodbye** [gʊd'baɪ] **'bye** [baɪ] **to see** [si:] **next** [nekst] **week** [wi:k] **See you** (next week)!	*opposite:* Hello. Goodbye. S~ next week!	auf Wiedersehen *etwa:* Tschüß! sehen nächste(r, s) Woche *(Abschiedsformel:)* Bis dann/bald! (Bis nächste Woche!)

Unit 1

1	**again** [ə'gen]	See you ~ next week.	wieder

2.1	**where** [weə]
	Where . . . from? [frɒm]
	Where are you from?
	
	from [frɒm]
	the [ðə], *vor Vokalen* [ði]
	the (United) States
	  *(of **America**)*
	  [ðə (ju:'naɪtɪd) 'steɪts (əv ə'merɪkə)]
	Are you English? ['ɪŋglɪʃ]
	Scotland ['skɒtlənd]
	British ['brɪtɪʃ]
	I'm British.
	
	so [səʊ]
	Canada ['kænədə]
	the USA [ðə ju: es 'eɪ]
	England ['ɪŋglənd]
	Wales [weɪlz]
	Northern Ireland ['nɔ:ðən 'aɪələnd]
	*Great **Britain*** [greɪt 'brɪtən]
	Ireland ['aɪələnd]
	Australia [ɒ'streɪljə, ɔ:'streɪljə]
	New Zealand [nju: 'zi:lənd]
		That's not Lucy. W~ is Lucy?
		
		I'm ~ Berlin. I'm not ~ Essen.
		the teacher; the English teacher
		= USA
		
		A~? – No, I'm not. I'm American.
		
		= England, Scotland and Wales
			wo
			Woher . . .?
			Wo sind Sie her;
			  Wo kommen Sie her?
			von; aus
			der; die; das
			die (Vereinigten) Staaten
			  (von Amerika)
			
			etwa: Sind Sie aus England?
			Schottland
			britisch
			Ich bin aus Großbritannien;
			  Ich bin Brite.
			hier: also
			Kanada
			die USA
			England
			Wales
			Nordirland
			Großbritannien
			Irland
			Australien
			Neuseeland

2.2	*France* [frɑ:ns] *French* [frentʃ] *Germany* ['dʒɜ:mənɪ] *German* ['dʒɜ:mən] *Italy* ['ɪtəlɪ] *Italian* [ɪ'tæljən] *Milan* [mɪ'læn]	 **[!]**: O o o **[!]**: o O o **[!]**: o O	Frankreich französisch Deutschland deutsch Italien italienisch *engl. für* Milano (Mailand)

2.3	**a** [ə]		ein(e)
	village [ˈvɪlɪdʒ]	Oberammergau is a ~ in Germany.	Dorf
	near [nɪə]	West Wickham is ~ London.	nahe; in der Nähe von
	Munich [ˈmjuːnɪk]		*engl. für* München
	it [ɪt]		es
	city [ˈsɪtɪ]	Berlin is a ~ and London is a ~, too.	(Groß-)Stadt
	town [taʊn]	Rothenburg is a ~, and Swansea is a ~, too.	Stadt
	in [ɪn]	Rothenburg is ~ Germany, Swansea is ~ Wales.	in
	Austria [ˈɒstrɪə, ˈɔːstrɪə]		Österreich
	Switzerland [ˈswɪtsələnd]		Schweiz
	but [bʌt]	I'm English, ~ my friend is German.	aber
	to live [lɪv]	I'm Austrian, but I ~ in Germany.	leben
	now [naʊ]	I'm from England, but I live in Germany ~.	jetzt
2.4	**Is that …?**		Ist das …?
	an	a teacher; ~ English teacher	*Form von* **a** *vor Selbstlauten;* ein(e)
	car [kɑː]	It's a Volkswagen. It's a German ~.	Auto
	No, it isn't.	Is that an American car? – N~, it's Italian.	Nein. (Das ist es nicht.)
	Yes it is.		Ja.
	to think [θɪŋk]	A Talbot? That's a French car, I ~.	denken; *hier:* glauben
	old [əʊld]	A Morris is an ~ English car.	alt
3.1	**can** [kæn]	Where is Lucy? C~ you see Lucy?	können; kann(st); könnt
	to spell [spel]	Can you ~ that, please? – Yes, M-O-R-R-I-S.	buchstabieren
3.2	**surname** [ˈsɜːneɪm]	I'm Peter Peters. My ~ is Peters,	Nachname; Familienname
	first name [fɜːst neɪm]	and my ~ is Peter.	Vorname
	double [ˈdʌbl]	RR is ~ R.	Doppel-
3.3	**hotel** [həʊˈtel]	[!]: o O; = *German*	Hotel
	to listen [ˈlɪsn]		(zu)hören
	guest [gest]	Is Mr Taylor a ~ in your hotel?	Gast
	the guest's name	What is ~?	der Name des Gastes
	he [hiː]	I – you – ~	er
	his [hɪz]	I – my; you – your; he – ~	seine
	nationality [næʃəˈnælətɪ]	[!]: o o O o o; What's your ~? – I'm British.	Staatsangehörigkeit; Nationalität
3.4	**I've got** [aɪv gɒt]	= I have got	ich habe
	reservation [rezəˈveɪʃn]	[!]: o o O o; I've got a hotel ~ for tonight in London.	Reservierung; Vorbestellung
	tonight [təˈnaɪt]	→ today	heute abend; heute nacht
	Vancouver [vænˈkuːvə]		(Stadt in Kanada)
	here [hɪə]	I live ~ in London, not in Swansea.	hier
	key [kiː]		Schlüssel
4.1	**job** [dʒɒb]	a guide, a teacher = ~s	Arbeit; Beruf
	bank [bæŋk]		Bank(haus)
	secretary [ˈsekrətərɪ]	[!]: O o o o	Sekretär/in
	waiter, waitress [ˈweɪtə, ˈweɪtrɪs]		Kellner, Kellnerin
	taxi driver [ˈtæksɪ ˈdraɪvə]		Taxifahrer/in
	hairdresser [ˈheədresə]		Friseur, Friseuse
	sales manager [ˈseɪlz ˈmænɪdʒə]		Verkaufsleiter/in
	she [ʃiː]	I – you – he – ~ – it	sie
	he's a waiter		er ist Kellner
	we [wiː]	I – you – he – she – it – ~	wir
	to write [raɪt]		schreiben
	to say [seɪ]	Please listen to what I ~.	sagen; sprechen
4.2	**What's your job?**	W~? – I'm a taxi driver.	Was sind Sie von Beruf?
	shop assistant [ˈʃɒp əˈsɪstənt]		Verkäufer/in
	student [ˈstjuːdnt]	[!]: O o; = *German*	Student/in; Kursteilnehmer/in
	housewife [ˈhaʊswaɪf]		Hausfrau
	engineer [endʒɪˈnɪə]		Ingenieur; Techniker
	to work [wɜːk]	What's your job? – I ~ in a bank.	arbeiten
	factory [ˈfæktərɪ]	The Volkswagen car ~ is in Wolfsburg.	Fabrik
	supermarket [ˈsuːpəmɑːkɪt]		Supermarkt
	shop [ʃɒp]	I work in a ~. I'm a shop assistant.	Geschäft
	office [ˈɒfɪs]	I work in an ~. I'm a secretary.	Büro
4.3	**to like** [laɪk]	I ~ Mozart.	mögen; gern haben
	How do you like B.?		Wie gefällt Ihnen B.?
	(I like it) very much [ˈverɪ ˈmʌtʃ]		sehr; außerordentlich (in Verbindung mit Verben)
	interesting [ˈɪntrəstɪŋ]	[!]: O o o	interessant
5.1	**How do you do?** [haʊdjʊˈduː]	How do you do? – How do you do?	(Redewendung bei Vorstellungen in einer formellen Situation; Antwort immer auch: 'How do you do?')
	family [ˈfæmɪlɪ]	[!]: O o o	Familie

5.3	*cowboy* ['kaʊbɔɪ]		Cowboy
	night [naɪt]	(→ tonight)	Nacht
	night club ['naɪt klʌb]		Nachtclub

6	opinion *Meinung*	like *wie z. B.*	to want *wollen*
	by *von*	kilt *Schottenrock*	to be like us *wie wir sein*
	that *daß*	hat *Hut*	most *die meisten*
	only *nur*	often *oft*	people *Leute*
	or *oder*	sometimes *manchmal*	to look at *ansehen*
	clothes *Kleidung*	to know *wissen*	animal *Tier*
	of course *natürlich*	last Sunday *vorigen Sonntag*	
	country *Land*	who *der, die; welche(r)*	

7	who *wer*	

Die Wörter in Blau dienen nur dazu, Ihnen das Textverständnis zu erleichtern. Sie sind kein Lernstoff; wenn ein solches Wort später noch einmal auftaucht, wird es so erklärt wie alle anderen neuen Wörter!

Unit 2

1.1	*damn it* ['dæmɪt]		verdammt
1.2	**how many** [haʊ 'menɪ]	H~ can you see? – I can see three.	wieviel(e)
	are there [ɑː ðeə]		sind; gibt es
	there is/there are ['ðeərɪz, 'ðeərɑː, 'ðeərə]		es gibt; da ist/da sind
	garden ['gɑːdn]	There are roses, irises and violets in the ~.	Garten
	only ['əʊnlɪ]	What's your job? – I'm '~' a housewife.	nur
	none [nʌn]	How many are there – three, four? – No, there are ~.	kein(e, s, er)
	right [raɪt]	Are you English? – Yes, that's ~, I'm from London.	richtig
	wrong [rɒŋ]	*opposite:* right	falsch
	you are right/wrong		Sie haben (nicht) recht
	to win [wɪn]	You can ~ DM 1,000,000 in the Lotto.	gewinnen
1.3	**telephone** ['telɪfəʊn]		Telefon
	number ['nʌmbə]	My telephone ~ is 854 106.	Nummer
	her [hɜː]	he – his; she – ~	ihr(e)
	double one ['dʌbl]	→ double R	*etwa:* zweimal die Eins
1.5	Is that you, John?		Bist du es, John?
	to speak [spiːk]	Can you ~ English? (≠ say)	sprechen
	Yes, speaking.		*etwa:* Ja, am Apparat.
	who [huː]	W~ are you? What's your name?	wer
1.7	**Directory Inquiries** [daɪ'rektərɪ ɪn'kwaɪərɪz]		(Telefon-)Auskunft
	which [wɪtʃ]	W~ town? – Coventry.	welche(r, s)
	then [ðen]		dann
	to find [faɪnd]	I cannot ~ the keys. Where are they?	finden
	the name **of the** hotel		den Namen des Hotels
	person ['pɜːsn]	[!]: O o; = German	Person
	telephone directory ['telɪfəʊn daɪ'rektərɪ]	His telephone number is not in the ~.	Telefonbuch
	to write down ['raɪt 'daʊn]	(→ write)	aufschreiben; notieren
1.8	**just** [dʒʌst]	≈ only	gerade; *hier:* nur
	moment ['məʊmənt]	[!]: O o; = German	Moment; Augenblick
	Just a moment.		Einen Augenblick.
	to take [teɪk]	Can I ~ your car?	nehmen
	or [ɔː]	Are you German ~ Austrian?	oder
	list [lɪst]		Liste
	neighbour ['neɪbə]		Nachbar/in
	to phone [fəʊn]	→ telephone	anrufen; telefonieren
	for Inge's number [fɔː, fə]		*hier:* wegen Inges Nummer
	night school ['naɪt skuːl]		Abendschule; „Volkshochschule"
	thing [θɪŋ]	What's that ~? What is it?	Ding
	to tell [tel]	T~ me your name. = Say what your name is.	sagen; erzählen
2.1	*Bingo* ['bɪŋgəʊ]		*eine Art Zahlenlottospiel*
	last [lɑːst]	Zarah is the ~ name on the list.	letzte(r, s, n)
	number ['nʌmbə]	Write down the ~s 45 – 83.	*hier:* Zahl
	to complete [kəm'pliːt]	Some of the names are not on this list. Can you ~ it, please?	vervollständigen
	to (complete)		um zu (vervollständigen)
2.3	*Buzz* [bʌz]		*Name eines Spiels, etwa:* „Summen"
	because [bɪ'kɒz]	Heidi and Marcel speak German and French ~ they are from Switzerland.	weil
	two **times** three [taɪmz]	Two ~ three is six.	2 mal 3

3.1	**their** [ðeə]	his friend + her friend = ~ friends		ihr(e)
	address [ə'dres]	[!]: ...dd...; Please write down your name, ~, and telephone number.		Adresse
	street [stri:t]	His address is 45, King S~.		Straße
	road [rəʊd]	the streets of London, but the ~ from Dover to London		Landstraße
	avenue ['ævənju:]	[!]: O o o; Av. or Ave.		Allee; „Prachtstraße"
	square [skweə]			(öffentlicher) Platz
	cinema ['sɪnəmə]			Kino
3.2	**to ask** [ɑ:sk]			fragen
	post code ['pəʊst kəʊd]			Postleitzahl
4	**they** [ðeɪ]	he + she = ~		sie (Mehrzahl)
	on [ɒn]	Where are my keys? – They are ~ the telephone directory.		auf; *hier:* im
	floor [flɔ:]			*hier:* Stock(werk); Etage
	first [fɜ:st]	*opposite:* last		erste(r, s)
	second ['sekənd]	His name is Philip Mark Rose. His ~ name is Mark.		zweite(r, s)
	third [θɜ:d]	Unit 3 = the ~ Unit		dritte(r, s)
	fourth [fɔ:θ]	Unit 4 = the ~ Unit		vierte(r, s)
	fifth [fɪfθ]	Unit 5 = the ~ Unit		fünfte(r, s)
	building ['bɪldɪŋ]	Can you tell me the name of that old ~? – Yes, it's Westminster Abbey.		Gebäude
	ground floor [graʊnd 'flɔ:]			Erdgeschoß
5.1	**left** [left]			links
	right [raɪt]			rechts
	to turn (left/right) [tɜ:n]			(links/rechts) abbiegen
	to go [gəʊ]			gehen
	straight ahead [streɪt ə'hed]	Go ~, turn left, and there it is.		immer geradeaus
5.2	**careful** ['keəfʊl]			sorgfältig
	to be [bi:]	I am, you are, he/she/it is		sein
	Be careful!	B~, there's a car!		Seien Sie vorsichtig!
	to stop [stɒp]	This is the street. Can you ~ here, please?		anhalten
	to go on [gəʊ 'ɒn]	I think the building is in the next street. Can you ~, please?		weitergehen/fahren; fortfahren
5.3	**to get to** ['get tʊ]	Can you tell me how to ~ Westminster Abbey, please?		(hin)kommen; gelangen
	bus [bʌs]	= *German*		Bus; Omnibus
	station [steɪʃn]			Bahnhof
	bus station			Omnibusbahnhof
	go straight **along** here [ə'lɒŋ]			*etwa:* gehen Sie hier geradeaus
	until [ʌn'tɪl]	I work from 9 ~ 5.		bis
	traffic light(s) ['træfɪk laɪts]			Verkehrsampel(n)
	post office Postamt			
	book shop Buchladen			
5.4	**to want** [wɒnt]			wollen
	you want to go to ...			Sie wollen zu(m, r) ... gehen
	corner ['kɔ:nə]			Ecke
	at the corner	The bank is ~ of King Street and London Road.		an der Ecke
	museum [mju:'zɪəm]	[!]: o O o; = *German*		Museum
	book shop ['bʊk ʃɒp]			Buchladen
	opposite ['ɒpəzɪt]	Dover is ~ Calais. Ludwigshafen is ~ Mannheim.		gegenüber (von)
	nearest ['nɪərɪst]			nächste(r, s)
	department store [dɪ'pɑ:tmənt stɔ:]	Harrods, Selfridges and Hertie are ~s.		Kaufhaus; Warenhaus
	next to ['nekstə]	The bank is ~ the book shop.		(direkt) neben(an)
	into ['ɪntʊ]	Go ~ that building, his office is on the 1st floor.		in (hinein)
	turn into X Street			biegen Sie in die X-Straße ein/ab
	on your left/right			auf Ihrer linken/rechten Seite; links/rechts
	entrance ['entrəns]	Where is the ~ to the bank?		Eingang
	park [pɑ:k]	= *German*		Park
	exit ['eksɪt]	*opposite:* entrance		Ausgang
	to know [nəʊ]			wissen
	... wants to know ...	Linda ~ where the post office is. Can you tell her?		möchte wissen
	post office ['pəʊst 'ɒfɪs]			Postamt
	school [sku:l]	→ night school		Schule
	restaurant ['restərɒŋ]	[!]: O o o; = *German*		Restaurant

Baker Street ['beɪkə striːt]	Wall Street ['wɔːl striːt]	Grand Hotel ['grænd həʊ'tel]
Columbo Street [kə'lʌmbəʊ striːt]	Dimple Street ['dɪmpl striːt]	Pizza Express ['piːtsə ɪk'spres]
Park Avenue [pɑːk 'ævənjuː]	Green Park ['griːn 'pɑːk]	Odeon ['əʊdɪən]
Dallas Street ['dæləs striːt]	Jeans Shop ['dʒiːnz ʃɒp]	boutique [buː'tiːk]
Bridge Street ['brɪdʒ striːt]	Bank of Arabia ['bæŋk əv ə'reɪbɪə]	bazaar [bə'zɑː]
Broad Street ['brɔːd striːt]	St. Martin's [snt 'mɑːtɪnz]	
Bourbon Street ['bɜːbən striːt]	Police Station [pə'liːs 'steɪʃn]	

8
town walk *Stadtrundgang*	picture *Bild*	furniture *Möbel*
to cross *überqueren*	time *Zeit*	large *groß*
to follow *folgen*	built *erbaut*	damaged *beschädigt*
to pass *vorbeigehen an*	century *Jahrhundert*	by fire *durch Feuer*
church *Kirche*	example *Beispiel*	door *Tür*
through *durch*	up *hinauf*	small *klein*
gate *Tor*	wall *Mauer*	take you back *versetzen Sie zurück*
which *welche(r, s)*	about *ca.*	that *welche(r, s)*
to give *geben*	with *mit*	found *fanden*

Unit 3

1
T-shirt ['tiːʃɜːt]	= German	T-shirt
suitcase ['suːtkeɪs]	What have you got in your ~?	Koffer
skirt [skɜːt]		Rock
suit [suːt]		Anzug *(für Herren od. Damen)*
shoe [ʃuː]		Schuh
socks [sɒks]	I can't find my shoes and ~.	Socken
pullover ['pʊləʊvə]	[!]: O o o; = German	Pullover
trousers ['traʊzəz]	Here's my pullover, but where are my ~?	Hose
umbrella [ʌm'brelə]	o O o	Regenschirm
dress [dres]		Kleid
blouse [blaʊz]	[!]	Bluse
coat [kəʊt]		Mantel
shirt [ʃɜːt]		Hemd
a pair of [ə 'peə(r) əv]	I've got ~ shoes for you.	ein Paar
jeans [dʒiːnz]	= German	Jeans

2.1
beautiful ['bjuːtəfʊl]	I think Rothenburg is a ~ town.	schön
over there ['əʊvə 'ðeə]	The key? It's ~, near the telephone.	dort drüben; da drüben
smart [smɑːt]	a beautiful dress, a ~ suit.	schick; elegant; fesch
quite [kwaɪt]		ziemlich
expensive [ɪk'spensɪv]	£500 is quite ~ for a coat.	teuer

2.2
very ['verɪ]	(→ I like it very much); very nice/smart/old	sehr *(bei Eigenschaftswörtern)*
too (expensive) [tuː]	St. Moritz is ~ expensive for me.	zu (teuer)

3.1
to wear [weə]		*(ein Kleidungsstück)* tragen
(she) is wearing	The Queen ~ a beautiful coat.	(sie) trägt *(gerade)*
grey [greɪ]		grau
red [red]		rot
green [griːn]		grün
blue [bluː]		blau
yellow ['jeləʊ]		gelb
brown [braʊn]		braun
black [blæk]		schwarz
white [waɪt]		weiß
made in ... [meɪd]	M~ Germany.	hergestellt in ...
by ... [baɪ]	The Messiah is ~ Handel.	von ...
100 % ['wʌn 'hʌndrəd pɜː'sent]	one hundred **per cent**	100 Prozent
wool [wʊl]		Wolle

3.2
cotton ['kɒtn]	a nice, white ~ blouse	Baumwolle
made of ['meɪd əv]	~ wool	hergestellt aus

4.1
to get [get]	You can ~ suitcases over there.	bekommen
to do the shopping ['duː ðə 'ʃɒpɪŋ]		einkaufen; Einkäufe machen
radio ['reɪdɪəʊ]	[!]: = German	Radio
TV ['tiː 'viː]	= television	TV; Fernseh-
department [dɪ'pɑːtmənt]	→ department store	Abteilung
record ['rekɔːd]	[!]: O o; It's a ~ by the Beatles, I think.	Schallplatte
cassette [kə'set]	[!]: = German	Kassette
sports wear ['spɔːts weə]		Sportbekleidung
child, children [tʃaɪld, 'tʃɪldrən]	My ~'s names are Tom, Susan and Caroline.	Kind, Kinder
children's wear		Kinderbekleidung
man, men [mæn, men]		Mann, Männer
men's wear	Pullovers, trousers, suits = ~	Herrenbekleidung
lady, ladies ['leɪdɪ, 'leɪdɪz]	the Queen = the first ~ in England	Dame, Damen
ladies' wear	skirts, blouses, dresses = ~	Damenbekleidung
book [bʊk]	→ book shop	Buch

	magazine [mægə'zi:n]	The 'Spiegel' and 'Stern' are German ~s.	Zeitschrift
	newspaper ['nju:zpeɪpə]	'The Washington Post' and 'The New York Times' are American ~s.	Zeitung
	souvenir [su:və'nɪə]	His ~ from Munich is a pair of Lederhosen.	Andenken; Souvenir
	camera ['kæmərə]	= German	Kamera; Fotoapparat
	film [fɪlm]	= German	Film
4.2	**to look for** ['lʊk 'fɔ:]	I ~ a suit. Can I get men's wear in this department?	suchen
	I'm looking for		ich suche
	picture **postcard** ['pəʊstkɑ:d]	Have you got a ~ of the Tower of London?	Ansichtskarte
	our ['aʊə]	I – my; we – ~	unser(e)
	store [stɔ:]	→ department store	großer Laden; Warenhaus
	you	Tom and Susan! Can ~ look for my umbrella, please?	ihr *(Mehrzahl)*; Sie; *auch:* man
	you can get	Y~ blouses in the ladies' wear department.	man kann bekommen
	to sell [sel]	Do you ~ jeans in this department?	verkaufen
	your [jɔ:]	[!]: I – my; we – our; you – ~	ihre; Ihr(e)
	Cassettes are on the . . . floor.		Kassetten gibt es im . . . Stock.
5.1	**you**		Ihnen
	to help [help]	Can I ~ you?	helfen
	size [saɪz]	My shoes are ~ 42.	Größe
	What size . . . ? [wɒt]	W~ are your shoes? 36 or 38?	Welche Größe . . . ?
	sure [ʃʊə]	I'm ~ it is 38 ≈ I know it is 38.	sicher
	I'm not quite sure.	→ quite expensive	Ich bin nicht ganz sicher.
	small [smɔ:l]	Size 32? That's very ~ for a lady's shoe.	klein
	colour ['kʌlə]	yellow, brown, green and blue are ~s	Farbe
	cannot, can't ['kænɒt, kɑ:nt]	Can you speak French? – No, I ~.	kann nicht
	to buy [baɪ]	*opposite:* to sell	kaufen
	the first **one** [wʌn]	King Street? It's ~ on the right.	der/die/das erste
	the second one	The first one is green, but ~ is blue.	der/die/das zweite
5.2	**a half** [ə 'hɑ:f]	five and a half	ein halb
5.3	**what about** . . .	W~ Jim? I think he can help you.	wie wär's mit . . .
	these [ði:z]	this book, ~ books	diese; die hier
	those [ðəʊz]	this – that, these – ~	jene; die da
	well [wel]		*(zögernd)* nun ja
	to try on [traɪ 'ɒn]	Can I ~ this pair of jeans?	anprobieren
	them [ðem, ðəm]	I – me; we – us; they – ~	sie
	certainly ['sɜ:tənlɪ]	Can you help me? – Yes, ~.	gewiß; sicher
	this one	You want to know the sizes? T~ is size 12 and ~ over there is size 14.	diese(r, s); diese(r, s) hier
	that one		jene(r, s); der, die das da/dort
	I'm afraid [aɪm ə'freɪd]	Can you help me? – No, ~ not.	ich fürchte
	big [bɪg]	*opposite:* small	groß
	long [lɒŋ]	The road is 5 kilometres ~.	lang
	short [ʃɔ:t]	*opposite:* long	kurz
	it is not the right colour	I'm afraid ~. I want green, not red.	*etwa:* es hat nicht die richtige Farbe
	all right [ɔ:l 'raɪt]	I'm afraid I cannot help you. – That's ~.	in Ordnung
6.1	**How much is it?/How much are they?** ['haʊ 'mʌtʃ]	This postcard, please. H~? – 20p.	Wieviel kostet es/kosten sie?
	It is . . ./They are . . .		*hier:* Es kostet/Sie kosten
	£ [paʊnd]		Pfund *(englische Währung)*
	p [pi:]	100 ~ = £ 1	Penny *(engl. Währung)*
	each [i:tʃ]	The postcards are 40p, they are 20p ~.	jede(r, s) *(aus einer kleinen Anzahl)*
	map [mæp]	It's near London; you can see it on the ~.	(Land-)Karte
	map of London	You can see Buckingham Palace on the ~.	Stadtplan von London.
6.3	**to change** [tʃeɪndʒ]	Can you ~ D-Marks into pounds, please?	*(Geld)* wechseln
	note [nəʊt]	There are 5, 10, 20 and 50 pound ~s.	(Bank-)Note; (Geld-)Schein
	there [ðeə]	→ over there	dort
	question ['kwestʃən]	'What's your name?' is a ~.	Frage
	can't [kɑ:nt]	= cannot	kann nicht
6.4	**another** [ə'nʌðə]	I'm afraid that's too expensive. Have you got ~ one?	ein(e) andere(r, s); noch ein(s, e, en)
	here you are	Can I have 2 postcards, please? – Certainly, ~.	Bitte (sehr). *(Wenn man etwas überreicht)*
	change [tʃeɪndʒ]	Two postcards for 20p each, and your ~: 60p.	Wechselgeld

love *mein Lieber*	*nearly* *beinahe*	*gave* *gab; habe gegeben*

I'd like [aɪd 'laɪk]	Can I help you? – Yes, ~ a map of London, please.	ich hätte gerne
poster ['pəʊstə]	[!]; *German*	Poster; Plakat
bridge [brɪdʒ]		Brücke
pen [pen]	I can't write a postcard, I haven't got a ~.	Kugelschreiber; Füller

7	flea market *Flohmarkt*		Greenland *Grönland*	
8	new *neu* was *war*		problem *Problem* price *(Kauf)Preis*	
9	favourite *Lieblings-* of course *natürlich* interesting *interessant* Reject China *(etwa:) Porzellan* mit kl. Fehlern Underground *U-Bahn*		selection *Auswahl* price *(Kauf-)Preis* wine *Wein* famous for *berühmt für* sweets *Süßigkeiten* chocolates *Pralinen*	home-made *selbst-/hausgemacht* cheese *Käse* spices *Gewürze* foods *Nahrungsmittel* probably *vielleicht* own *eigen(e)*

Unit 4

date [deɪt]   Datum

1.1   six **o'clock** [sɪks ə'klɒk]   6.00   sechs Uhr
       half past six ['hɑːf pɑːst]   = 6.30   halb sieben
       eight thirty   8.30   acht Uhr dreißig; halb neun

1.2   **have you got ...?** [hæv juː gɒt]   haben Sie ...?
       time [taɪm]   Zeit
       Have you got the time, please?   H~? – Yes, it's six o'clock.   *etwa:* Wie spät ist es, bitte?
       answer ['ɑːnsə]   Have you got an ~ to my question?   Antwort
       almost ['ɔːlməʊst]   5.58 = It's ~ six o'clock.   fast; beinahe

1.3   **What's the time, please?**   = Have you got the time, please?   *etwa:* Wie spät ist es?
       Can you tell me the time,   *etwa:* Können Sie mir sagen,
         please?   wie spät es ist?

1.4   **when** [wen]   wann
       open ['əʊpən]   When is the post office ~?   offen; geöffnet
       Norwich ['nɒrɪdʒ]   *Stadt in Südost-England*
       cathedral [kə'θiːdrəl]   [!]: o O o   Kathedrale
       what time   ≈ when   wann
       pub [pʌb]   where you can meet friends for a drink   Kneipe; Lokal; Wirtshaus
       still [stɪl]   It's only 5 o'clock, the shops are ~ open.   noch
       after ['ɑːftə]   The post office is not open ~ 6 o'clock.   nach *(zeitlich)*
       (at) midnight ['mɪdnaɪt]   24.00/0.00   Mitternacht

       from ... to ...   I work in an office ~ 9 ~ 5.   von ... bis ...
       in the morning   am Morgen; am Vormittag
       till [tɪl]   = until   bis
       in the evening   I go to night school ~.   am Abend
       afternoon [ɑːftə'nuːn]   12.00 – 18.00   Nachmittag
       in the afternoon   I only work ~, from 2 to 6:30.   am Nachmittag

       a.m. [eɪ 'em]   [!]: o O; = in the morning   morgens; vormittags
       p.m. [piː 'em]   [!]: o O; = in the afternoon/evening   nachmittags; abends; nachts
       castle museum ['kɑːsl mjuː'zɪəm]   Schloß-/Burgmuseum
       Tourist Information Centre   [!]: O o   o O o   O o   Informationszentrum für
         ['tʊərɪst ɪnfə'meɪʃən 'sentə]   Touristen

2.1   **(a) quarter past/to**   12.15 = ~ twelve./11:45 = ~ twelve.   Viertel nach/vor
         [ə 'kwɔːtə pɑːst/tʊ]
       five **to** eleven   10.55 (eleven o'clock – 5 minutes)   fünf vor elf
       minute ['mɪnɪt]   [!]: O o; It's five to ten. = It's five ~s to ten.   Minute
       five **past** eleven [pɑːst]   11.05 (eleven o'clock + 5 minutes)   fünf nach elf

2.2   **What time is it?**   = What's the time?   Wie spät ist es?
       really ['rɪəli]   I think it's a good film. – Yes, it's ~ good.   wirklich
       I have to ['hæv tʊ]   I ~ go, it's almost midnight.   ich muß
       to leave [liːv]   I work from 9 to 5, and I ~ the office at 5.10.   verlassen; *hier:* abfahren
       at (six o'clock) [æt]   I'm afraid the pubs aren't open ~ midnight.   um (sechs Uhr)
       my bus leaves at ...   mein Bus geht um ...
       What time is your bus?   Wann geht Ihr Bus?
       train [treɪn]   (Eisenbahn-)Zug
       home [həʊm]   I leave the office at 5. – I go ~ at 5.   nach Hause
       work [wɜːk]   → to work   Arbeit
       your train **to work**   Ihr Zug zur Arbeit
       to go by car/train/bus   I ~ to work ~ bus,   mit dem Auto/Zug/Bus fahren
       to walk [wɔːk]   but I ~ to town.   (zu Fuß) gehen

2.3   **to** Norwich   *opposite:* from   nach Norwich
       the six-o-five train   the 6.05 train   der Zug um sechs Uhr fünf
       departure [dɪ'pɑːtʃə]   *Abkürzung:* dep.   Abfahrt
       arrival [ə'raɪvəl]   *Abkürzung:* arr.   Ankunft

3	to plan [plæn]		planen
	Monday ['mʌndɪ]		Montag
	Tuesday ['tjuːzdɪ]		Dienstag
	Wednesday ['wenzdɪ]		Mittwoch
	Thursday ['θɜːzdɪ]		Donnerstag
	Friday ['fraɪdɪ]		Freitag
	Saturday ['sætədɪ]		Sonnabend, Samstag
	Sunday ['sʌndɪ]		Sonntag
	weekend [wiːk'end]	[!]: o O, *auch* O o; Saturday and Sunday = the ~	Wochenende
	Dear ... [dɪə]		Liebe(r, s) ...; Sehr geehrte(r, s) ...
	shall we (go)? [ʃæl wiː]	S~ go to the cinema or ~ go to a pub?	Sollen wir (gehen)?
	on (Sunday)	I can't do the shopping ~ Sunday.	am (Sonntag)
	Yours, ...		Dein(e), Ihr(e)
	let's (go) [lets]	We have to do it, ~ do it now.	Laß(t) uns (gehen)
	to go to (the cinema/Blickling Hall)		in(s Kino) gehen; nach (...) fahren
	I'm going to		*hier:* ich werde gehen (fahren); ich gehe
	with		mit
	after that	We can do the shopping, then we can visit the museum, and ~ we can go to the cinema.	danach
	could [kʊd]	We ~ go and meet our friends at the weekend.	könnte(n)
	Boat [bəʊt]	When you go to England by car, you have to go by ~, too.	Boot; Schiff
	trip [trɪp]	a ~ to London	Ausflug; Reise
	to go on a boat trip		einen Bootsausflug machen
	idea [aɪ'dɪə]	[!]: o O o; Let's go on a boat trip. – That's a good ~.	Idee
	(to be) interested in ['ɪntrəstɪd]	[!]: O o o; I'm not ~ museums. Let's go to the cinema.	sich interessieren für
	instead [ɪn'sted]	I'm not interested in a boat trip. Let's go to a pub ~.	stattdessen
	day [deɪ]	*opposite:* night	Tag

never   *niemals*
daily   *täglich*
American Theme Park [ə'merɪkən 'θiːm 'pɑːk]   *(etwa:) Vergnügungspark mit amerikanischen Motiven*
theatre ['θɪətə]   *Theater*
Swan Lake ['swɒn 'leɪk]   *„Schwanensee"*
Norfolk Broads ['nɔːfək 'brɔːdz]   *breite seenartige Flußmündung im Südosten Englands*

4.1	birthday ['bɜːθdeɪ]		Geburtstag
	month [mʌnθ]		Monat
	January ['dʒænjʊərɪ]		Januar
	February ['febrʊərɪ]		Februar
	March [mɑːtʃ]		März
	April ['eɪprəl]	[!]: O o	April
	May [meɪ]		Mai
	June [dʒuːn]		Juni
	July [dʒʊ'laɪ]	[!]: o O	Juli
	August ['ɔːgəst]	[!]: O o	August
	September [sep'tembə]		September
	October [ɒk'təʊbə]		Oktober
	November [nəʊ'vembə]		November
	December [dɪ'sembə]		Dezember
4.2	on the first of June	We can meet ~ (= 1 June).	am ersten Juni
	husband ['hʌzbənd]	I am Helen White and this is Peter White, my ~.	Ehemann
	wife [waɪf]	I am her husband; she is my ~.	Ehefrau
	year [jɪə]		Jahr
	in that year		in jenem Jahr
	was [wɒz, wəz]		war
	(s)he has to	→ I have to	sie/er muß
	to find out ['faɪnd 'aʊt]	Can you ~ when the train gets to London? (→ to find)	herausfinden
	in (January)	We can meet again ~ January.	im (Januar)
	son [sʌn]	This is my wife, Helen, this is our ~ Peter,	Sohn
	daughter ['dɔːtə]	and this is our ~ Linda.	Tochter
5.1	present ['preznt]	[!]: O o; I've got a nice ~ for my friend's birthday.	Geschenk
	(s)he has got	→ I have got	sie/er hat
	(for) him [hɪm]	It's Frank's birthday today. Have you got a present for ~?	(für) ihn
	whose [huːz]	W~ car is that? Is it Peter's?	wessen *(Fragewort)*
	..., isn't it?	It's your birthday today, ~?	*(angehängt an einen Satz mit 'It is ....')* nicht wahr?
	what presents		was für Geschenke
	(for) her	Is this for Pat? – No, it's not for ~.	(für) sie
	nothing ['nʌθɪŋ]	What have you got for Pat? – N~.	nichts
	yet [jet]	I'm only 20. I'm not 21 ~.	*hier:* noch; bis jetzt
	nothing yet		noch nichts

	(for) **me**	There are 4 postcards for my wife, but there's nothing for ~.	(für) mich
	(for) **you**	I – for me; you – for ~	(für) dich/Sie
	(for) **us**	It's for Peter and me. It's for ~.	(für) uns
	(for) **them**	It's for Peter and Helen. It's for ~.	(für) sie *(Mehrzahl)*
5.2	**already** [ɔːˈredɪ]		schon
	to talk to [tɔːk]	Peter hasn't got a telephone, but he works in my office, so I can ~ him on Monday.	mit jemandem reden/ sprechen
	about [əˈbaʊt]	Tell me ~ your job.	über
	own [əʊn]	I've got my ~ car. ≈ It's my car.	eigene(r, s)
	no [nəʊ]	There are ~ books here. Where are they?	*hier:* kein(e)
	I've got no idea.	→ idea	*etwa:* Ich habe keine Ahnung.
5.3	*cassette recorder* [kəˈset rɪˈkɔːdə]		Cassettenrecorder
6	flexitime *gleitende Arbeitszeit, „Gleitzeit"*	early *früh*	back home *zu Hause*
		about *(hier:) über*	come back *zurückkommen*
	finish *beenden*	late *spät*	make dinner *das Abendessen zubereiten*
	reader *Leser/in*	other *andere(r, s)*	
	more *mehr*	urgent *dringend, eilig*	take ... off *(hier:) frei nehmen*
7	news *Nachrichten*	letter *Brief*	
	conducted by *dirigiert von*	bedtime *Bett-/Schlafenszeit*	
8	room *Zimmer; Raum*	actress *Schauspielerin*	
	world *Welt*	to play *spielen*	
	Woman's Hour *(wörtl.: Frauenstunde), Frauenprogramm*	adventure *Abenteuer*	
		during *während*	

Unit 5

1.1	**would** [wʊd]		würde(st, n); möchte(st, n)
	would you like ...		möchten Sie/möchtest du (gerne) ...
	to come [kʌm]	*opposite:* to go	kommen
	to come over [ˈkʌm ˈəʊvə]	Can you ~ and meet some friends from Canada?	herüber kommen
	Would you like to come over?		Möchten Sie herüber kommen?
	drink [drɪŋk]	Whisky and Coca Cola are ~s.	Getränk
	for a drink		*etwa:* und etwas mit uns trinken
	invitation [ɪnvɪˈteɪʃn]	I've got an ~ to see the Queen next week!	Einladung
	to fill in [ˈfɪl ˈɪn]	F~ in your first name and then your surname.	ausfüllen; eintragen
	to do [duː]	What can we ~ on Sunday?	tun
	What are you doing?		Was tun/machen Sie *(gerade eben oder in naher Zukunft)*?
	this evening	→ evening	heute abend
1.2	**dinner** [ˈdɪnə]	We've got time for a drink, ~ is at 8 p.m.	Abendessen
	to have dinner [hæv ˈdɪnə]	We ~ at 8 p.m.	zu Abend essen
	to love	≈ to like very much	lieben, gern etwas tun
	I'd love to.		*etwa:* Liebend gern.
	See you then.		*etwa:* Bis dann.
	tomorrow [təˈmɒrəʊ]	Today is Monday, ~ is Tuesday.	morgen
	at the weekend	on Saturday or on Sunday = ~	am Wochenende
	some friends		*etwa:* Freunde; ein paar Freunde
	party [ˈpɑːtɪ]	= German	Party; Feier
	with me		mit mir
	concert [ˈkɒnsət]	[!]: O o; a ~ with the London Philharmonic Orchestra	Konzert
	to invite [ɪnˈvaɪt]	→ invitation	einladen
2.1	**why** [waɪ]	W~? – Because ...!	warum
	homework [ˈhəʊmwɜːk]	After school children have to do ~.	Hausaufgaben
	to leave for ...	What time do you ~ London?	aufbrechen, losgehen zu(m, r)/nach ...
2.2	I'm sorry	→ sorry	es tut mir leid
	to paint [peɪnt]		malen; *hier:* anstreichen
	bathroom [ˈbɑːθrʊm]		Bad(ezimmer)
	to have a party	I'm ~ing ~ on my birthday.	eine Party feiern
	to wash [wɒʃ]	In the morning you ~ in the bathroom.	waschen; sich waschen
	that's a pity [ˈpɪtɪ]	We can't come over this evening. – Oh, ~.	das ist schade
	to watch [wɒtʃ]	My husband and I ~ TV on Saturday evenings. (see ≠ ~)	(an)sehen; betrachten
	on TV		im Fernsehen
	to play [pleɪ]	After their homework the children ~ in the garden.	spielen
	to drink [drɪŋk]	→ a drink	trinken

	glass [glɑːs]	a ~ of whisky	Glas
	wine [waɪn]	Beaujolais is a French ~.	Wein
2.3	**other** [ˈʌðə]	Here are two postcards. One is for you and the ~ one is for me.	andere(r, s)
	if they can come [ɪf]	They want to know ~ you can help.	*hier:* ob
	If an answer is 'Yes', ...		*hier:* wenn
	glad [glæd]	Hello, I'm ~ to meet you.	froh
	I'm glad you can come.		Ich bin froh, daß Sie kommen können. *(Dieses „daß", engl.: that, wird im Engl. sehr häufig weggelassen!)*
	never mind [ˈnevə ˈmaɪnd]	I'm afraid I can't come over tonight. – N~, you can come tomorrow.	etwa: das macht nichts, machen Sie sich nichts daraus; schon gut
	holiday(s) [ˈhɒlɪdeɪ(z)]		*Einz.:* Feiertag; *Einz. oder Mehrz.:* Ferien; Urlaub
	to go on holiday	We ~ in June or September, not in July or in August.	in (die) Ferien fahren/gehen; Urlaub machen
	late [leɪt]	It's too ~ to go to the pub. It's 11 p.m.	spät
	to work late		(bis) spät (in die Nacht) arbeiten
	people	How many ~ are there in your family?	Leute; Menschen
	as many people **as** you can		so viele Leute wie Sie können
	class [klɑːs]	How many students are there in your English ~?	Klasse; *hier:* Lerngruppe
2.4	**pleasant** [ˈpleznt]	I think Peter is very nice. – Yes, he's very ~.	angenehm
	at the moment	→ moment	im Augenblick; gerade
	it's a pity you can't come		..., daß ...
	video [ˈvɪdɪəʊ]	[!]; = *German*	Video(film)
	to sit [sɪt]	You can ~ over there to watch the TV.	sitzen
	theatre [ˈθɪətə]	[!]: O o o; Let's go to the ~ tonight and see 'Hamlet'.	Theater
	extra [ˈekstrə]		extra; überzählig; *hier:* zuviel
	ticket [ˈtɪkɪt]	How much are the ~s for the theatre?	(Eintritts-, Fahr-)Karte
	to come along [kʌm əˈlɒŋ]	→ come over/go along	mitkommen
	sometimes [ˈsʌmtaɪmz]	S~ I watch television and ~ I go to the cinema.	manchmal
	to need [niːd]	You ~ (= have to have) a pen to write a postcard.	brauchen
	perhaps [pəˈhæps]	I'm not quite sure. P~ Helen can help us.	vielleicht
	hour [ˈaʊə]	60 minutes = one ~	Stunde
	for an hour		für eine Stunde
	to look after [ˈlʊk ˈɑːftə]	When we go to the theatre our neighbours ~ the children.	sich kümmern um; nach ... sehen
	baby [ˈbeɪbɪ]	= *German*	Baby, Kleinkind
	tennis [ˈtenɪs]	= *German*	Tennis
	instead of me [ɪnˈsted əv]	→ instead	an meiner Stelle; für mich
	take me to ...	I haven't got a car. Would you ~ the station, please?	mich zum/zur ... bringen
	airport [ˈeəpɔːt]	Heathrow is a London ~.	Flughafen
2.5	**hair** [heə]	→ hairdresser	Haar(e)
3.1	**picture** [ˈpɪktʃə]	Henry is painting a ~ of our garden.	Bild
	to learn [lɜːn]	Why are you ~ing English?	lernen
	to use [juːz]	You ~ a pen to write a postcard.	benutzen; gebrauchen
	home computer [ˈhəʊm kəmˈpjuːtə]		Heimcomputer
	letter [ˈletə]	Not a postcard again! Let's write him a ~.	Brief
	to read [riːd]	*opposite:* to write; You ~ books, newspapers and magazines.	lesen; *hier:* vorlesen
	to listen to a record	→ to listen	eine Schallplatte hören
3.2	**summer** [ˈsʌmə]	= June, July and August	Sommer
	course [kɔːs]	You are learning English in an English ~.	Kurs
	they like going ...		sie lieben (es), ... zu gehen
	hobby [ˈhɒbɪ]	= *German*	Hobby
	something [ˈsʌmθɪŋ]	I can see ~ next to the TV. What is it?	etwas
	new [njuː]	*opposite:* old	neu; *hier:* Neues
	college [ˈkɒlɪdʒ]	Peter and Tom are 14; they go to school. Linda and Eric are 18; they go to ~.	*(in Amerika)* höhere Lehranstalt mit meist vierjährigem Lehrplan, den Übergang bildend zwischen der höheren Schule (high school) und dem Universitäts- oder Berufsstudium
	in front of [ɪn ˈfrʌnt əv]	Where's your car? – It's ~ the hotel.	vor
	main [meɪn]	Our summer holiday is our ~ holiday.	Haupt-
	creative writing [krɪˈeɪtɪv]	[!]: o O o O o	kreatives Schreiben
	group [gruːp]	My English class is a nice ~ of people.	Gruppe
	story	I know the ~, I've got the book.	Geschichte
	modern [ˈmɒdən]	[!]: O o; = *German*	modern
	literature [ˈlɪtrətʃə]	[!]: O o o; = *German*	Literatur
	comic [ˈkɒmɪk]	= *German*	Comic; Bildgeschichte

Sie wollen möglichst oft Englisch hören und sprechen?

Dazu der erste Vorschlag:
Zwei Übungscassetten mit begleitendem Textheft

Auf der gegenüberstehenden Seite 16 sehen Sie rechts zwei Zeichen: ▷ AB5 · CC und ▷ AB6 · CC. Sie zeigen Ihnen – wie an vielen anderen Stellen des Lehrbuchs –, daß es zu diesem Abschnitt unter der gleichen Nummer eine oder mehrere Übungen auf den Übungscassetten zu TAKE OFF 1 gibt. Es handelt sich meist um einfache Nachsprechübungen zu Wörtern und Redewendungen, um Grammatikübungen oder um kleine Rollenspiele zu Alltagssituationen. Wenn Sie diese Übungen im Anschluß an die jeweilige Lehrbuchübung einige Male durchnehmen, werden Sie die neuen Wörter und Sätze auch im Unterricht und später sicherer benutzen können.

Das den beiden Übungscassetten beiliegende Textheft hilft Ihnen, sich schnell in den Tonaufnahmen zurechtzufinden. Viele Übungen sind in Dialogform oder als Hörspiel angelegt. Hier können Sie nach zwei vorangegangenen Beispielen selbst eine Rolle übernehmen. Entsprechende Pausen sind für Sie auf den Cassetten freigehalten. Ein Blick in das Textheft zeigt Ihnen den Übungsaufbau – und dann können Sie mit den immer sprechbereiten Partnern trainieren, so oft Sie wollen.

Und der zweite Vorschlag:
Die Höraufgaben-Cassette

Diese Cassette bietet Beispiele dafür, wie sich Engländer oder Amerikaner miteinander unterhalten. Sie sprechen Ihnen alle neuen Redewendungen vor, die in den Units von TAKE OFF 1 eingeführt werden. Die entsprechende Stelle im Lehrbuch ist an dem blauen Cassettensymbol mit eingedruckter Ziffer zu erkennen. Alle Höraufgaben-Texte sind im Anhang dieses Buches ab Seite 142 abgedruckt. Sie können diese Cassette zusätzlich verwenden, um sich noch intensiver in die englische Sprache einzuhören.

Zwei weitere interessante Vorschläge finden Sie auf der Rückseite dieses Informationsblatts.

Bestellkarte

Hiermit bestelle ich die im Kästchen angekreuzten Arbeitsmittel zur Lieferung **gegen Nachnahme** direkt an umseitige Anschrift oder durch die nachstehend angegebene Buchhandlung:

_____

_____

☐ **2 Übungscassetten** zum Lehrbuch TAKE OFF 1
Laufzeit ca. 150 Minuten, mit 40seitigem Textheft. 49,80 DM. Bestellnummer 49043.

☐ **1 Höraufgabencassette** zum Lehrbuch TAKE OFF 1
Laufzeit 50 Minuten. Unverbindliche Preisempfehlung 23,90 DM Bestellnummer 49027.

☐ **1 Englische Grammatik für Erwachsene.** Von W. Hüllen, 112 Seiten, zweifarbig, kartoniert. 16,80 DM. Bestellnummer 5259.

☐ **1 Leseheft "Have you got a minute?"**
56 Seiten, zweifarbig, kartoniert. 11,90 DM. Bestellnummer 32370.

☐ **1 Arbeitsbuch** zum Lehrbuch TAKE OFF 1
92 Seiten, zweifarbig, DIN A4, kartoniert. 21,90 DM. Bestellnummer 49000.

Stand der Preisangaben vom 1.1.1993. Änderungen vorbehalten.

Name und Anschrift bitte umseitig eintragen!

Zu Hause lernen bringt Sie voran ...

Der dritte Vorschlag:
Englische Grammatik für Erwachsene

Dieses Grammatikbuch von Prof. Dr. W. Hüllen steht in enger Verbindung mit Ihrem Lehrbuch TAKE OFF. Wenn Sie hier Seite 106 (Grammatikanhang) aufschlagen, finden Sie rechts neben jeder Zwischenüberschrift einen Paragraphen-Hinweis. Er bezieht sich auf die entsprechenden Abschnitte des zusätzlichen Grammatikbuches, in dem Sie weitere, ausführlichere Informationen bekommen. Bespielsätze in leicht verständlichem Englisch verdeutlichen die Regeln, die in deutscher Sprache angeboten werden. Dabei wird immer dort, wo es sinnvoll ist, zum Vergleich auf grammatikalische Erscheinungen der deutschen Sprache hingewiesen. Zahlreiche Verweise im Buch helfen Ihnen, Ihre Kenntnisse selbständig zu erweitern.

Inhalt der „Englischen Grammatik für Erwachsene":
Der einfache Satz. Das Prädikat. Modale Hilfsverben. Gebrauch der Zeiten und der Verlaufsform. Fürwörter. Eigenschaftswörter. Umstandswort. Satzmuster mit der Grundform und der ing-Form. Aktiv und Passiv. Untergeordneter Satz. Indirekte Rede. Zahlen und Zahlenangaben.

Zuletzt noch ein Lektüre-Vorschlag:
Leseheft
"Have you got a minute?"

Schon mit geringen Vorkenntnissen können Sie dieses interessante und abwechslungsreich gestaltete Heft ohne fremde Hilfe lesen. Es werden viele aktuelle Themen angesprochen, Informationen über Großbritannien gegeben und in bunter Folge Bildgeschichten, Spiele, Rätsel und Denksportaufgaben eingeschoben. Sie werden feststellen: Englisch lesen ist gar nicht so schwer und macht Vergnügen.

Bitte wählen Sie unter diesen Vorschlägen und benutzen Sie die vorbereitete Bestellkarte.

Postkarte

Bitte als Postkarte freimachen

Cornelsen Verlagsgesellschaft
Postfach 87 29
4800 Bielefeld 1

Versandanschrift

Name   Best.-Dat.

Vorname

Straße/Hausnummer

PLZ   Ort

| PR-SU | RA | URA | SA | MA | Text | NBKZ | E |

	painting workshop [ˈpeɪntɪŋ ˈwɜːkʃɒp]		Malerei-Arbeitsgruppe/Seminar
	piano [pɪˈænəʊ] = *German*		Piano; Klavier
	to play **the** piano		Klavier spielen
	photography [fəˈtɒɡrəfɪ] [!]: o O o o; = *German*		Photographie
	to take a picture Would you ~ of me and my wife with our camera, please?		ein Bild/Photo machen/ aufnehmen; knipsen
	while [waɪl] I can do the shopping ~ you are watching TV.		während
	to bring along [ˈbrɪŋ əˈlɒŋ] You can come to our party and ~ your friends.		mitbringen

4	offer *anbieten*	Lab Fee *(etwa:) Werkstattgebühr*	like *wie*
	spend *verbringen*	crime *Kriminalität*	such as *wie*
	beach *Strand*	print *drucken*	value *Wert*
	art *Kunst*	lesson *Unterricht, Lektion, Stunde*	pressure *Druck*
	develop *entwickeln*	level *Niveau*	introduction *Einleitung, Einführung*
	still life *Stilleben*	chamber music *Kammermusik*	world *Welt*
	landscape *Landschaft*	further *weitere(r, s)*	enough *genug*
	different *verschiedene; unterschied- liche*	call *anrufen*	operate *betätigen*
		century *Jahrhundert*	solve *lösen*

Unit 6

1.1	*usual* [ˈjuːʒʊəl]	In England it is ~ to have dinner at 7 or 8 p.m.	gewöhnlich; üblich
	unusual [ʌnˈjuːʒʊəl]	'Rumpelstiltskin' is an ~ name.	ungewöhnlich
	first [fɜːst]	F~ they do their homework, then they watch TV.	zuerst
	What does he do?		Was tut er?
	the last thing he does		das letzte, was/das er tut (*das* 'that', *das* in engl. Neben- sätzen hier stehen könnte, wird oft weggelassen)
	to answer [ˈɑːnsə]	Can you ~ this question?	(be-)antworten
	in German	'answer' is 'Antwort' ~	auf deutsch
	bottle [ˈbɒtl]	Would you like a ~ of wine or two glasses of wine?	Flasche
	beer [bɪə]	I'd like a bottle of white wine and 3 bottles of ~.	Bier
	snack [snæk]	In the office I only have a ~ because I have a big dinner at home.	Imbiß
	I have a snack.		Ich esse eine Kleinigkeit.
	paper [ˈpeɪpə]	*Kurzform von* newspaper	Zeitung
	bed [bed]	Would you like a room with 2 ~s?	Bett
	to go to bed	I sometimes ~ very late – at 2 or 3 o'clock in the morning.	ins Bett gehen

1.2	the first thing you do		das erste, was/das …
	to go for a run [rʌn]		laufen gehen
	shower [ˈʃaʊə]	Is there a ~ in your bathroom?	Dusche
	to have a shower [ˈʃaʊə]		(sich) duschen
	to make [meɪk]	I usually ~ the dinner for my family on Sundays.	machen
	cup [kʌp]	you drink from it, but not beer or wine	Tasse
	tea [tiː]	a cup of ~	Tee
	breakfast [ˈbrekfəst]		Frühstück
	to have breakfast	→ to have a dinner/a snack; I ~ at 7 a.m.	frühstücken
	music [ˈmjuːzɪk]	[!]: O o; = *German*	Musik
	I listen to some music		ich höre (ein wenig) Musik
	news [njuːz]	→ newspaper	Nachrichten
	usually [ˈjuːʒʊəlɪ]	I ~ leave the office at 5, but today I'm leaving at 6.	(für) gewöhnlich
	often [ˈɒfn]	*opposite:* sometimes	oft; häufig
	always [ˈɔːlweɪz]	sometimes = not ~	immer

1.3	day in, day out		Tag für Tag; tagtäglich
	every [ˈevrɪ]	~ day = on Monday, Tuesday, Wednesday etc.	jede(r, s)
	to get up [ˈɡet ˈʌp]	I usually ~ at 7 to go to work, but on Saturday and Sunday I ~ at 8.	aufstehen
	to drive [draɪv]	→ taxi driver	fahren
	to town	Do you have to drive ~ to do the shopping, or is there a supermarket near your office?	in die Stadt

1.4	**life** [laɪf]	We live a very pleasant ~ in the summer!	Leben
	milkman [ˈmɪlkmən]		Milchmann *(der morgens die Milch ausfährt)*
	Gatwick [ˈɡætwɪk]		*Flughafen im Süden Londons*
	doctor [ˈdɒktə]	= *German*	Arzt
	hospital [ˈhɒspɪtl]	[!]: O o o; = *German*	Hospital; Krankenhaus
	to start [stɑːt]	*opposite:* to stop	anfangen; beginnen
	to get home	I leave the office at 5 and I ~ at 6.	nach Hause kommen
	to go out	We often watch TV from Monday to Friday, but on Saturday we always ~; we often go to the cinema or the theatre.	ausgehen
	to tell about [ˈtel əˈbaʊt]	In the story he ~s us ~ his life in London.	erzählen von/über

1.5	to go and see friends		*etwa:* Freunde besuchen gehen
	Why do you think **so**?		Warum denken Sie das?
2.1	**friendly** [ˈfrendlɪ]	→ friend	freundlich
	personality [pɜːsəˈnælɪtɪ]	I like him. He has got a very pleasant ~.	Persönlichkeit
	to be good at		(etwas) gut können
	sport(s) [spɔːts]	→ sports wear	Sport
	foreign [ˈfɒrɪn]		ausländisch; fremd
	language [ˈlæŋgwɪdʒ]	Which foreign ~s can you speak?	Sprache
	where [weə]	W~ are you going for your next holidays?	*hier:* wohin
	all [ɔːl]	= German; ~ my friends = each of my friends	alle
	between [bɪˈtwiːn]	B is ~ A and C.	zwischen
	animateur [ænɪməˈtɜː]	[!]; = German	Unterhalter; Animateur
	the person we are looking for		..., die wir suchen
	at [æt]	Our holiday ~ the holiday club was very nice.	*hier:* im
2.2	*pop* music [ˈpɒp ˈmjuːzɪk]	[!]: O O o; = German	Schlagermusik
	jazz [dʒæz]	[!]; = German; Ella Fitzgerald, the Queen of ~.	Jazz
	classical music [ˈklæsɪkl]	Beethoven's, Mozart's music = ~ music	klassische Musik
	going to the cinema		ins Kino zu gehen; *(wörtlich: das Ins-Kino-Gehen)*
	to go for a walk		spazierengehen
	to do sports		Sport treiben
	fast [fɑːst]	A Porsche is a very ~ car.	schnell
	animal [ˈænɪml]		Tier
2.3	you are on holiday		Sie machen Ferien
	among [əˈmʌŋ]	2,8,3,22,4,5; 22 is the double number ~ these numbers	*(mitten)* unter *(mehreren)*
	Venice [ˈvenɪs]		Venedig
	card [kɑːd]	→ postcard	Karte
	who to look for		nach wem Sie suchen sollen
	similar [ˈsɪmɪlə]	The name 'Browne' is very ~ to 'Brown'.	ähnlich
	squash [skwɒʃ]	[!]; = German	Squash *(tennisartiges Spiel auf einem mit hohen Wänden umgebenen Spielfeld, wobei die Spieler nebeneinander stehen)*
	ICC [ˈaɪ siː ˈsiː]		erfundener Firmenname
	volleyball [ˈvɒlɪbɔːl]	[!]; = German	Volleyball; Flugball
	driving *sports-cars*		Sportwagen zu fahren
	painting [ˈpeɪntɪŋ]	→ to paint; painting workshop	Malerei; das Malen
	football [ˈfʊtbɔːl]	Franz Beckenbauer was very good at ~.	Fußball
2.4	**dream** [driːm]		Traum
	partner [ˈpɑːtnə]	= German	Partner/in
	to look like [ˈlʊk ˈlaɪk]		aussehen wie ...
	favourite [ˈfeɪvrɪt]	[!]: O o; What is your ~ sport – tennis or football?	Lieblings-
	film star [ˈfɪlm stɑː]	Marilyn Monroe was my favourite ~.	Filmstar
	everything [ˈevrɪθɪŋ]	*opposite:* nothing (→ something)	alles
	to (find out)		um zu; (um herauszufinden)
	to try [traɪ]	I know you can do it if you ~.	versuchen; probieren
	to remember [rɪˈmembə]	I can't ~ his name. Is it Jim or Peter?	sich erinnern an
	who [huː]	W~ are you? What's your name?	wer
	the **same** [seɪm]	3 + 2 is the ~ as 2 + 3	das gleiche
	game [geɪm]	a ~ of tennis, a ~ of football	Spiel
	as [æz]		wie
	(kangaroo) farm [(kæŋgəˈruː) ˈfɑːm]		(Bauern-)Hof; Gut; Farm
	company [ˈkʌmpənɪ]	[!]: O o o	Gesellschaft, Firma
	rugby [ˈrʌgbɪ]	= German	Rugby
	Scotch whisky [ˈskɒtʃ ˈwɪskɪ]	= German	Schottischer Whisky
	golf [gɒlf]	= German	Golf
	gin and tonic [ˈdʒɪn ənd ˈtɒnɪk]	= German	Gin Tonic
2.5	**ideal** [aɪˈdɪəl]	[!]: o O o; = German; He's the ~ husband, he does the shopping and the housework and he's got a job.	ideal
	boss [bɒs]	he tells you what you have to do at work	Chef; Vorgesetzter; Boss
	things an ideal boss does		..., die ...
	what he is like	Can you tell me ~? Is he nice, is he pleasant?	wie er ist
	housework [ˈhaʊswɜːk]	My wife goes to work, too; I do the shopping and she does the ~,	Hausarbeit
	to take (a person) out	and at the weekend I always ~ her ~ for dinner.	jemanden ausführen
	never [ˈnevə]	*opposite:* always	nie(mals)
3.1	*present* [ˈpreznt]	[!]: O o	*hier:* gegenwärtig
	(train) services [ˈsɜːvɪsɪz]	There are no ~ on Sunday; you have to go by bus or by car.	(Eisenbahn-)Verbindungen
	interview [ˈɪntəvjuː]	[!]: O o o; = German	Interview
	passenger [ˈpæsɪndʒə]	[!]: O o o; This bus can take 70 ~s and one driver.	Passagier; Fahrgast

	how often		wie oft
	to travel ['trævəl]	How do you ~ to work? By bus, by car or by train?	reisen; fahren
	from time to time	→ sometimes; from . . . to . . .	ab und zu
	journey ['dʒɜːnɪ]	The ~ from Hamburg to Munich by train is very long.	Reise
	before [bɪ'fɔː]	B~ I get up I drink a cup of tea in bed.	vor *(zeitlich)*
	How long does it **take**?	H~ from Hamburg to Munich by train?	Wie lange dauert es?
	more [mɔː]	If I go to the office by car, it takes 10 minutes. If I go by bus, it takes 20 minutes ~.	mehr; *hier:* länger (= mehr als eine Stunde)
	to change (trains) [tʃeɪndʒ]	If you go from Manchester to Dover by train, you have to ~ in London.	*(in einen anderen Zug)* umsteigen
	once [wʌns]	You only live ~!	einmal
	twice [twaɪs]	I go to the cinema every Monday and Tuesday, that's ~ every week.	zweimal
	three **times**	→ 2 times 2 = 4	dreimal
3.2	**centre** ['sentə]	→ Tourist Information Centre	Zentrum; Mitte
	to leave the house	→ to leave for . . .	das Haus verlassen
	at work		bei ihrer Arbeitsstelle
	to get back (home) ['get 'bæk]	→ to get home	*(nach Hause)* zurückkommen
	to spend (time) [spend] on (trains/buses)	I ~ an hour each day on the bus to work.	(Zeit) verbringen im (Zug/Bus)
	underground ['ʌndəgraʊnd]	The 'Metro' is the name of the ~ in Paris.	U-Bahn
	to ask about ['ɑːsk ə'baʊt]	→ to tell about	fragen nach
4.1	**to hear** [hɪə]	≠ to listen!	hören
	I'm sorry to hear that.	→ I'm sorry	Es tut mir leid (, das zu hören).
	What's the matter (with you)? [wɒts ðə 'mætə]	– Ouch, oh! – W~?	Was ist los (mit Ihnen)?
	to feel [fiːl]	I ~ sorry ≈ I am sorry	(sich) fühlen
	terrible ['terɪbl]	very bad	schrecklich
	early ['ɜːlɪ]	*opposite:* late	früh
	pint [paɪnt] a pint of the usual	I'd like a ~ of beer, please.	*Maßeinheit:* 0,568 l „ein Gläschen (vom üblichen)"
	unpleasant [ʌn'pleznt]	→ pleasant	unangenehm
	to forget [fə'get]	*opposite:* remember; What's his name? I always ~ it.	vergessen
	Oh, dear! [əʊ 'dɪə]		*etwa:* O je!
	pay [peɪ]	Is the ~ good in your job? How much do you get?	Bezahlung; Lohn
4.2	How nice for you!		Wie schön für Sie!
	I'm glad to hear that!	→ glad	*etwa:* Ich bin froh, dies zu hören.
	Congratulations! [kəŋgrætjʊ'leɪʃnz]	[!]: o o o O o; It's your birthday? C~!	(Herzlichen) Glückwunsch!
	good/bad news	→ news	gute/schlechte Neuigkeiten/ Nachrichten
	firm [fɜːm]	Which ~ do you work for?	Firma
	to send [send]	Please ~ me a postcard from London.	senden; schicken
	Qatar [kə'tɑː]		*(Staat am Persischen Golf)*
	(you) do not like	*Kurzform:* don't like	(Sie) mögen nicht
	about your job		an ihrer Arbeit
	at night	He works ~; from 6 p.m. to 2 a.m.	in der Nacht; nachts
	too much work		zuviel Arbeit
	a lot of [ə 'lɒt əv]	There's ~ work, but not too much for me.	viel(e)
	to mix [mɪks]	You have to ~ the cards before you play.	mischen
	some of them		einige davon
	what they feel for you		was sie für Sie empfinden/fühlen

5	meals on wheels *Essen auf Rädern*	vegetable *Gemüse*	was born *wurde geboren*
	to pick up *(hier:) abholen*	enough *genug*	next door *nebenan*
	church *Kirche*	get cold *werden kalt*	to smoke *rauchen*
	to cook *kochen*	only *einzige*	repairs *Reparaturen*
	to put . . . into *in . . . stellen/tun*	I am worried about her *ich mache mir Sorgen um sie*	left her *hinterließ ihr*
	round *Runde*		quickly *schnell*
	customer *Kunde*	ill *krank*	he never washes *er wäscht sich nie*
	has died *ist gestorben*	also *auch*	
	meat *Fleisch*	difficult *schwierig*	

Unit 7

1.1	**way** [weɪ]		*hier:* Art und Weise
	What's the best way of getting to H.?		Welches ist die beste Art und Weise, nach H. zu kommen?
	reception [rɪ'sepʃn]	[!]: o O o; At a hotel you get your key at the ~.	Rezeption; Empfang
	to recommend [rekə'mend]	I can ~ this book. It's very interesting.	empfehlen
	the tube [tjuːb]	= the underground in London	*(umgangssprachlich)* die Londoner Untergrundbahn

	taxi ['tæksɪ]	= German	Taxi
	to **take** (the bus/a taxi/...)	to travel by (bus/...) ≈ to ~ the bus	... nehmen
	about [ə'baʊt]	27-33 people = ~ 30 people	ungefähr; ca.
	faster ['fɑːstə]	It's 10 minutes by car and 20 minutes by bus. It's ~ by car.	schneller
	you **should** [ʃʊd]	You ~ take the tube if you want to get there fast.	Sie sollten
1.2	**tourist** ['tʊərɪst]	[!]: O o; = German; → T~ Information Centre	Tourist
2.1	**cheap**, cheaper	*opposite: expensive*	billig, billiger
	comfortable, more comfortable ['kʌmfətəbl]	[!]: O o o o; = German; It's faster by car, but it's more ~ by train.	bequem, bequemer
	travel agent ['trævl 'eɪdʒənt]	The ~ can tell you the best way of travelling to the USA.	Reiseagentur
	flight [flaɪt]	Lufthansa ~ LH 030 from London to Frankfurt is at 8.40.	Flug
	much faster		viel schneller
	to **fly** [flaɪ]	If you go to England from Germany, you have to ~ or to go by boat.	fliegen
	plane [pleɪn]		Flugzeug
	to go by plane	~ ≈ to fly	fliegen; mit dem Flugzeug reisen
2.2	to **prefer** [prɪ'fɜː]	Which would you ~, white wine or red wine?	vorziehen; etwas lieber tun
	coach [kəʊtʃ]	a comfortable bus	Reisebus
	safe [seɪf]	By car? Oh no, it's ~r to travel by train or by plane.	sicher *(vor Gefahren)*
	convenient [kən'viːnjənt]	There's a bus station near my office: it's very ~ for me to travel by bus.	praktisch; bequem
	Spain [speɪn]		Spanien
	sight-seeing ['saɪtsiːɪŋ]	to go ~ = to go and see a town, a city, old buildings etc.	Besichtigung
2.3	mph = miles per hour *Meilen pro Stunde*	fare [feə] *Fahrpreis*	during ['djʊərɪŋ] *während*
		door [dɔː] *Tür*	to cost *kosten*
	even ['iːvn] *sogar*	without [wɪ'ðaʊt] *ohne*	more than *mehr als*
	example [ɪg'zɑːmpl] *Beispiel*	per gallon [pɜː 'gælən] *mit einer Gallone (= ca. 4,5 l)*	petrol ['petrəl] [!]: O o *Benzin*
	one way [wʌn weɪ] *(nur die) Hinfahrt*		to fill up *(das Auto) volltanken*
	mile [maɪl]		Meile (= 1,609 km zu Land)
	kilometre ['kɪləmiːtə]	[!]: O o o o, *sometimes:* o O o o [kɪ'lɒmətə]	Kilometer
	gallon ['gælən]	= 8 pints	Gallone (= 4,5459 l in GB; 3,7853 l in USA)
	litre ['liːtə]	= German	Liter
	weekday ['wiːkdeɪ]	Monday – Friday = ~s; → weekend	Wochentag
	one way only ['wʌn 'weɪ 'əʊnlɪ]		nur die Hinfahrt
	so that ['səʊ ðæt, ðət]		so daß
	special ['speʃl]	[!]: O o; = German	besondere(r, s); Spezial-; Sonder-
	fare [feə]	How much is the ~ from London to Birmingham by train?	Fahrpreis; Tarif
	I'd go	= I would go	ich würde fahren
	at a travel agent's		im Reisebüro
	single/return ticket ['sɪŋgl/rɪ'tɜːn 'tɪkɪt]		Einzel-/Rückfahrkarte
	the cheapest/fastest		das billigste/schnellste
2.4	**famous** ['feɪməs]	A lot of people know him, he's very ~.	berühmt
	place [pleɪs]		Ort
	what you think is the best way of getting there		wie man Ihrer Meinung nach dort am besten hinkommt
	regular ['regjʊlə]	There are usually 3 ~ buses and 2 special buses at this time of the evening.	regelmäßig
3.1	most elegant *eleganteste(n)*	century ['sentʃərɪ] *Jahrhundert*	resort [rɪ'zɔːt] *Erholungs-/Urlaubsort*
	seaside ['siːsaɪd] *See-*	dolphinarium [dɒlfɪ'neərɪəm] *Delphinarium*	
	built [bɪlt] *erbaut*		those who *jene, die*
	pleasure pier ['pleʒə pɪə] *Vergnügungspier*	largest ['lɑːdʒɪst] *größte(r, s)*	peaceful ['piːsfʊl] *friedlich*
		seat [siːt] *Sitzplatz*	
	lane [leɪn] *Gasse*	port [pɔːt] *Hafen(stadt)*	
	to **compare** [kəm'peə]	If you ~ the train fare with the bus fare, the bus is cheaper.	vergleichen
	it **seems** to be [siːmz]	I~ bigger, but it isn't really bigger.	es scheint zu sein
	quiet ['kwaɪət]	It's a very ~ street. There are no cars.	ruhig
	attractive [ə'træktɪv]	Bamberg is an ~ town, but Rothenburg is more beautiful.	attraktiv; anziehend
	better ['betə]	good – ~ – best	besser
	(A is cheaper) **than** (B) [ðæn, ðən]	It's cheaper to travel by train ~ by plane.	(A ist billiger) als (B)
	more [mɔː]	→ it takes 20 minutes more	mehr

	entertainment [entəˈteɪnmənt]	There's a lot of ~. = There are night clubs, pubs, cinemas etc.		Unterhaltung
	nearer to [ˈnɪərə tʊ]	→ near – nearer – nearest		näher bei
	to agree [əˈgriː]	I ~ = I think so, too.		zustimmen; übereinstimmen
	I'm sorry, I don't agree.			Es tut mir leid, (aber) ich stimme da nicht zu.
	(A is just) **as** (nice) **as** (B.) [dʒʌst əz ... əz]	Which is nicer, Paris or London? – I think Paris is just ~ nice ~ London.		(A ist eben)so (hübsch) wie (B.)
	a two week holiday	We're going on ~, from 14-28 July.		ein zweiwöchiger Urlaub
	which one you think is better			welcher Ihrer Meinung nach besser ist
	as [æz, əz]	He's not a very pleasant person, I would not like to have him ~ a friend.		als
	holiday resort [ˈhɒlɪdeɪ rɪˈzɔːt]	Westerland is a famous ~ on Sylt.		Ferien-/Urlaubsort
	which of them			welchen von ihnen
	do you find nicer			finden Sie netter
3.2	has set standards *hat Maßstäbe gesetzt*	tea making facilities [fəˈsɪlɪtɪz] *Möglichkeiten zum Teekochen*	lounge [laʊndʒ] *Aufenthaltsraum* without [wɪˈðaʊt] *ohne*	
	since *seit*	full [fʊl] *voll(ständig)*		
	bedroom *(Schlaf-)Zimmer*	room [ruːm, rʊm] *Zimmer*		
	shopping centre [ˈʃɒpɪŋ ˈsentə]	→ do the shopping; Tourist Information Centre		Einkaufszentrum
	beach [biːtʃ]	On holiday I spend most of the time on the ~.		Strand
3.3	in town	Luigi's is the best restaurant ~.		in der Stadt
	quietest [ˈkwaɪətɪst]	→ quiet		ruhigste
	the **most** comfortable [məʊst ˈkʌmfətəbl]	comfortable – more comfortable – the ~		bequemste
4.1	**single** [ˈsɪŋgl]			Einzel-
	room [ruːm, rʊm]	How is your hotel ~? – Very comfortable.		Zimmer
	double [ˈdʌbl]	→ double R; → double 5; (opposite: single)		Doppel-
	private [ˈpraɪvɪt]	[!]: O o; = German		privat; (hier: nicht zu übersetzen)
	anything [ˈenɪθɪŋ]	→ something; → nothing		irgendetwas
	free [friː]	Have you got a single room ~ for tonight?		frei
	possible [ˈpɒsɪbl]	Five people in one room? I'm afraid that's not ~.		möglich
	to cost [kɒst]	How much does it ~ to send a postcard to Germany?		kosten
	per [pɜː]	The room costs £30 ~ night.		pro
	without [wɪˈðaʊt]	With or ~ a private bathroom?		ohne
	bath [bɑːθ]	Would you like a room with shower or with ~?		Bad
	I'll take			ich werde ... nehmen
	WC [ˈdʌbljuːˈsiː]			WC; Toilette
4.2	**Dear Sirs,** [dɪə ˈsɜːz]			Sehr geehrte Herren,
	manager [ˈmænɪdʒə]	[!]; = German		*hier:* Geschäftsführer
	to reserve [rɪˈzɜːv]	Can you ~ a double room and two single rooms for 21 January, please? (→ reservation)		reservieren
	in my name			auf meinen Namen
	at the back	There's a street in front of the hotel and a park ~.		auf der Rückseite; nach hinten hinaus
	to confirm [kənˈfɜːm]	If you reserve a hotel room by telephone, you usually have to ~ the reservation by letter.		bestätigen
	booking [ˈbʊkɪŋ]	If you reserve a room or flight, you have a ~.		Buchung
	soon [suːn]	He's not coming at the weekend, but I know he's coming ~.		bald
	as soon as	I have to answer this letter ~ possible.		so bald wie
	Yours sincerely, [ˈjɔːz sɪnˈsɪəlɪ]			Mit freundlichen Grüßen,
	page [peɪdʒ]	The sports ~ is often at the back of the newspaper.		Seite
	to ask	Could I ~ you to help me with this, please?		*hier:* bitten
4.3	booking	*hier: Form von* **to book**		buchen
	to arrive [əˈraɪv]	→ arrival; What time does the train ~ in London?		ankommen
	has just arrived			ist gerade angekommen
	view [vjuː]	We have got a beautiful ~ of the beach from our hotel room.		Ausblick; Aussicht
	OK [ˈəʊˈkeɪ]	= all right		OK; in Ordnung
	front room [ˈfrʌnt ˈrʊm]	*opposite:* a room at the back		Raum nach vorne hinaus/zur Straße
	to put up [ˈpʊt ˈʌp]			*hier:* aufstellen
	sign [saɪn]	Can you see the 'Exit' ~ over there?		Schild; Zeichen
	the others [ðɪ ˈʌðəz]	We want to go to the theatre, but ~ want to go to the cinema.		die anderen
	round [raʊnd]	to walk round		umher
	so many ... that	There are ~ people here ~ we cannot find rooms for all of them.		so viele ..., daß
	everybody [ˈevrɪbɒdɪ]	→ everything		jeder
	the [ðiː]	They say that beer is ~ German drink.		*(betonte Form: andere Aussprache)*

5
coast *Küste*	steel *Stahl*	enough *genug*
picturesque *malerisch*	out of work *arbeitslos*	made *machte*
area *Gebiet*	poor *arm*	island *Insel*
rich *reich*	anywhere else *irgendwo anders*	on the other hand *andererseits*
agricultural *Agrar-; landwirtschaftlich*	difficult *schwierig*	reason *Grund*
highly industrialised *hoch industriell*	to overcome *überwinden*	will change *wird sich ändern*
part *Teil; Gebiet*	lake *(Binnen-)See*	in the next few years *in den kommenden Jahren*
world *Welt*	legal *Rechts-*	trade *Handel*
a hundred years ago *vor hundert Jahren*	independence *Unabhängigkeit; Selbständigkeit*	

Unit 8

food [fuːd] — Essen; Nahrungsmittel

1.1
for breakfast [fə ˈbrekfəst] — I usually have only tea ~. — zum Frühstück
to look at [ˈlʊk ˈæt] — → to watch — (sich) ansehen; betrachten
to order [ˈɔːdə] — *hier:* bestellen
menu [ˈmenjuː] — [!]: O o; You look at it before you have dinner in a restaurant. — Speisekarte

fruit [fruːt] — Frucht; Frucht-
juice [dʒuːs] — No wine or beer for me, please – just fruit ~. — Saft
tomato [təˈmɑːtəʊ] — [!]; T~es are red. — Tomate
  pl.: tomatoes
cornflakes [ˈkɔːnfleɪks] — [!]; = German — Cornflakes
bacon [ˈbeɪkn] — Frühstücksspeck; Schinken(speck)
egg [eg] — In Britain they often have bacon and ~s for breakfast. — Ei

sausage [ˈsɒsɪdʒ] — Wurst
toast [təʊst] — = German — Toast
bread [bred] — Brot
butter [ˈbʌtə] — = German — Butter
jam [dʒæm] — You usually eat it on white bread. — Marmelade (Konfitüre) *(sofern nicht aus Orangen oder Zitronen)*

marmalade [ˈmɑːməleɪd] — [!]: O o o — Marmelade *(aus Orangen oder Zitronen)*

coffee [ˈkɒfɪ] — Tea or ~ with your breakfast? — Kaffee

1.2
(they) were visiting us *(sie) besuchten uns*	table *Tisch*	
said *sagte*	was, were *war, waren*	
lovely *(etwa:) herrlich; nett*	thought *dachte*	
	pinta (= pint of)	

orange [ˈɒrɪndʒ] — [!]: O o; = German — Orange; Apfelsine
madam [ˈmædəm] — [!]: O o; Yes, sir, yes, ~, can I help you? — gnädige Frau *(Anrede für eine Dame, benutzt von Kellnern, Verkäufern etc.)*

else [els] — Would you like anything ~, or is that all, madam? — (auch) noch
boiled [bɔɪld] — Would you like bacon and eggs or a ~ egg? — gekocht

2.1
vegetable *Gemüse*	C'mon (= come on) *(etwa:) mach' schon*	
you have a choice of *du hast die Wahl zwischen*	to decide *(sich) entscheiden*	
pea *Erbse*	just *(etwa:) einfach*	
spinach *Spinat*	I'll have . . . *Ich werde . . . nehmen*	

2.2
lunch [lʌntʃ] — We usually have ~ between 12.30 and 1. — Mittagessen
as they order — wie sie . . . bestellen
table [ˈteɪbl] — The coffee is on the ~. — Tisch
Which table . . . at? — An welchem Tisch . . .? *(häufige Wortstellung in Fragen: die Präposition steht am Satzende)*

soup [suːp] — Would you like tomato juice or ~ to start with? — Suppe
roast **chicken** [ˈrəʊst ˈtʃɪkɪn] — Brathähnchen/-hühnchen
chips [tʃɪps] — Pommes frites
steak [steɪk] — = German — Steak
potato [pəˈteɪtəʊ] *pl.:* potatoes — You make chips from ~es. — Kartoffel
ice-cream [ˈaɪs ˈkriːm] — Children love to eat ~ in the summer. — (Speise-)Eis

2.3
salad [ˈsæləd] — [!]: O o; No potatoes with the steak, just a ~. — *(angemachter)* Salat
to follow [ˈfɒləʊ] — to come after — folgen
What would you like to follow? — *etwa:* Und danach?
vegetable [ˈvedʒtəbl] — In the garden we have flowers and ~s. — Gemüse
as a vegetable — als Gemüse
pea [piː] — a small, green vegetable — Erbse
dry [draɪ] — Red wines from France are usually quite ~. — trocken

	Liebfraumilch		*(in England beliebter Konsumwein deutscher Herkunft)*
	lager ['lɑ:gə]		*(Export-)*Bier
	mineral **water** ['mɪnərəl 'wɔ:tə]	[!]: O o o O o; No beer or wine for me please, just a fruit juice or ~.	Mineralwasser
	to take orders		Bestellungen aufnehmen

	for any two courses *für 2 beliebige Gänge*	cold cuts [kəʊld 'kʌts] *Aufschnitt*	sirloin steak ['sɜ:'lɔɪn steɪk] *Lendensteak*
	Anglesey Eggs ['æŋglsɪ] *(walisische Eierspezialität)*	sideboard *Büffet*	price [praɪs] *Preis*
	charcoal ['tʃɑ:kəʊl] *Holzkohle*	choice of ... ['tʃɔɪs əv] ... *nach Wahl*	baked potatoes [beɪkt pə'teɪtəʊz] *im Backofen gebackene Kartoffeln*
	trout [traʊt] *Forelle*	dip [dɪp] *Soße; Tunke*	Peelouts (skins) ['pi:laʊts] *Pellkartoffeln (ungepellt)*
	joint [dʒɔɪnt] *Braten (oft: Keule)*	corn [kɔ:n] *Mais*	sour cream [saʊə kri:m] *saurer Rahm*
	pie [paɪ] *Pastete*	wrapped in [ræpt ɪn] *eingewickelt in*	chive dressing [tʃaɪv 'dresɪŋ] *Schnittlauchdressing*
	Good Shepherd's Pye ['ʃepədz] *(Name eines trad. Gerichts, bestehend aus Hackfleisch, Gemüse und überbackenem Kartoffelpüree)*	corn tortilla [kɔ:n 'tɔ:tɪjə] *Maisfladen*	award winning *preisgekrönt*
		covered with ['kʌvəd wɪθ] *bedeckt mit*	to choose [tʃu:z] *wählen*
		cheese [tʃi:z] *Käse*	cole slaw ['kəʊl slɔ:] *Krautsalat*
	Lancashire Hot Pot ['læŋkəʃə] *Ragout (mit Kartoffeln aus der Grafschaft Lancashire)*	minced beef [mɪnst bi:f] *Hackfleisch*	crispy ['krɪspɪ] *knackig*
		lettuce ['letɪs] *grüner (Kopf-)salat*	full slab ['fʊl 'slæb] *etwa: ein dicker Klacks*
	Bangers and Mash ['bæŋgəz n'mæʃ] *Würstchen mit Kartoffelpüree*	B.B.Q. *Barbecue-; gegrillt*	blueberry ['blu:bərɪ] *Heidel-/Blaubeere*
		bean [bi:n] *Bohne*	
	onion gravy ['ʌnjən 'greɪvɪ] *Zwiebelsoße*	bowl [bəʊl] *Schüssel*	
	pease pudding ['pi:z 'pʊdɪŋ] *Erbsenbrei*	hot [hɒt] *hier: scharf*	
		side salads [saɪd 'sælədz] *Salatbeilagen*	
		fries [fraɪz] *Pommes frites*	
		smoked [sməʊkt] *geräuchert*	
2.4	cheeseburger ['tʃi:zbɜ:gə] *Hamburger mit Käse*	sparkling ['spɑ:klɪŋ] *sprudelnd; "-Limonade"*	thick [θɪk] *dick*
	bun [bʌn] *Brötchen*	hot apple pie [hɒt 'æpl paɪ] *heißer Apfelkuchen*	milk shake ['mɪlkʃeɪk]
	quarterpounder ['kwɔ:təpaʊndə] *Viertelpfünder*	pure [pjʊə] *rein*	chocolate ['tʃɒklət]
			strawberry ['strɔ:bərɪ] *Erdbeere*

	meal [mi:l]	Breakfast, lunch and dinner are ~s.	Mahlzeit; Essen
	nothing to write on		nichts, um darauf zu schreiben
	to come back	→ get back; to come	zurückkommen
	to serve [sɜ:v]	Would you ~ breakfast in our room tomorrow, please?	servieren
3.1	**Have a drink.**		*etwa:* Möchten Sie etwas trinken?
3.2	**some** [sʌm, səm]	I'd like ~ fruit juice and ~ cornflakes.	etwas; ein wenig; ein paar *(oft aber ohne deutsche Entsprechung)*
	sweet [swi:t]	Jam is too ~ for me, I prefer marmalade.	süß
	medium ['mi:djəm]	It wasn't big or small, it was ~.	mittel
	half a pint	→ pint	*ca. 0,25 l*
	ice [aɪs]	→ ice-cream	Eis
4.1	**bill** [bɪl]	When you want to pay in a restaurant, the waiter brings you the ~.	Rechnung
4.2	How did you like ...?		*etwa:* Hat's geschmeckt?
	meat [mi:t]		Fleisch
	was/wasn't		war/war nicht
	cooked [kʊkt]	This steak is still red, it isn't ~.	gekocht; *hier:* gar
	fish [fɪʃ]	What would you like? F~ or meat?	Fisch
	cold [kəʊld]	It's very ~ in Finland in December and January.	kalt
	fresh [freʃ]	This fish is not ~, it's ten days old.	frisch
	warm [wɔ:m]	[!]; = German	warm
5.1	**to eat** [i:t]	What would you like to ~? Fish or meat?	essen
	more and more		immer mehr; mehr und mehr
	to go camping ['kæmpɪŋ]	[!]; = German	zelten gehen; Camping machen
	to cook [kʊk]	→ cooked	kochen
	Have we got **any** ... left? ['enɪ]		*(„any" in Fragen hat im Deutschen meist keine Entsprechung)*
	... **left** [left]	Whave to buy some more meat, there isn't any ~.	übrig
	not any	There is ~ milk left.	kein(e)
	apple ['æpl]	A~s and oranges are fruit.	Apfel
	pear [peə]	[!]; P~s are fruit, too.	Birne
	salt [sɒlt]		Salz
	sugar ['ʃʊgə]	A lot of ~ , please. I love sweet coffee.	Zucker
	cream [kri:m]	Would you like sugar and ~ in your coffee?	Sahne
	milk [mɪlk]	I like cream in my coffee and ~ in my tea.	Milch
	cheese [tʃi:z]	Gorgonzola is the only ~ I don't like.	Käse
5.2	Is there **any** sugar ...?		*(hier etwa:)* Steht Zucker ...?

6

business *Geschäft; Betrieb*	well-loved *sehr beliebt*	public *öffentlich*
owner *Eigentümer/in*	cleanliness *Sauberkeit*	jukebox *Musikbox*
met *traf; kennenlernte*	value *Wert*	fruit machine *Spielautomat*
even *(hier:) sogar*	customer *Kunde/Kundin*	seat *Sitzgelegenheit*
father *Vater*	sold *verkaufte*	to enjoy *genießen*
to afford *sich leisten*	a billion A.E. = 1,000,000,000	important *wichtig*
clean *sauber*	B.E. = 1,000,000,000,000	country *Land*
sea food *Meeresfrüchte*	. . . dollars worth of *im Wert von*	to understand [ʌndəˈstænd]
taco *Mexikanischer Maisfladen*	. . . Dollar	*verstehen*
gefüllt mit gewürztem Hackfleisch	in sales *(etwa:) durch Verkäufe*	to become [bɪˈkʌm] *werden*
pancake *Pfannkuchen*	to employ *beschäftigen*	popular [ˈpɒpjʊlə] [!] : O o o
advertising *Werbung*	security *Sicherheit*	*populär*

Unit 9

	past [pɑːst]		*Vergangenheit*
1.1	with love		*etwa: mit besten Grüßen*
	wonderful [ˈwʌndəfʊl]	better than very good	*wundervoll*
	* went [went]	to go – ~	*gingen; fuhren*
	* spent [spent]	to spend – ~	*verbrachten*
	last week	~ – this week – next week	*vorige Woche; letzte Woche*
	to give, gave [gɪv, geɪv]	Can I have a beer? ≈ G~ me a beer, please.	*geben, gab*
		opposite: to take	
	kiss [kɪs]	I always give my husband a ~ before I leave for the office.	*Kuß*
	yesterday [ˈjestədeɪ]	~ – today – tomorrow	*gestern*
	Everglades [ˈevəgleɪdz]		*(Sumpflandschaft;*
			Nationalpark in Florida)
	alligator [ˈælɪgeɪtə]	[!] : O o o o; = German	*Alligator*
	* ate [et] *auch:* [eɪt]	to eat – ~	*aß; fraß*
	weather [ˈweðə]	The ~ is beautiful today. It's really warm and pleasant.	*Wetter*
	Love, . . . [lʌv]		*(vertraulicher umgangssprachl.*
			Briefschluß, etwa:) Beste Grüße, . . .
	to visit [ˈvɪzɪt]	We like to ~ interesting old towns when we are on holiday.	*besuchen*
	we did not like it		*wir mochten es nicht*
	although [ɔːlˈðəʊ]	[!] : o O; A~ he's English he speaks very good German.	*obgleich*
	a lot [əˈlɒt]	very many	*eine Menge*
	to show [ʃəʊ]	If you don't like that coat, madam, I can ~ you another one.	*zeigen*
	moon [muːn]		*Mond*
	best wishes [best ˈwɪʃɪz]		*(mit) besten Wünschen*
1.3	two years **ago** [əˈgəʊ]	It's now 1985, and that was in 1983, so that was ~.	*vor zwei Jahren*
	* did [dɪd]	do – ~	*tat*
	I did a lot of sight-seeing		*ich besichtigte vieles*
	to swim, swam [swɪm, swæm]	In summer when it's really warm I like to go to the beach to ~.	*schwimmen, schwamm*
	all day	What does he do ~? – Nothing, really.	*den ganzen Tag*
2.1	* took out [ˈtʊk ˈaʊt]	to take out – ~	*führte aus*
2.2	things people do		*Dinge, die Leute tun*
	* read [red]	to read – ~	*las*
	at home		*zu Hause*
	* had [hæd]	to have – ~	*hatte*
	* won [wʌn]	to win – ~	*gewann*
	* made [meɪd]	to make – ~	*machte*
	* met [met]	to meet – ~	*traf*
	* drove [drəʊv]	to drive – ~	*fuhr*
	to rob [rɒb], robbed	to ~ a bank	*(be)rauben*
	tried [traɪd]	to try – ~	*versuchte*
	last night	~ – tonight – tomorrow night	*gestern abend*
	you weren't **in**		*du warst nicht zu Hause*
	Me?		*Ich?*
	all evening		*den ganzen Abend*
	Did you?		*(leicht erstaunt) Hast du das getan?*
	Come on! [kəm ˈɒn]		*Nur sachte!*
3.1	text [tekst]	= German	*Text*
	while listening [waɪl]		*während Sie zuhören*
	to leave out	→ leave	*aus-/weglassen*

* = *„unregelmäßige" Vergangenheitsformen: Liste S. 112!*

filler ['fɪlə]	→ fill in		Füllsel
speaker ['spi:kə]	→ speak, speaking		Sprecher
listener ['lɪsnə]	→ listen (to)		Zuhörer
I mean [mi:n]			ich meine
you know [jə 'nəʊ]			wissen Sie/weißt du
you see [jə 'si:]			*etwa:* ... ja?/... gell?
sort of ['sɔ:təv]			*etwa:* so'ne Art ...
kind of ['kaɪndəv]			*etwa:* so'ne Art ...
actually ['æktʃʊəlɪ]	[!]: O o o		wirklich
by the way ['baɪ ðə 'weɪ]			übrigens
to flirt [flɜ:t]	[!]; = German		flirten
one day			eines Tages
if I could baby-sit ['beɪbɪsɪt]			ob ich auf das Baby aufpassen könnte
dead [ded]	Mozart is ~, and Goethe is ~.		tot
3-year-old			3 Jahre alt
all alone [ə'ləʊn]	My family is not here, I'm ~.		ganz allein
to go over [gəʊ 'əʊvə]	→ to come over		hinüber gehen
house [haʊs]	They live in a ~ with a nice garden.		Haus
was all in a mess [mes]			war in einer fürchterlichen Unordnung
to clean [kli:n]	Mr Brown likes to ~ his car every Saturday.		säubern
* **came** [keɪm]	to come – ~		kam
even ['i:vn]	They all came to watch it, ~ Jim, who doesn't usually like TV.		sogar; noch
before [bɪ'fɔ:]	Did you paint the kitchen? It looks nicer than ~.		vorher
to look round [lʊk 'raʊnd]			sich umsehen; umhersehen
* **said** [sed]	to say – ~		sagte
to smile [smaɪl]	Look at the camera and ~, please.		lächeln
the next time			das nächste Mal
* **sat** [sæt]	to sit – ~		saß
ill [ɪl]	*opposite:* well; He can't go to the office today because he feels ~.		krank
for a week			eine Woche lang
* **bought** [bɔ:t]	to buy – ~		kaufte
sweets [swi:ts]	Their children eat too many ~.		Süßigkeiten
that [ðæt, ðət]	It was so cheap ~ I bought it.		*hier:* daß
to go back [gəʊ 'bæk]	*opposite:* to come back		zurückgehen/fahren
* **thought** [θɔ:t]	to think – ~		dachte
was over [wəz 'əʊvə]	When the film ~, they all went home.		war vorbei
* **wrote** [rəʊt]	to write – ~		schrieb
driving lessons ['draɪvɪŋ 'lesənz]	→ lesson		Fahrstunden
instructor [ɪn'strʌktə]	[!]: o O o; a teacher		(Fahr-)Lehrer/in
* **felt** [felt]	to feel – ~		fühlte (mich)
nervous ['nɜ:vəs]	[!]: O o; = German		nervös
mistake [mɪ'steɪk]	[!]; 'He go', is not right; it's a ~.		Fehler
* **told** [təʊld]	to tell – ~		erzählte; sagte
male [meɪl]	It says 'Mr', so the person is ~.		männlich
would have been better			besser gewesen wäre
the driving			das Fahren
or me			oder ich
together [tə'geðə]	[!]: o O o; I live ~ with my family in a small house in a village near London.		zusammen
test [test]	= German		Test; Prüfung
to pass a test [pɑ:s]			eine Prüfung bestehen
to guess [ges]	I've got a present for you, ~ what it is!		raten

3.2
at a dance [dɑ:ns]			bei einem Tanz
boy [bɔɪ]	(*opposite:* girl) My son is not very old, he's still a ~.		Junge
love [lʌv]	→ with love, Love ...		Liebe; *hier:* Liebes-

4
things to remember			Dinge, an die man sich erinnern sollte/erinnert
parents ['peərənts]	Are you the ~ of these children?		Eltern
bike [baɪk]	Do your children walk to school or do they go on their ~s?		Fahrrad
smoke [sməʊk]	You can ~ in some cinemas in England, but not in theatres.		rauchen
cigarette [sɪgə'ret]	[!]: o o O; He smokes more than 40 ~s a day.		Zigarette
in 1950	I think that was ~.		(im Jahre) 1950

reunion *(Wieder-)Treffen*	to earn *verdienen*		to forget *vergessen*
noisy *geräuschvoll*	odd jobs *Gelegenheitsarbeiten*		suddenly *plötzlich*
cheerful *fröhlich*	important *wichtig*		happily married *glücklich verheiratet*
slim *schlank*	unexpected *unerwartet*		to realize *sich bewußt werden; einsehen*
success *Erfolg*	for example *zum Beispiel*		
to marry *heiraten*	as ever *wie immer; wie je zuvor*		
business *Geschäft; Betrieb*	to understand *verstehen*		
to become (an engineer) *Ingenieur werden (Vergangenheitsform:* became*)*	once *einst* little *klein*		

Unit 10

1.1	what they feel like	→ what he is like		wie sie sich fühlen
1.2	quite well			ganz gut
	to complain [kəmˈpleɪn]	He likes to ~, even when everything is fine and he is having a good time.		sich beschweren

nobody [ˈnəʊbədɪ]   *niemand*

2.1	**a headache** [ˈhedeɪk]	Have you got an aspirin? I've got a terrible ~.	Kopfschmerz(en)
	tablet [ˈtæblɪt]	[!]: O o; = German	Tablette
	to see a doctor	If you don't feel better tomorrow, you should ~.	einen Arzt aufsuchen
	to stay [steɪ]	On Sunday mornings I like to ~ in bed until 11.	bleiben
2.2	**every** four hours	→ every day	alle 4 Stunden
	medicine [ˈmedsɪn]	[!]: O o; = German	Medizin
	15 tablets **a** day		15 Tabletten pro Tag
	without asking . . .		ohne . . . zu fragen
	under [ˈʌndə]	*opposite:* on; It's not on the table, it's ~ the table.	unter

pain	*Schmerz*	dose	*Dosis*	advice	*Rat*
cold	*Erkältung, Schnupfen*	unless	*wenn nicht*	to repeat	*wiederholen*
flu	*Grippe*	directed	*angewiesen*	to contain	*enthalten*
adult	*Erwachsener*	except on	*außer auf*	to persist	*anhalten; andauern*

2.3	**to hope** [həʊp]	I ~ you can come and see us next year.	hoffen
	I hope you'll **get better** soon		ich hoffe, es geht Ihnen bald besser; Gute Besserung!
	(a) cold [kəʊld]	In winter a lot of people get ~s.	Erkältung; Schnupfen
	the 'flu [fluː]	*short for* influenza [ɪnfluˈenzə]. Have you got a cold, or is it ~?	Grippe
	to hurt [hɜːt], hurt	Be careful with that umbrella. You could ~ somebody with it.	(sich) verletzen
	foot [fʊt]	→ football	Fuß
	leg [leg]	He can't walk very fast, he has got short ~s.	Bein
	back [bæk]	→ back of the hotel	Rücken
	somebody [ˈsʌmbədɪ]	a person	jemand
	serious [ˈsɪərɪəs]		ernst
	a temperature [ˈtemprətʃə]	[!]: O o o; 39°? You've got ~.	Fieber
	the people you meet		die Leute, die Sie treffen
3.1	*tip* [tɪp]	= German	Hinweis; Tip
	south [saʊθ]		Süd; Süden
	Europe [ˈjʊərəp]	[!]: O o	Europa
	things to remember		Dinge, an die man denken sollte
	happy [ˈhæpɪ]	He always complains. He's never ~.	glücklich
	if you want it to be a happy one		wenn Sie wollen, daß es ein glücklicher (Urlaub) wird
	water [ˈwɔːtə]	Would you like ~ and ice in your whisky?	Wasser
	tap [tæp]	Use the red ~ if you want warm water.	Wasserhahn
	without washing it		ohne es zu waschen
	sun [sʌn]	On holidays I like spending as much time as possible in the ~.	Sonne
	to leave [liːv], left [left]	You can ~ your suitcase over there, it's quite safe.	*hier:* lassen
	baggage [ˈbægɪdʒ]	[!] O o; How much ~ have you got? – Only this suitcase.	Gepäck
	money [ˈmʌnɪ]	Pounds and pence are English ~.	Geld
	traveller's cheque [ˈtrævələz tʃek]	→ travel; I haven't got any English money, but I've got £100 in ~s.	Reisescheck
	valuable [ˈvæljʊəbl]		wertvoll
	to carry [ˈkærɪ]	I've got 3 suitcases. Could you ~ one for me, please?	*(eine Sache/Last mit den Händen)* tragen
	cash [kæʃ]	I've got £100 in traveller's cheques and $20 in ~.	Bargeld
	swim wear [ˈswɪm weə]	→ sports wear	Badekleidung
	church [tʃɜːtʃ]	Do you go to ~ every Sunday?	Kirche
	photo [ˈfəʊtəʊ]	Would you like to come over and see the ~s of our summer holidays?	Fotografie
	to take photos	→ to take pictures	fotografieren
3.2	who		. . ., der/die/das . . .
	true [truː]	A lot of English people speak German. – That's not ~.	wahr
3.3	to look happy		glücklich aussehen
	to be in love with somebody		in jemanden verliebt sein
	noisy [ˈnɔɪzɪ]	Our house is next to a main road, so it's very ~.	laut; geräuschvoll
	dirty [ˈdɜːtɪ]	It's ~. Can you clean it for me, please?	schmutzig

	to steal, stole, [stiːl, stəʊl]	They robbed the bank and ~ all the money.	stehlen
	passport [ˈpɑːspɔːt]	If you go to America, you have to take your ~ with you.	(Reise-)Paß
	woman, women [ˈwʊmən, ˈwɪmɪn]	(≠ lady; ≠ wife; ≠ madam) This job is for a man or a ~.	Frau, Frauen
	problem [ˈprɒbləm]	[!]: O o; = German	Problem
	to happen [ˈhæpən]		geschehen; passieren
	how **could** that happen?		wie konnte das passieren?
	What a pity! [wɒt ə ˈpɪtɪ]	I'm sorry, I can't come to your party. – Oh, ~!	Wie schade
	write a letter to …		einen Brief schreiben an …
	police [pəˈliːs]	[!]: o O; Look, they're robbing the bank! Phone the ~!	Polizei

4.1
cool [kuːl]	Even in summer the nights are sometimes ~.	kühl
cloudy [ˈklaʊdɪ]	You can't see the sun, it's ~.	wolkig; bewölkt
sunny [ˈsʌnɪ]	It's ~, you can see the sun.	sonnig
rainy [ˈreɪnɪ]	On ~ days I just stay at home and watch TV or read a book.	regnerisch
foggy [ˈfɒgɪ]	It's really ~, I can't see a thing.	neblig

hot *heiß*	*sun sets/rises* [ˈraɪzɪz] *Sonne geht unter/auf*	*ins* [ˈɪntʃɪz] = *inches*
risk *Risiko*	*lighting-up time* *Zeit des Einschaltens der Straßenbeleuchtung*	*around* (= *round*)
shower [ˈʃaʊə] *(Regen-)Schauer*	*high* [haɪ] *hoch*	*coast* [kəʊst] *Küste*
spell *Perioden*	*wet* *naß*	
thunderstorm [ˈθʌndəstɔːm] *Gewitter; Unwetter*		

4.2
snow [snəʊ]		Schnee
north [nɔːθ]	*opposite:* south; Kiel is in the ~ of Germany.	Nord; Norden
there will be …		es wird … geben
in the north		im Norden
west [west]		West; Westen
east [iːst]	*opposite:* west	Ost; Osten
rain [reɪn]	→ rainy	Regen
storm [stɔːm]	[!]; = German	Sturm
wind [wɪnd]	[!]; = German	Wind
fog [fɒg]	What terrible weather. I can't see a thing in this ~.	Nebel
weather forecast [ˈweðə ˈfɔːkɑːst]	I always listen to the news and the ~.	Wetterbericht
temperature [ˈtemprətʃə]	[!]: O o o; = German	Temperatur
°C (= degrees Celsius) [dɪˈgriːz ˈselsɪəs]		Grad Celsius

4.3
sunshine [ˈsʌnʃaɪn]		Sonnenschein
winter [ˈwɪntə]	*opposite:* summer	Winter

4.4
something to talk about		etwas, über das sie sich unterhalten (können)
key **word** [ˈkiː ˈwɜːd]		Schlüsselwort

4.5
a bit [ə ˈbɪt]	It's ~ expensive. ≈ It's expensive, but not very expensive.	ein bißchen; ein wenig
hot [hɒt]	It's very ~ in Africa.	heiß
wet [wet]	*opposite:* dry; Water is ~.	naß
to put, put [pʊt]	P~ the books on the table, please.	legen; stellen
team [tiːm]	= German	Team; Mannschaft

5
mother *Mutter*	shelter *Schutz*	pursuit of happiness *Streben nach Glück (Begriff aus der US-Verfassung)*
little *klein*	through *durch*	
drag *(etwa:) Belastung*	busy *(hier:) geschäftig, arbeitsreich*	a bore *etwas Langweiliges*
kid *(umgangssprachlich:) Kind*	instant cake *Fertigkuchen*	to die, dying *sterben, Sterbe-*
different *verschieden*	to burn *verbrennen*	
to hear *hören*	frozen *(hier:) Tiefkühl-*	
to calm down *beruhigen*	outside *draußen vor*	

Alphabetische Wortliste

a, an 1/2.3, 1/2.4, 10/2.2
about
 ask ~ 6/3.2
 like ~ 6/4.2
 talk ~ 4/5.2
 tell ~ 6/1.4
about (= ca.) 7/1.1
actually 9/3.1
address 2/3.1
afraid, I'm ~ 3/5.3
after 4/1.4
 after that 4/3
afternoon 4/1.4
again 1/1
ago 9/1.3
agree 7/3.1
ahead 2/5.1
airport 5/2.4
all 6/2.1
 ~ day 9/1.3
all right 3/5.3
alligator 9/1.1
almost 4/1.2
alone 9/3.1
along
 bring ~ 5/3.2
 come ~ 5/2.4
 go ~, straight ~ 2/5.3
already 4/5.2
although 9/1.1
always 6/1.2
am 0/1.1, 0/1.2
a.m. 4/1.4
America 1/2.1
among 6/2.3
and 0/1.1
animal 6/2.2
animateur 6/2.1
another 3/6.4
answer n 4/1.2
answer v 6/1.1
any 8/5.1, 8/5.2
anything 7/4.1
apple 8/5.1
are 0/1.2, 0/2.2
 A~ you English? 1/2.1
arrival 4/2.3
arrive 7/4.3
as (= als) 7/3.1
as (= wie) 6/2.4
as ... as 5/2.3, 7/3.1
ask (= fragen) 2/3.2
ask (= bitten) 7/4.2
at
 ~ home 9/2.2
 ~ the corner 2/5.4
 ~ the club 6/2.1
 ~ the back of the hotel 7/4.2
 ~ 6 o'clock 4/2.2
 ~ the weekend 5/1.2
 ~ the moment 5/2.4
 ~ night 6/4.2
 ~ work 6/3.2
be good ~ 6/2.1
attractive 7/3.1
avenue 2/3.1

baby 5/2.4
baby-sit 9/3.1
back
 come ~ 8/2.4
 get ~ 6/3.2
 go ~ 9/3.1
back (of the hotel) 7/4.2
back (=Rücken) 10/2.3
bacon 8/1.1
bad 0/2.3
baggage 10/3.1
bank 1/4.1
bath 7/4.1
bathroom 5/2.2
be 7/3.1
 B~ careful! 2/5.2
 ~ in love with 10/3.3
beach 7/3.2
beautiful 3/2.1
because 2/2.3
bed 6/1.1
beer 6/1.1
before (= vor) 6/3.1
before (= vorher) 9/3.1
best 0/2.2
 ~ wishes 9/1.1
better 7/3.1
between 6/2.1
big 3/5.3
bike 9/4
bill 8/4.1
birthday 4/4.1
bit, a ~ 10/4.5
black 3/3.1
blouse 3/1
blue 3/3.1
boat 4/3
boiled 8/1.3
book n 3/4.1
book v 7/4.3
book shop 2/5.4
booking 7/4.2
boss 6/2.5
bottle 6/1.1
boy 9/3.2
bread 8/1.1
breakfast 6/1.2, 8/1.1
bridge 3/6.4
bring 5/3.2
Britain 1/2.1
British 1/2.1
brown 3/3.1
building 2/4
bus 2/5.3
bus station 2/5.3
but 1/2.3
butter 8/1.1
buy 3/5.1
by
 ~ (= von) 3/3.1
 ~ car 4/2.2
 ~ plane/train/... 7/2.1
 ~ the way 9/3.1
bye 0/3

camera 3/4.1
camping 8/5.1
can 1/3.1
cannot 3/5.1

car 1/2.4
card 6/2.3
careful 2/5.2
carry 10/3.1
cash 10/3.1
cassette 3/4.1
cassette recorder 4/5.3
castle 4/1.4
cathedral 4/1.4
centre 6/3.2
 shopping ~ 7/3.2
 Tourist Information C~ 4/1.4
certainly 3/5.3
change v
 ~ money 3/6.3
 ~ trains 6/3.1
change n 3/6.4
cheap 7/2.1
cheese 8/5.1
chicken 8/2.2
child, children 3/4.1
chips 8/2.2
church 10/3.1
cigarette 9/4
cinema 2/3.1
city 1/2.3
class 5/2.3
classical music 6/2.2
clean v 9/3.1
cloudy 10/4.1
coach 7/2.2
coat 3/1
coffee 8/1.1
cold adj 8/4.2
cold n, a ~ 10/2.3
college 5/3.2
colour 3/5.1
come
 ~ along 5/2.4
 ~ back 8/2.4
 ~ over 5/1.1
come on 9/2.2
comfortable 7/2.1
comic 5/3.2
company 6/2.4
compare 7/3.1
complain 10/1.2
complete v 2/2.1
concert 5/1.2
confirm 7/4.2
congratulations 6/4.2
convenient 7/2.2
cook v 8/5.1
 cooked 8/4.2
cool 10/4.1
corner 2/5.4
cornflakes 8/1.1
cost v 7/4.1
cotton 3/3.2
could 4/3, 10/3.3
course 5/3.2
cowboy 1/5.3
cream 8/5.1
creative writing 5/3.2
cup 6/1.2

damn it 2/1.1
dance 9/3.2
date 4/(Überschrift)

daughter 4/4.2
day 4/3
dead 9/3.1
dear n, Oh, ~! 6/4.1
dear adj
 D~ Jenny, ... 4/3
 ~ Sirs, ... 7/4.2
degree 10/4.2
department 3/4.1
department store 2/5.4
departure 4/2.3
dinner 5/1.2
directory 2/1.7
 D~ Inquiries 2/1.7
dirty 10/3.5
do, does (Hilfsverb) (in Fragen) 6/2.1, 6/2.3, 6/3.2
 (bei Verneinung) 6/4.2
How do you like ...? 1/4.3
What does (he do)? 6/1.1
do, does (Vo!lvb.) 5/1.1, 6/1.1
 ~ the shopping 3/4.1
 ~ sight-seeing 9/1.3
 ~ sports 6/2.2
How do you do? 1/5.1
doctor 6/1.4
double (Buchstaben) 1/3.2
 (Zahlen in Tel.-Nr.) 2/1.3
adj 7/4.1
down, write ~ 2/1.7
dream 6/2.4
dress 3/1
drink n 5/1.1
 Have a ~ 8/3.1
drink v 5/2.2
drive 6/1.3
driving lesson 9/3.1
dry 8/2.3

each 3/6.1
early 6/4.1
east 10/4.2
eat 8/5.1
egg 8/1.1
else 8/1.3
engineer 1/4.2
England 1/2.1
English 0/1.1
 Are you ~?; I'm ~. 1/2.1
entertainment 7/3.1
entrance 2/5.4
Europe 10/3.1
even 9/3.1
evening 0/1.1
every (= jede,r,s) 6/1.3
every (two hours) (= alle) 10/2.2

everybody 7/4.3
everything 6/2.4
excuse v, E~ me, ... 0/1.2
exit 2/5.4
expensive 3/2.1
extra 5/2.4
factory 1/4.2
family 1/5.1
famous 7/2.4
fare 7/2.3
farm 6/2.4
fast 6/2.2
favourite 6/2.4
feel 6/4.1
 ~ like 10/1.1
fill in 5/1.1
filler 9/3.1
film 3/4.1
film star 6/2.4
find 2/1.7
 ~ out 4/2.2
fine, I'm ~. 0/2.3
firm 6/4.2
first (= erste,r,s) 2/4
first (= zuerst) 6/1.1
first name 1/3.2
fish 8/4.2
flight 7/2.1
flirt 9/3.1
floor 2/4
flower 0/2.2
flu 10/2.3
fly 7/2.1
fog 10/4.2
foggy 10/4.1
follow 8/2.3
food 8/(Überschrift)
foot 10/2.3
football 6/2.3
for
 ~ (= für) 0/2.2
 ~ (= wegen) 2/1.8
to leave ~ 5/2.1
 ~ an hour/a week 5/2.4, 9/3.1
 ~ breakfast 8/1.1
forecast, weather ~ 10/4.2
foreign 6/2.1
forget 6/4.1
free 7/4.1
fresh 8/4.2
friend 0/2.2
friendly 6/2.1
from 1/2.1
from ... to ... 4/1.4
front, in ~ of 5/3.2
front room 7/4.3
fruit, ~ juice 8/1.1

game 6/2.4
gallon 7/2.3
garden 2/1.2
get 3/4.1
 ~ back 6/3.2
 ~ better 10/2.3
 ~ home 6/1.4
 ~ to 5/2.3
 ~ up 6/1.3
gin and tonic 6/2.4

girl 0/2.2
give 9/1.1
glad 5/2.3
glass 5/2.2
go 2/5.1
 ~ and see friends 6/1.5
 ~ back 9/3.1
 ~ for a run/walk 6/1.2, 6/2.2
 ~ on 2/5.2
 ~ on holiday 5/2.3
 ~ on a trip 4/3
 ~ out 6/1.4
 ~ over 9/3.1
 ~ to 4/3
 ~ to bed 6/1.1
golf 6/2.4
good 0/1.1
 G~ evening/morning. 0/1.2
good at, be ~ 6/2.1
goodbye 0/3
Great Britain 1/2.1
green 3/3.1
grey 3/3.1
ground floor 2/4
group 5/3.2
guess 9/3.1
guest 1/3.3
guide 0/1.1

hair 5/2.5
hairdresser 1/4.1
half
 five and a ~ 3/5.2
 ~ past 4/1.4
 ~ a pint of 8/3.2
happen 10/3.3
happy 10/3.1
have
 ~ breakfast/dinner 6/1.2, 5/1.2
 H~ a drink! 8/3.1
 ~ a party 5/2.2
 ~ a snack 6/1.1
 ~ a shower 6/1.2
have got 1/3.4, 4/1.2
has got 4/5.1
hat 1/6
have to 4/2.2
has to 4/4.2
he 1/3.3
headache 10/2.1
hear 6/4.1
hello 0/1.1
help v 3/5.1
her 2/1.3, 4/5.1
here 1/3.4
H~ you are. 3/6.4
Hi! 0/2.2
him 4/5.1
his 1/3.3
hobby 5/3.2
holiday
 go on ~ 5/2.3
 be on ~ 6/2.3
home adv 4/2.2
at ~ 9/2.2
get ~ 6/1.4
home computer 5/3.1
homework 5/2.1
hope v 10/2.3

hospital 6/1.4
hot 10/4.5
hotel 1/3.3
hour 5/2.4
house 9/3.1
housewife, ... wives 1/4.2
housework 6/2.5
how 1/4.3
 H~ are you? 0/2.2
 H~ do you do? 1/5.1
 H~ long? 6/3.1
 H~ many? 2/1.2
 H~ much is it/ are they? 3/6.1
 H~ nice! 6/4.2
 H~ often? 6/3.1
hurt 10/2.3
husband 4/4.2

I 0/1.1
I'd like 3/6.4
I'd love to 5/1.2
I'm afraid 3/5.3
I'm fine 0/2.3
I'm sorry 5/2.2, 6/4.1
I've got no idea 4/5.2
ice 8/3.2
ice-cream 8/2.2
idea 4/3
ideal 6/2.5
if (= ob), (= wenn) 5/2.3
ill 9/3.1
in 1/2.3
 ~ the morning/ afternoon/evening 4/1.4
 ~ January 4/4.2
 ~ 1940 9/4
 ~ German 6/1.1
 ~ my name 7/4.2
 you were not ~ 9/2.2
in front of 5/3.2
instead (of) 4/3, 5/2.4
instructor 9/3.1
interested in 4/3
interesting 1/4.3
interview 6/3.1
into, turn ~ 2/5.4
invitation 5/1.1
invite 5/1.2
is 0/1.1
isn't it? 4/5.1
it 1/2.3
jam 8/1.1
jazz 6/2.2
jeans 3/1
job 1/4.1
journey 6/3.1
juice 8/1.1
just
 ~ a moment 2/1.8
 ~ (= ebenso) 7/3.1

key 1/3.4
key word 10/4.4
kilometre 7/2.3
kind of 9/3.1
kiss 9/1.1
know 2/5.4
 you ~ 9/3.1

lady 3/4.1
lager 7/2.3
language 6/2.1

last (= letzte,r,s) 2/2.1
 ~ week/ night 9/1.1, 9/2.2
late 5/2.3
learn 5/3.1
leave (= abfahren) 4/2.2
 ~ for 5/2.1
leave (= verlassen) 6/3.2
leave (= lassen) 10/3.1
leave out 9/3.1
left (= links) 2/5.1, 2/5.4
left (= übrig) 8/5.1
leg 10/2.3
let's 4/3
letter 5/3.1
life 6/1.4
like v 1/4.3
 ~ doing 5/3.2
 I'd ~ 3/6.4
 Would you ~ ...? 5/1.1
like adv
 What's he ~? 6/2.5
 look ~ 6/2.4
 feel ~ 10/1.1
list 2/1.8
listen (to) 1/3.3, 5/3.1
listener 9/3.1
literature 5/3.2
litre 7/2.3
live 1/2.3
long 3/5.3
look
 ~ after 5/2.4
 ~ at 8/1.1
 ~ for 3/4.2
 ~ happy 10/3.3
 ~ like 6/2.4
 ~ round 9/3.1
lot, a ~ of 6/4.2
 a ~ 9/1.1
love v 5/1.2
love n 9/3.2, 10/3.3
 Love, ... 9/1.1
 ... with ~ 9/1.1
lunch 8/2.2

madam 8/1.3
made in/of 3/3.1, 3/3.2
magazine 3/4.1
main 5/3.2
make 6/1.2
male 9/3.1
man, men 3/4.1
manager 7/4.2
 sales ~ 1/4.1
many 4/3
 How ~? 2/1.2
map 3/6.1
marmalade 8/1.1
matter, What's the ~? 6/4.1
me 0/1.2, 4/5.1, 5/1.2
me (= ich) 9/2.2
meal 8/2.4
mean, I ~ 9/3.1
meat 8/4.2
medicine 10/2.2
medium 8/3.2
meet 0/1.1
menu 8/1.1
mess 9/3.1
midnight 4/1.4
mile 7/2.3

milk 8/5.1
milkman 6/1.4
mineral water 8/2.3
minute 4/2.1
Miss 0/2.1
mistake 9/3.1
mix 6/4.2
modern 5/3.2
moment 2/1.8
money 10/3.1
month 4/4.1
moon 9/1.1
more 6/3.1, 7/2.1, 7/3.1
 ~ and ~ 8/5.1
morning 0/2.1
most 7/3.3
Mr 0/1.1
Mrs 0/2.1
much
 very ~ 1/4.3
 How ~? 3/6.1
 too ~ 6/4.2
 ~ faster 7/2.1
museum 2/5.4
music 6/1.2
my 0/1.1

name 0/1.1
 in my ~ 7/4.2
nationality 1/3.3
near 1/2.3
nearest 2/5.4
need 5/2.4
neighbour 2/1.8
nervous 9/3.1
never 6/2.5
never mind 5/2.3
new 5/3.2
news (= Nachrichten) 6/1.2
news (= Neuigkeiten) 6/4.2
newspaper 3/4.1
next 0/3
next to 2/5.4
nice 0/1.1
 N~ to meet you. 0/1.1
night 1/5.3
 at ~ 6/4.2
 last ~ 9/2.2
night club 1/5.3
night school 2/1.8
no (= nein) 0/1.2
no (= kein) 4/5.2
noisy 10/3.3
none 2/1.2
north 10/4.2
not 0/1.2
 not any 8/5.1, 8/5.2
note (= Geldschein) 3/6.3
nothing 4/5.1
now 1/2.3
number 2/1.3, 2/2.1

OK 7/4.3
o'clock 4/1.1
of
 some ~ my friends 0/2.2
 the name ~ the hotel 2/1.7
 the 5th ~ March 4/4.2
 a pair ~ shoes 3/1
 a map ~ London 3/6.1
 a bottle ~ beer 6/1.1
 a cup ~ tea 6/1.2

office 1/4.2
often 6/1.2
old 1/2.4
on
 ~ the first floor 2/4
 ~ the left/right 2/5.4
 ~ Saturday 4/3
 ~ 4th May 4/4.2
 ~ TV 5/2.2
 ~ holiday 6/2.2
 ~ trains 6/3.2
 nothing to write ~ 8/2.4
once 6/3.1
one, the first ~ 3/5.1
this/that ~ 3/5.2
one day 9/3.1
one-way 7/2.3
only 2/1.2
open adj 4/1.4
opposite 2/5.4
or 2/1.8
orange n 8/1.3
order v 8/1.1
order n 8/2.3
other 5/2.3
our 3/4.2
out
 find ~ 4/4.2
 day in, day ~ 6/1.4
 go ~ 6/1.4
 take a person ~ 6/2.5
over, come/go ~ 5/1.1, 9/3.1
over (= vorbei) 9/3.1
over there 3/2.1
own adj 4/5.2

p 3/6.1
page 7/4.2
paint 5/2.2
painting 6/2.3
painting workshop 5/3.2
pair, a ~ of 3/1
paper (= newspaper) 6/1.2
parents 9/4
park 2/5.4
partner 6/2.4
party 5/1.2
pass, ~ a test 9/3.1
passenger 6/3.1
passport 10/3.3
past, half ~ 4/1.1
5 minutes ~ 5 4/2.1
pay n 6/4.1
pea 8/2.3
pear 8/5.1
pen 6/4.1
pence 3/6.1
penny 3/6.1
people 5/2.3
per 7/4.1
per cent 3/3.1
perhaps 5/2.4
person 2/1.7
personality 6/2.1
phone v 2/1.8
photo 10/3.1
photography 5/3.2
piano 5/3.2
picture (= Bild) 5/3.1
picture (= Foto) 5/3.2
 take a ~ 5/3.2

picture postcard 3/4.2
pint 6/4.1
pity
 That's a ~. 5/2.2
 What a ~! 10/3.3
place 1/4.1
plan v 4/3
plane 7/2.1
play v 5/2.2
pleasant 5/2.4
please 0/1.1
p.m. 4/1.4
police 10/3.3
pop music 6/2.2
possible 7/4.1
post code 2/3.2
post office 2/5.4
postcard 3/4.2
poster 3/6.4
potato 8/2.2
pound (= £) 3/6.1
prefer 7/2.2
present (= Geschenk) 4/5.1
present adj 6/3.1
private 7/4.1
problem 10/3.3
pub 4/1.4
pullover 3/1
put 10/4.5
 ~ up 7/4.3

quarter, (a) ~ past/ to 4/2.1
question 3/6.3
quiet 7/3.1
quite 3/2.1
 ~ well 10/1.2

radio 3/4.1
rain n 10/4.2
rainy 10/4.1
read 5/3.1
really 4/2.2
reception 7/1.1
recommend 7/1.1
record 3/4.1
red 3/3.1
regular 7/2.4
remember 6/2.4
reservation 1/3.4
reserve 7/4.2
resort 7/3.1
restaurant 2/5.4
return (ticket) 7/2.3
right, you are ~ 2/1.2
right (= rechts) 2/5.1, 2/5.4
road 2/3.1
roast 8/2.2
rob 9/2.2
room 7/4.1
round
 walk ~ 7/4.3
 look ~ 9/3.1
rugby 6/2.4
run n, go for a ~ 6/1.2

safe adj 7/2.2
salad 8/2.3
sales manager 1/4.1
salt 8/5.1
same 6/2.4
sausage 8/1.1
say 1/4.1
school 2/5.4
 night ~ 2/1.8

second (= zweite,r,s) 2/4
secretary 1/4.1
see (= sehen) 0/3
 ~ you next week 0/3
 you ~ 9/3.1
see (= besuchen) 6/1.5
 ~ a doctor 10/2.1
seem 7/3.1
sell 3/4.2
send 6/4.2
serious 10/2.3
serve 8/2.4
service, train ~ 6/3.1
Shall we ...? 4/3
she 1/4.1
shirt 3/1
shoe 3/1
shop 1/4.2
shop assistant 1/4.2
shopping centre 7/3.2
short 3/5.3
should 7/1.1
show v 9/1.1
shower (= Dusche) 6/1.2
sight-seeing 7/2.2
 do ~ 9/1.3
sign 7/4.3
similar 6/2.3
sincerely, Yours ~ 7/4.2
single
 ~ room 7/4.1
 ~ ticket 7/2.3
sir 7/4.2
sit 5/2.4
size 3/5.1
skirt 3/1
small 3/5.1
smart 3/2.1
smile 9/3.1
smoke 9/4
snack 6/1.1
snow n 10/4.2
so (= so) 0/2.3
 Why do you think ~? 6/1.6
so (= also) 1/2.1
so-so 0/2.3
so that 7/2.3
socks 3/1
some (= einige) 0/2.2
some (= etwas/ein paar) 8/3.2
somebody 10/2.3
something 5/3.2
sometimes 5/2.4
son 4/4.2
soon, as ~ as 7/4.2
sorry 0/1.2
 I'm ~. 5/2.2
 I'm ~ to hear that. 6/4.1
sort of 9/3.1
soup 8/2.2
south 10/3.1
souvenir 3/4.1
speak 2/1.5
speaking 2/1.5
speaker 9/3.1
special 7/2.3
spell 1/3.1
spend (time) 6/3.2
sport(s) 6/2.1
sports-car 6/2.3
sports wear 3/4.1
square n 2/3.1

one hundred and forty-one 141

squash 6/2.3
start 6/1.4
station 2/5.3
stay 10/2.1
steak 8/2.2
steal 10/3.3
still *adv* 4/1.4
stop *v* 2/5.2
store 3/4.2
storm 10/4.2
story 5/3.2
straight ahead 2/5.1
straight along 2/5.3
street 2/3.1
student 1/4.2
sugar 8/5.1
suit 3/1
suitcase 3/1
summer 5/3.2
sun 10/3.1
sunny 10/4.1
sunshine 10/4.3
supermarket 1/4.2
sure 3/5.1
surname 1/3.2
sweet 8/3.2
sweets 9/3.1
swim 9/1.3
swim wear 10/3.1

table 8/2.2
tablet 10/2.1
take (= *nehmen, ein-/aufnehmen*)
~ a book 2/1.8
~ a bus/a taxi 7/1.1
~ orders 8/2.3
~ a picture 5/3.2
~ a photo 10/3.1
~ a tablet 10/2.1
take (= *bringen*)
~ a person to ... 5/2.4
take (= *benötigen*)
It ~s two hours. 6/3.1

take a person out 6/2.5
talk (to) 4/5.2
tap 10/3.1
taxi 7/1.1
taxi driver 1/4.1
tea 6/1.2
teacher 0/1.1
team 10/4.5
telephone 2/1.3
telephone directory 2/1.7
tell 2/1.8
~ about 6/1.4
temperature
~ (= C°) 10/4.2
a ~ (= *Fieber*) 10/2.3
tennis 5/2.4
terrible 6/4.1
test 9/3.1
text 9/3.1
than 7/3.1
thank you, thanks 0/2.3
that (= *der/die/das da, jene,r,s*) 0/1.3
that (= *daß*) 9/3.1
so ~ 7/2.3
the 1/2.1
in ~ evening 4/1.4
play ~ piano 5/3.2
[ði:] 7/4.3
theatre 5/2.4
their 2/3.1
them 3/5.3, 4/5.1
then 2/1.7
there 3/6.3
over ~ 3/2.1
~ is/are 2/1.2
these 3/5.3
they 2/4
thing 2/1.8
think 1/2.4
third 2/4
this 0/1.3
~ evening 5/1.1

those 3/5.3
ticket (= *Eintrittskarte*) 5/2.4
ticket (= *Fahrkarte*) 7/2.3
till 4/1.4
time 4/1.2
What's the ~? 4/2.2
What ~ is it? 4/1.3
time (= *Mal*) 9/3.1
times (= *mal*) 2/2.3, 6/3.1
tip 10/3.1
to 0/1.1
5 – 8 4/2.1
~ work 4/2.2
~ London 4/2.3
listen ~ 5/3.1
a letter ~ 10/3.3
to (= *um zu*) 2/2.1, 6/2.4
toast 8/1.1
today 0/2.2
together 9/3.1
tomato 8/1.1
tomorrow 5/1.2
tonight 1/3.4
..., too (= *auch*) 0/1.2
too (= *zu*) 3/2.2
~ much 6/4.2
tourist 7/1.2
Tourist Information Centre 4/1.4
town 1/2.3
to ~ 6/1.3
in ~ 7/3.3
traffic light(s) 2/5.3
train 4/2.2
travel 6/3.1
travel agent 7/2.1
traveller's cheque 10/3.1
trip 4/3
trousers 3/1
true 10/3.2
try 6/2.4

try on 3/5 3
T-shirt 3/1
tube (= *Londoner U-Bahn*) 7/1.1
turn *v*
~ left/right 2/5.1
~ into X St. 2/5.4
TV 3/4.1
twice 6/3.1

umbrella 3/1
under 10/2.2
underground 6/3.2
unpleasant 6/4.1
until 2/5.3
unusual 6/1.1
up
get ~ 6/1.3
put ~ 7/4.3
us 4/5.1
use 5/3.1
usual 6/1.1
usually 6/1.2

valuable 10/3.1
vegetable 8/2.3
very 3/2.2
very much 1/4.3
video 5/2.4
view 7/4.3
village 1/2.3
visit 9/1.1
volleyball 6/2.3

WC 7/4.1
waiter, waitress 1/4.1
walk *v* 4/2.2
walk *n* 6/2.2
want 2/5.4
warm 8/4.2
was 4/4.2
wash 5/2.2
watch 5/2.2
water 10/3.1
mineral ~ 8/2.3

way (= *Art/Weise*) 7/1.1
one-~ (= *Hinfahrt*) 7/2.3
by the ~ 9/3.1
we 1/4.1
wear *v* 3/3.1
wear *n*
sports ~, children's ~ 3/4.1
weather 9/1.1
weather forecast 10/4.2
week 0/3
weekday 7/2.3
weekend 4/3
well (= *gut*), very/quite ~ 10/1.2
Well, ... 3/5.3, 9/3.1
west 10/4.2
wet 10/4.5
what 0/1.1
W~'s your name? 0/1.1
W~ size? 3/5.1
W~ about ...? 3/5.3
W~ time is it? 4/2.2
W~ time (= *when*) 4/1.4
W~'s the time? 4/1.3
W~'s the matter? 6/4.1
W~ a pity! 10/3.3
when (= *wann*) 4/1.4
when (= *wenn*) 6/1.4
where (= *wo*) 1/2.1
where (= *wohin*) 6/2.1
where from 1/2.1
which 2/1.7
while 5/3.2
whisky 6/2.4
white 3/3.1
who (= *wer*) 2/1.5

who (= *wen, wem*) 6/2.3
who (= *der, die, das*) 6/2.4
whose 4/5.1
why 5/2.1
wife, wives 4/4.2
will, 'll 7/4.1, 10/4.2
win 2/1.2
wind 10/4.2
wine 5/2.2
winter 10/4.3
wish, best ~es 9/1.1
with 4/3
without 7/4.1
woman, women 10/3.3
wonderful 9/1.1
wool 3/3.1
word 10/4.4
work *v* 1/4.2
work *n* 4/2.2
workshop 5/3.2
would 5/1.1
write 1/4.1
~ down 2/1.7
wrong, You are ~. 2/1.2

year 4/4.2
yellow 3/3.1
yes 0/1.2
yesterday 9/1.1
yet 4/5.1
you (= *du, Sie*) 0/1.2
you (= *dich, Sie*) 0/1.1
you (= *euch, Sie, Ihnen*) 3/5.1, 4/5.1
you (= *man*) 3/4.2
you are right/wrong 2/1.2
your 0/1.1
Yours, ... 4/3
Yours sincerely, ... 7/4.2

Höraufgaben-Texte

UNIT 0

2.1 Good morning, Mrs Finch. – Good morning, Miss Miller.

(1) – Good morning, Mrs Finch.
 – Good morning.
(2) – Hi, Sue!
 – Hi, Tony! How's life?
(3) – Good morning, Mrs Brown.
 – Morning.
(4) – Hello, Julia.
 – Hello.

2.4 How are you?

(1) – Hello, Peter.
 – Hello, Simon. How are you?
 – Fine, thanks. And you?
(2) – Good morning, Mrs Baker.
 – Good morning.
 – How are you today?
 – Well, not so bad.
 – Oh.

(3) – Hello, Tony. How are you?
 – Thank you, I'm fine. And you?
 – Fine, too, thanks.
(4) – Hi, Barbara. How are you?
 – Hm. So-so.
 – Oh.

UNIT 1

2.1 Where are you from?

(1) – And, er, where are you from?
 – I'm from the States.
 – – erm, yeah, where from in the States?
 – – er, – Denver, Colorado.
 – Ah. I see.
(2) – Er, Fitzgerald. That's an Irish name, isn't it?
 – Well, yes, it is, but I'm English, I'm from Liverpool.
 – Ah, I see . . .
(3) – Are you English?
 – Oh no, I'm from Australia.

(4) – Are you American?
 – No, I'm from Canada. From Toronto.
 – Ah.
(5) – You're English?
 – No, – British. I'm from Scotland.
(6) – Are you from Australia?
 – No, I'm not. I'm from New Zealand.

3.1 Can you spell that, please?

(1) – What's your name, please?
 – Yates. Y – A – T – E – S.
 – Thank you.
(2) – And your name, please?
 – Woods.
 – W – double O-D-S?
 – Yes, that's right.
 – Thank you.
(3) – And what's your name, please?
 – Bankes.
 – B–A–N–K–S?
 – No, B–A–N–K–E–S. With an 'e'.
 – Right. Thank you.

3.3 In a hotel in England.

– Good evening. Er, I've got a reservation for tonight. My name is Miller.
– Ah, yes. Good evening, Mr Miller. What's your first name, please?
– Er, Oliver.
– Oh, thank you. Are you American?
– Yes. I'm from New York.

5.1 This is Nancy MacDonald

Text = Seite 15
Schlüssel: 1. Glasgow 2. Sales Manager 3. Toronto 4. Scotland 5. London

7. Who is it?

– Hello.
– Hello. This is Jill Browne. Can I speak to Mrs Grey, please?
– I'm sorry, but she isn't in. She's in London.

– Oh. Can you tell her I called, please?
  It's Jill Browne, Browne with an 'e'.
– With an 'e'?
– Yes: B–R–O–W–N–E. Jill Browne
  from Manchester.
– All right. I'll tell her you called.
– Thank you. Bye-bye.
– Goodbye.

UNIT 2

1.1 Ten, nine, eight, . . .

– nine – eight – seven – six – five –
  four – three – two – one – zero –
  damn it!!

1.3 What's his telephone number?

(1) – . . . and what's your telephone
    number, please?
  – It's 474 6490.
  – Thanks.
(2) – What's your telephone number?
  – *erm*, double 4, 3 – 2, double 1, 5.
  – double 4, 3 – 2, double 1, 5.
    Thanks.

1.5 Hello, John.

Text = Seite 20
Schlüssel: (1) 335 3032   (2) Helen

1.7 Directory Inquiries. Which town, please?

(1) – Directory Inquiries. Which town,
    please?
  – Margate, please. The Arosa Hotel.
  – Just a moment, please. . . .
    That's the Arosa Hotel,
    5, Second Avenue.
  – Yes, that's right.
  – The number is Thanet 21 905.
  – 2, 1, 9, 0, 5. Thanks.
(2) – Directory Inquiries. Which town?
  – Ashford.
  – The name, please?
  – Pyke, John Pyke.
  – Can you spell that, please?
  – P–Y–K–E.
  – Just a moment, please. . . .
    The number is 50843.

2.1 Bingo!

4 – 5 – 10 – 16 – 17 – 70 – 71 – 72 –
73 – 66 – 88 – 89 – 47 – 46 – 45 –
44 – 7 – 8

3.1 What's his address?

(1) – My address? My address is 22
    Oxford Street, London.
(2) – And your address, please?
  – 125 London Road.
  – This town?
  – Yes, Coventry.
(3) – *Er*, Brown and Co. –
    What's their address?
  – – *erm* – it's 12 Park Avenue,
    Dover.
  – Aha, thanks.
(4) – And, and where is the cinema?
  – Oh, it's in College Square, near
    the post office.
  – Ah, yes, thanks.

5.3 Excuse me, can you tell me how to get to the bus station?

(1) – Excuse me, where's the
    Central Hotel, please?
  – *Erm*, Central Hotel?
    Erm, – Go along King Street
    here, and it's on your left.
  – Thank you.
(2) – Excuse me.
  – Yes?
  – Can you tell me how to get to
    the post office, please?
  – The post office? Yes. Straight
    ahead, straight along King Street
    until you get to the traffic lights.
    Then turn right, and it's on your
    left, opposite the bus station.
(3) – Excuse me, can you tell me
    where Miller's book shop is?
  – Yes, certainly. It's in London
    Road. Straight along here until
    you get to the traffic lights, then
    turn left, and it's on your left,
    opposite the Rex.
  – Aha, thanks.

6. Is there a supermarket?

– This holiday club is very nice.
  And the guests are nice, too.
– Is there a supermarket in the club?
– Yes, there is. It's here, next to the
  main hotel building. The entrance is
  opposite the self service restaurant.
– So that's the self service restaurant.
– Yes, in the hotel building on the
  ground floor, on the right. And there's
  a lot of entertainment in the club.
  There's a night club on the fourth
  floor of the hotel building.
– Hmhm.
– And the Rendezvous Bar near the
  swimming pool is open all day.
  And there's a pub in the Old
  Farmhouse, too.
– The Old Farmhouse?
– Yes, this building here. There's the
  pub, and there's a ladies' hairdresser
  on the first floor, and there's a
  souvenir shop, too.
– Oh, there's a ladies' hairdresser's,
  too?
– Yes, on the first floor, and one for
  men in the main hotel building.
– And how can I get to the village from
  the club?
– There are taxis just opposite the
  entrance to the club.

UNIT 3

2.1 That's a beautiful dress over there!

(1) – That's a beautiful dress.
  – The one over there?
    Next to the . . .
  – Yes. It's beautiful, isn't it?
  – Hm. Yes.
(2) – And that coat over there?
  – Beautiful! Very elegant.
(3) – And there's a nice pullover for
    you.
  – The brown and beige one? Hmm.
    Well. Hmm. It's quite expensive.
  – Yes, it is. You're right.
    But it's very smart.
(4) – That's a nice blouse.
  – Hm, yes – quite nice.

3.1 She's wearing a beautiful grey blouse . . .

And here's Sandra. Sandra's wearing a
beautiful red blouse – a very French
blouse from Paris – very 'chic', very
elegant – and a beautiful blue skirt.
Christian Dior design, of course.
Now – here's Violetta – she's from Italy.
She's wearing a black coat – made in
Italy by Cerruti, – very elegant, and very
sexy! And a very smart pullover! It's a
beautiful grey and 100 % wool.
Thank you, Violetta.
And this is Holly. She's from Japan, and
she's wearing a dress by Kenzo, a disco
green dress, and yellow shoes. Very
'avantgarde' – **the** dress for a cocktail
party.

4.1 Where can we get jeans?

– Ah, look, there. . . . The T-shirt for
  Billy – where can we get the T-shirt
  for Billy?
– Children's wear is on the third floor.
– Good. Third floor.
– And I think you can get your sports
  shoes there, too.
– Yes, you're right. I can. Sports wear is
  on the third floor, too.
– And the socks?
– Well, I think you can get them in the
  sports department, too.
  On the third floor.
– And a film for my camera, – where
  can we get films?
  On the ground floor?
– Yes, you can get a film on the
  ground floor.
– And the video cassette for Charles?
– *Er* . . . . The radio and TV
  department is on the fourth floor.

5.1 Can I help you?

– Can I help you?
– *Er*, yes, please. I'm looking for a
  blouse.
– Blouses are over there, madam.
– What size, please?
– *Erm*, 10? 12? I'm not quite sure.
– The size 10 blouses are here.
– What about this one? It's very smart.
– Well, yes, but it's too small.
  It's size 8.
– Oh, I'm sorry. Here's a size 10.
– It's nice, isn't it?
– Yes, but it's not the right colour.

6.1 How much is it?

(1) – I'm looking for an umbrella.
    How much is that one over there,
    please?
  – *Erm*, let me see, five pounds, sir.
  – Ah, thank you.
(2) – How much is a postcard to
    Germany, please?
  – 22p.
  – These two postcards, please.
    How much are they?
  – 10p each. That's 20p please,
    madam.
  – Here you are.
  – Thank you.
(4) – This is the best map of London
    you can get.
  – How much is it?
  – It's two pounds and ninety-nine p.
  – What?!?!

6.3 Can you change a £50 note, please?

(1) – Fares, please.
  – Can you change a £50 note,
    please?
  – A £50 note?! What do you think
    this is – a bus or the
    Bank of England?
(2) – *Erm*, – excuse me. Can you, can
    you change this, please?
    50 pounds?
  – *Erm*, – no, I'm sorry, I can't, sir.
    Try the bank in North Street.
  – Ah, yes. Thanks.

8. It's from Macy's.

– That's a nice blouse you're wearing,
  Carol.
– Oh, do you like it? It's from Macy's in
  New York.
– In New York?
– Yes, I was there in July. Macy's is
  fantastic, it really is. It's the biggest
  department store in New York – it's
  like Harrods.
– Is it expensive, shopping in New York?
– No, not really – London prices, but not
  really expensive. Sizes are a problem,
  though.
– Oh?
– They haven't got British sizes. Our
  size 10 is size 8 in America, for
  example.
– Oh, really?

UNIT 4

1.1 It's six o'clock.

1 It's six o'clock. Here is the news
   read by John Davenport.
2 Radio 4. Two o'clock and time for
   Woman's Hour.
3 Radio 4. And now at ten thirty
   it's time for Morning Story.
4 Seven o'clock. The news on Radio 3.
5 This is Radio 4. The six o'clock
   news.
6 It's eleven thirty. Open University.
7 It's twelve o'clock and you're
   listening to Radio 2. Music while
   you work.
8 Six thirty on Radio 3. Jazz Today.
9 It's 8.30. Country Club – direct
   from Texas!
10 It's midnight. Late news and
   weather on Radio 4.

1.2 Have you got the time, please?

(1) – Excuse me.
  – Yes?
  – Have you got the time, please?
  – *Er*, ten. It's almost ten o'clock.
  – Ten o'clock. Thank you.
(2) – Excuse me. What's the time,
    please?
  – It's – *er* – half past three.
  – Thanks.
(3) – Excuse me. Can you tell me the
    time, please?
  – The time? *Erm*, just a moment.
    It's six – almost six o'clock.
  – Thank you.

2.1 It's a quarter past eight.

(1) – Excuse me, what's the time,
    please?
  – *Erm*, five past four.
  – Thanks.
(2) – Have you got the time?
  – Yes. Just a moment – it's three
    minutes past ten.
  – Oh, thank you.
(3) – I really must go.
  – What time is it?
  – It's a quarter to nine, and my bus
    is at nine.
(4) – Excuse me, can you tell me the
    time, please?
  – *Er*, it's ten to nine.
  – Thank you.
(5) – Have you got the time, please?
  – Yes, it's twenty-two minutes
    to seven.
  – Thanks.

2.3 When's the next train to Norwich?

The train now arriving at platform 4 is
the 5.25 to King's Lynn, calling at
Cambridge and Ely.
The next train from platform 6 is
the 5.30 to Norwich, calling at Ipswich
only.

4.1 When's your birthday?

1 It's on the 25th of April.
2 *Erm* – on the 27th of August.
3 On the 2nd of May. Why? –
   What have you got for me?
4 It's on July 21. Why?
5 On the 13th of December, and
   that's a Friday!
6 It's on the 29th of February, so I'm
   only 16, really!

5.1 Birthday presents

Text = Seite 47
Schlüssel: 1. a Louis Armstrong
record   2. Linda's 13th birthday.

7 Listen, please.

And now for tonight's programme on
Radio 4.
After the six o'clock news, 'Music from
America' at 6.30 with the BBC
Philharmonic Orchestra, conducted by
Gunther Schuller – in stereo.
At 7.25 it's time again for Alistair
Cooke's 'Letter from America', followed
by the 'News' at 8 and 'Jazz Today' at
8.10: Charles Fox presents the best of
modern jazz on records.
At 8.40 – 'Checkpoint', our new series
about listeners' problems. The Vienna
Philharmonic Orchestra, conducted by
Eugen Jochum, plays Bruckner's
Symphony No 7 in E at nine o'clock on
Radio 4. At 10, 'The World Today',
followed by 'Radio Active' at 10.30.
The 'Book at Bedtime', today at
11 o'clock, is Sir Walter Scott's 'Anne of
Geierstein'. On long wave only, we end
the day with 'Today in Parliament' at
11.30, followed by the 'News and
Weather' at midnight.

UNIT 5

1.1 Would you like to come over for a drink?

(1) – Hi, Gill. What are you doing this
    evening?
  – Nothing, really.
  – Would you like to come over and
    listen to my old Beatles records?
  – Yeah, great.
(2) – Hello, Brenda, it's Fred. What are
    you doing this evening?
  – This evening? Oh, nothing, really.
  – Well, would you like to come to
    the cinema?
  – Hm. What's on?
(3) – What are you doing this evening,
    Jack?
  – Nothing, really, Jim.

– Would you like to come over to the pub for a drink?
– Yes, fine. Where are you? What pub?
(4) – What are you doing this evening?
– Nothing really.
– We're having a party. Would you like to come over?

2.1 Why can't they come?

(1) – Hello, is that you Betty?
– Oh, hello. Robert.
– What are you doing at the moment? Would you like to come and have dinner with us?
– Oh, I'm sorry – I'd love to, but I'm helping Janet with her homework.
– Oh, that's a pity.
(2) – We're going to the pub tonight. Would you like to come, too?
– I'm sorry, Bob, I can't. I'm working tonight.
– Oh, that's a pity.
(3) – Well, we can go to the cinema, if you like.
– Hm.
– Well, – would you like to?
– Well, I'm just leaving for night school.
– Oh, that's a pity. What about tomorrow, then?
(4) – 35062.
– Hi, Kate. This is Ellen.
– Hi, how are you?
– Fine thanks. Would you like to come over and meet some friends from Canada?
– I'm sorry, I can't. I'm having dinner with John tonight.

UNIT 6

1.1 A usual morning for an unusual person . . .

Well, er, the first thing I do in the morning is – I go home. I have a snack and I drink a bottle of beer. Then I read the morning paper and go to bed. A bit unusual, perhaps, but not if you work as a . . .

3.1 What do you think about the present train and bus services?

– Can I ask you some questions about the present bus services, please?
– Are you from the City Transport Department?
– Yes, that's right.
– Yes, all right.
– How often do you travel by bus?
– *Erm*, well, every day in winter.
– Hmhm. And when do you usually start your journey?
– Between quarter past eight and eight thirty. I have to be in the office at 9.
– So, how long does each journey take?
– Oh, about 20 minutes, I'd say.
– And how often do you have to change?
– Once. Only once.
– What do you think about the present services?
– What do I think? – Well, they're all right – could be better: one or two more buses in the morning, so that you always find a seat . . .

6 Twenty Questions

– And our next competitor is Fred Alderton from Greenwich. Good evening, Fred. Come and sit down here.
– Good evening. Thank you.
– Do you work indoors?
– Yes, I do.
– In a factory?
– No, . . .
– Do you work in an office?
– Yes, well, – in a kind of office.
– Do you buy and sell things?
– No, not really.
– Do you offer a service?
– Yes, I do.
– Do you work with people?
– Ye-es, I do.
– Do you help people with problems?
– Yes, I do.
– Psychological problems?
– No.
– Do you work in a hospital?
– No, I don't.
– Are people afraid of you?

– Some people, yes.
– Are you a (*bleep*)?!
– Yes, I am.
– Sorry, Fred. The team wins again! Thank you for coming. Now, perhaps you'd like to tell us about yourself . . .

UNIT 7

1.1 What's the best way of getting to Heathrow?

Text = Seite 68
Schlüssel: Airbus

2.1 Cheaper, faster, more comfortable

(1) – Do you always travel by train?
– Yes, when I've got the time. It's cheaper and more comfortable than travelling by car.
(2) – How are you travelling to France this summer, by train or by plane?
– By train.
– Do you always travel by train?
– Not always, but it's cheaper.
(3) – Well, a flight to Paris is more expensive, but it's much more comfortable than travelling by boat and train, or by car. And much faster, of course – only an hour.

4.1 I'm looking for a single room.

– Park Hotel, good evening.
– Good evening. I'm looking for a double room for two nights. Have you got anything free?
– With private bathroom or shower?
– With shower, if possible.
– Yes, that's possible.
– How much does it cost?
– £18 per night.
– Hm. Haven't you got anything cheaper?
– Only without bath or shower.
– All right. I'll take one without bath.

UNIT 8

1.1 What would you like for breakfast?

– What would you like for breakfast?
– Have you got any tomato juice?
– Yes, and what would you like to eat?
– I'd like some eggs and tomato and toast, please.
– No bacon or sausages?
– No, thanks.
– Would you like coffee or tea?
– Coffee, please.

2.2 What do they order?

– Can I take your order, sir?
– Yes. For me tomato soup to start with, and roast chicken. What about you, Tom?
– What's the fruit juice?
– Orange, sir.
– Then I'll take the tomato soup, too. And the roast chicken.
– Two tomato soups and two roast chicken and chips.
– Oh, no, not for me. Boiled potatoes for me. What about you, Tom?
– I'll have boiled potatoes, too.
– Fine. Two roast chicken with boiled potatoes. And after the chicken –
– Ice-cream and coffee.
– Me, too.

3.1 Have a drink!

– What would you like, Jean?
– I'd like a sherry.
– Dry or sweet?
– Medium, please.
– And what about you, Mary?
– I'd like a dry white wine.
– Right. And you, Peter?
– A pint of lager, please.
– So, that's a medium sherry, a dry white wine, and two pints of lager, please.

4.1 Can I have the bill, please?

– Can I have the bill, please?
– That's eight pounds 45. How did you like your meal, sir?
– Well, the fish was quite good, but the wine was much too warm, I'm afraid.
– Oh, I'm sorry about that.

5.1 What do we need?

– Have we got any sugar left?
– Yes, we've got quite a lot of sugar, but we need some cream.
– Cream – and milk. There isn't any milk left.
– Hmhm. And what about fruit? Have we got any apples or pears?
– I don't think so. Let's buy some apples. They're cheaper than pears.
– Yes, and we need vegetables, too. Let's get some potatoes and tomatoes.
– And what about cheese?
– Do we need any cheese?
– Yes. Let's get some Camembert and Gorgonzola.
– Well, that's it then, I think.

7 What's number 8, please?

– Yes, madam.
– What's number 8, please?
– Rogan Josh – that's mutton, madam.
– Mutton?
– Yes, mutton – sheep –
– Oh, I see.
– – with curry and vegetables.
– Peas and carrots?
– Yes, – and cauliflower. Very hot. Very good.
– *Er*, yes. Well, I think I'll take number 8. Yes, number 8, please.
– And would you like some rice?
– Or, can I have potatoes?
– Well, that's in the curry. Peas, potatoes, carrots . . .
– Oh, I see. And is the rice extra?
– Yes, madam. The pilau rice is very good. That's rice with peas.
– Fine, I'll have some – what did you call it?
– Pilau.
– Pilau. Yes, I'll have pilau rice.
– And would you like chutney?
– Yes, mango chutney, please.
– Certainly, madam. Anything else?
– No, thank you, that's all.
– Would you like papadums?
– No, thank you.
– Thank you, madam.

UNIT 9

1.2 Where did you spend your holidays?

– Hello, Bob.
– Harry! Good to see you again. Did you have a good holiday?
– Yes, thanks. Wonderful.
– Spain again?
– No, not Spain this year.
– Oh, where did you go to then? To Italy?
– No, Scotland.
– Scotland?
– Yes, a small place near Inverness. What about you?
– Oh, we went to the States this year.
– Hm. Where did you go? New York?
– Well, we spent a week in New York, and then we went on to Florida.
– And how did you like it in . . .

2.1 I took Joan Collins out to dinner.

(1) – What did you do last night?
– I painted the bathroom.
– Oh, did you? The bathroom?
(2) – You didn't come to the club last night.
– No I didn't. I was at home. I invited Brenda over for a glass of wine.
– Oh, really?
(3) – I tried to phone you last night, but you weren't in.
– Me? But I **was** in.
– Oh, really?
– Yes, – in bed with a really good book.
(4) – I saw you in your car last night. Where did you go?
– I went to the cinema.

– Oh, what did you see?
– Dr Zhivago.
– Dr Zhivago. I love Dr Zhivago.
(5) – I tried to phone you last night, but you weren't at home.
– You phoned me? But I **was** at home.
– You didn't answer the phone. Where were you?
– Oh, come on. I took Joan Collins out to dinner.
– You did what?
– I . . . . Look, I really **was** at home. I watched TV all evening.
– Hmph.

3.1 Where I met my partner.

Text = Seite 90

UNIT 10

1.1 How are you?

(1) – Good morning, Jim. How are you this morning?
– So – so, thanks. Can't complain.
(2) – Hi, Mary. How are you?
– Oh, I feel terrible. It's the weather, you know.
– Oh, I'm sorry to hear that.
(3) – Good morning, Mrs Sheridan. How are you?
– Very well, thank you. And how are you?
– Thank you, I'm fine.

2.1 I've got a headache.

(1) – Hello, Julia.
– Hi, Joe.
– You don't look very well today.
– I don't **feel** very well.
– What's the matter?
– I've got a headache.
– You should take some tablets.
(2) – You look terrible this morning.
– Yeah. I **feel** terrible. I drank too much last night.
– You should stay in bed.
– I can't. I have to go to work.
(3) – Atishoo!
– Bless you! Have you got a cold?
– Yeah.
– You should drink a bottle of whisky and stay in bed for a day or two.
– Ha, ha!

4.2 There will be snow in the north . . .

And now the weather. It will be cool in all parts of the British Isles today with temperatures between 8 degrees Celsius in the North to 12 degrees Celsius in the South. After a foggy start in the South-East, it will be sunny in the early afternoon. A cold front moving in from the North-West will reach Scotland and the North-West by midday. There will be rain in most parts of northern England and some snow in Scotland later in the day. And now the outlook for the weekend . . .

4.4 Talking about the weather

(1) – Good morning.
– Morning.
– Lovely morning, isn't it?
– Yes, it is. Real holiday weather. It's a pity we have to go to work.
– Yes. By the way – when are you going on holiday?
– Well – I don't know yet. . . .
(2) – Hello . . .
– Hi, Peter.
– What a beautiful day.
– Ah well, too hot. Especially when you have a long drive in front of you.
– Oh, where are you going?
– I have to visit a firm in Brighton.
(3) – Morning.
– Morning. Terrible weather!
– Yes, it's always like this at the weekend.
– Yes. Just when I wanted to work in the garden.
– Hm. – Ah, what I wanted to ask you was – the roses – what do you do with roses when . . .